China and US Foreign Investment Laws and Practices

The book is a comparative study of the national security review of foreign investment laws in China and the US.

The author establishes a theoretical framework to explain the dominant role of ideas on national security and foreign investment rooted in China and the US, as well as the oriented role of China-US investment interaction. She concludes that it is difficult for China and the US to reach a consensus on national security review due to their different internal ideas on national security and foreign investment. By comparing the similarities and differences in the development of national security review in China and the US, she also proposes a feasible approach to facilitate bilateral investment practices.

The book will attract scholars of international economic law, investment law, and Sino-US relations.

Liu Ziyu is a lecturer at China Foreign Affairs University. Her research area covers international investment law, Chinese law, and in particular, Chinese foreign investment law and comparative law. She holds a PhD in law from the University of Hong Kong. Prior to her doctorate, she obtained a master's degree in law from National University of Singapore and a bachelor's degree in law and a bachelor's degree in philosophy from Renmin University of China.

China and US Foreign Investment Laws and Practices

A Theoretical Explanation of National Security Review

Liu Ziyu

Routledge
Taylor & Francis Group
LONDON AND NEW YORK

First published 2025
by Routledge
4 Park Square, Milton Park, Abingdon, Oxon OX14 4RN

and by Routledge
605 Third Avenue, New York, NY 10158

Routledge is an imprint of the Taylor & Francis Group, an informa business

British Library Cataloguing in Publication Data
A catalogue record for this book is available from the British Library

Library of Congress Cataloging in Publication Data
Names: Liu, Ziyu, 1994– author.
Title: China and US foreign investment laws and practices : a theoretical explanation of national security review / Ziyu Liu.
Other titles: China and United States foreign investment laws and practices
Description: Abingdon, Oxon [UK] ; New York, NY : Routledge, 2024. | Includes bibliographical references and index.
Identifiers: LCCN 2024032409 (print) | LCCN 2024032410 (ebook) | ISBN 9781032669069 (hardback) | ISBN 9781032901121 (paperback) | ISBN 9781003543749 (ebook)
Subjects: LCSH: Investments, Foreign—Law and legislation—China. | Investments, Foreign—Law and legislation—United States. | National security—Law and legislation—China. | National security—Law and legislation—United States.
Classification: LCC K3830 .L589 2024 (print) | LCC K3830 (ebook) | DDC 346.5107—dc23/eng/20240714
LC record available at https://lccn.loc.gov/2024032409
LC ebook record available at https://lccn.loc.gov/2024032410

ISBN: 978-1-032-66906-9 (hbk)
ISBN: 978-1-032-90112-1 (pbk)
ISBN: 978-1-003-54374-9 (ebk)

DOI: 10.4324/9781003543749

Typeset in Times New Roman
by Apex CoVantage, LLC

Contents

Figures

Tables

Acknowledgements

This book is based on my doctoral research and the dissertation, *A Comparative Study of National Security Review in China and US Foreign Investment Laws and Practices*, in the Faculty of Law at the University of Hong Kong (HKU). This book would not have been possible without the assistance of the following people to whom I am deeply grateful:

First, my primary supervisor, Prof. Yun Zhao, to whom I must express my deepest gratitude for his comprehensive guidance throughout my PhD studies. I would never have been able to complete the book without the advice and criticism he offered during countless discussions. He encouraged me to attend a number of conferences which were of great educational benefit to me, not only in the area of law, but also in those of international relations and politics. In addition to providing invaluable research training, he was kind and generous in his support for my personal well-being and career development. I would like to express my deep gratitude to my co-supervisor, Prof. Xianchu Zhang. I could not have proceeded this far without his profound insights and continual encouragement. I am sincerely thankful to Prof. Jiangyu Wang, Prof. Douglas Arner, Dr. Angela Zhang, and Prof. Marco Wan, for their invaluable comments on the drafts of this book. I owe my deepest appreciation to Professor Fu Hualing, Professor He Xin, and Prof. Chan Johannes for their constructive questions on this writing proposal. I owe a special debt of gratitude to Prof. Iain MacNeil and Dr. Zhang Chi of the University of Glasgow, Dr. Zhao Huimiao of Beijing University of Chemical Technology, and Dr. Kang Yumei of Beijing Foreign Studies University, for their encouragement and support of my academic research. I would also like to thank the Faculty of International Law, China Foreign Affairs University, in general, and my colleagues at the university in particular for their support and guidance.

I would like to acknowledge the generous support of China Foreign Affairs University, which provided the funds for the research and writing of the book under the Fundamental Research Funds for the Central Universities (Grant Number 3162022ZYQB01). My sincere thanks also go to HKU for its financial support on my doctoral research.

Last but not least, my deepest gratitude and appreciation are reserved for my parents and husband for their long-term love and support. I was fortunate enough to become pregnant and give birth to a son during the writing of this book. Thank you to my precious son for accompanying me throughout the writing process. You have brought me yet more love and strength.

All errors and mistakes in this book remain my personal responsibility. Any comments and criticism are warmly welcome.

1 Theoretical Structure

A Constructivist Approach to Idea Dominance and Process Orientation in National Security Review

1.1 National Security in Constructivism Theory

The term "constructivism" was first coined in international relations theory in 1989 by Nieholas Onuf, who contended that sovereign states are the actors in a world in which social facts are made by human action, a proposition stemming from the philosophical thoughts of Wilhelm Dilthey, Ludwig Wittgenstein, and R. G. Collingwood.[1] Constructivism—in contrast to realism and liberalism, which have focused particularly on the question of "how the behavior of agents generates outcomes"—employs a sociological perspective in relation to world politics, which is concerned with the significant role of ideational factors, such as concepts, norms, and culture in constituting interests and action.[2] At the most general level, constructivism in international relations assumes that human interaction is not shaped by material factors but primarily by ideational ones. The most significant ideational factors in this context are "intersubjective" beliefs as shared collective understanding, and these beliefs construct the actors' identities and interests.

Countering the realist position, which perceives national interests as "objects that have merely to be observed or discovered", Weldes conceptualizes national interests as "social constructions" created by the nation-state itself, mainly by its officials and elites, simply to "enable to make a decision or to act in a particular situation", and argues that the representations created by state officials "make clear both to those officials themselves and to others who and what we are, who and what our enemies are, in what ways we are threatened by them, and how we might best deal with those threats" by means of cultural and linguistic sources.[3] On the basis of George and Keohane's definition, Wendt develops national interests into four types: physical survival, autonomy, economic well-being, and collective self-esteem.

In international relations theory, national security is always an essential concept. In the view of traditional realists, the main force of international politics is the internal power of a state within the structure, and national security depends on the extent of the power enjoyed by the state. In contrast, neo-idealism holds that national security can also be ensured through international cooperation and the promotion of interdependence among states, in order to eliminate the effects of

DOI: 10.4324/9781003543749-1

power on national security. Inspired by a social constructivist approach, however, an emerging ideational change holds that national security cannot be separated from ideological factors such as social ideas and culture. Walling believes that constructivist accounts of norms and ideas also matter significantly and contends that "interests are shaped by normative values". Cho is concerned mainly with comparing conventional and critical constructivism and provides a concluding remark that "identities are often regarded as explanatory variables for certain security phenomena in conventional constructivism, but in critical constructivism the identities themselves are to be explained to make sense of the cultural productions of insecurities". Haas, further, argues that ideological distance—the degree of ideological similarity and difference—among actors plays a crucial role in leaders' perceptions of threat and shaping of national interests. Drawing lights on such a constructivist perspective, identity, and insecurity are produced and reproduced in a mutually constitutive process, and security matters are perceived as social and cultural products, rather than natural facts.

It is generally recognized that security is the core element shaping international behavior, and international behavior and international relations also affect national security. Constructivism also emphasizes the interaction between international actors and international structure, which is used to analyze the actions of sovereign states in relation to big power relations in the context of foreign investment. Constructivists hold that national security, which is largely constituted by national security, which is largely constituted by national identities and national interests, is closely linked with relationships among major international powers, and the field of foreign investment is no exception to this.

1.2 A Constructivist Approach to Explaining National Security Review

In the view of constructivists, the meaning of the distribution of power in international politics is constituted in important part by the distribution of interests and the content of interests is in turn constituted in important part by ideas, which are constitutive.[4] Wendt argues that power and interest are just as important and determinative as before, and that such a constructivist approach does not hold that ideas are more important than power and interest or independent of power and interest, but that power and interest have the effects they do by virtue of the ideas of which they are composed.[5] In terms of national security, where realism focusing on power and politics has traditionally predominated, there is an emerging constructivist approach that could make up for the dilemma of insecurity when explaining national security.

Such a constructivist approach lends itself to explaining and comparing cognition and decision-making in relation to national security in foreign investment laws and practices among big powers, which is also of great reference significance for research on the regulatory mechanism of national security review in relation to foreign inward investment. The perception of national security in foreign inward investment builds the social structure concerning such investment, which indicates that it lays the foundation for national security review in relation to foreign inward investment. For several reasons, it is the idea—rather than interest or other material factors—that plays a direct and dominant role in the evolving process of national security review in foreign inward investment laws and practices. First, when formulating national security review, in spite of the fact that critical technology causes material profits and wealth increases, the perception that critical technology is closely related to national security is constituted by identities. As the US is a technological leader in the global economy and desires to maintain that position, for example, it deems critical technology an essential factor in the context of its national security. It can be imagined that if the US did not conceive of itself as the most advanced technological country, it might be less sensitive than it is about foreign investment in the field of critical technology and might encourage foreign inward investment in advanced technology as China has done in the past. Second, in the enforcement of national security review, it is a normal phenomenon that similar investments from different countries might result in different national security review outcomes. This indicates that purely material factors are not the most determinative or directly influential. Rather, only when these material factors are associated with beliefs and desires, such as national identities and national interests, can material factors make significant contributions. That is to say that material forces are part of the idea, only work through the subjective understanding and interpretation of leaders and lawmakers, and in national security reviews are also ideational.

To be specific, the impacts of reform and enforcement of national security review in US foreign investment practices have varied in terms of the origin of the investment. As regards foreign investment in rapidly developing countries which are not US allies, such as China and Russia, the Committee on Foreign Investment in the United States (CFIUS), which conducts national security reviews in relation to foreign inward investment, adopts a relatively strict policy while, for allies, such as the UK, Canada, and Australia, the CFIUS may be more lenient. The bidder, Dubai Ports World (DPW), for example, raised the CFIUS's concerns in 2006 to acquire a British shipping company—P&O Steam Navigation (P&O)—with US ports, while the previous transaction conducted by the P&O to acquire these US ports was allowed without the launch of national security review. Both DPW and P&O were state-owned enterprises. Generally speaking, there should be no difference if the right to operate a country's critical infrastructure is transferred from one foreign state-owned enterprise to another, while different origins of acquirers lead to different threats on national security. In the DPW case, however, the new bidder, Dubai Ports World (DPW), raised the CFIUS's concerns, because it comes from the sensitive Middle East.[6] The difference in treatment indicates that national security reviews in relation to foreign investment laws and practices are largely affected by how the host country perceives the country of origin of the investment, and such a judgment is perceptional and ideational.

In the era of globalization, the US has been sensitive to actual or potential power and often adopted measures to block potential challengers. In the face of China's economic growth, the US perceived threats from China and even came to regard China as its greatest competitor. Nowadays, the relationship between China and the US is becoming more complex, with interdependence and competition in economic fields and mutual distrust in relation to national security.[7] National security reviews in relation to nation-states' foreign investment laws also reflect the international relations factors to be considered in legal texts. The Foreign Investment Risk Review Modernization Act (FIRRMA), for example, clearly stipulates a number of factors which must be taken into account when reviewing foreign inward investment in relation to foreign state-owned enterprises: whether the foreign government and the US are consistent in foreign policy and whether they are consistent in multilateral counterterrorism, nuclear technology proliferation, and export restrictions.[8] These factors vary with the different relationships enjoyed by different foreign countries, which leads in turn to different perceptions of national security threats caused by investments from different countries.

1.3 Internal Structure

1.3.1 The Role of Ideas

As a broad phenomenon, ideas in constructivism relating to international relations are common and collective products of beliefs and desires offered by an intentional explanation, which can be either publicly or privately shared.[9] A belief is *about* something, while a desire is *for* something.[10] Desire is a matter of passion or motivation, not cognition, but beliefs activate and channel desires as cognition, which cannot become desires.[11] The arguments of D' Andrade, Howe, and others concerned with the relationship between desire and belief refer mostly to individuals rather than groups, while Wendt argues that certain groups, including states, also have desires. Private ideas consist of beliefs and interests that one individual holds but others do not, while private ideas about a nation are shared by its people.

The beliefs of a nation-state about itself constitute its national identity, while its desires for itself constitute its national interest. According to Gilbert, beliefs can be ascribed to a group or even a nation that are not merely shared by individuals at any given moment but are inherently historical phenomena which are kept alive through the generations by an ongoing process of socialization and ritual enactment, as long as the individuals within the group or nation accept the legitimacy of the group or nation's decisions and the obligation to act in accordance with its results. Such beliefs, which are often inscribed in "collective memory", constitute who a group is and how it relates to others and will be available as a resource for mobilizing collective action even if they are not believed, in a phenomenological sense, by individuals, and in that way, they can help explain patterns in aggregate behavior.[12] As a result of struggles and wars caused by foreign countries in Chinese history, for example, at the earliest stage of the establishment of the People's Republic of China (PRC), the Chinese people, including their leaders, regarded the behavior toward China of foreign countries as inimical to and unhealthy for China's socialist development.

In other words, the idea of national security is the intersubjective belief about identity and desire for security shared by a nation's people, which generates a microlevel pattern in individual behaviors over time, and is constituted by its national identity and national interest. The Chinese, for example, have all shared for thousands of years a historical memory governed by the Confucian paradigm, which stresses nonviolent strategies and the equivalency of the role of emperor with that of Heaven (*tian*), a role broadly comparable to that of God in Western beliefs. It was therefore normal in China for imagery of the emperor and his bureaucracy to appear everywhere. As the internal stability of the family and the nation lies at the core of Confucianism, Chinese were satisfied with their *status quo* and resistant to encounters with the external world. This could explain the Chinese people's traditional conservativism and suspicion regarding foreign things, including foreign investment, which might threaten the nation's internal stability and security. China's national identity was formed under the guidance of the emperor and his bureaucracy, with the support of the people's beliefs. China's struggle of the past hundred years has strongly stimulated its people's sensitivity towards every aspect of national security, strengthening its resistance to foreign phenomena, including foreign investment. In other words, the Chinese have been relatively conservative in relation to foreign phenomena, and such conservatism in relation to national security has mainly been determined by subjective feelings, especially the dignity of the "self" and fear of the "other", concerning the pursuit of internal stability free from any potential foreign threats. China has its interest, furthermore, in achieving its promise to develop socialism, and the US has interests in promoting its values in every aspect, including both economic and political fields, in order to maintain its power in the global context. It is undeniable that China and the US, as sovereign states, not only have their own national identities, which include, respectively, socialism and capitalism, but also have different national interests, and this is true in the field of foreign investment as much as in other fields.

It may seem that there is no need to discuss and compare the ideas of national security in China and the US, as it is obvious that ideas on national security and foreign investment, or on national security reviews in China and the US are different. As this view is taken for granted most of the time, however, national security review in relation to Chinese and US investments in each other's countries are facing a security dilemma. Only when shared expectations are violated or international rules or customs are breached among nation-states can the significance of ideas in constituting who they are and what they want to do be realized.[13] Because of historical differences, however, it is hard to imagine that China and the US, starting from extremely contradictory positions and pulling in opposite directions might share a common path if determining factors leading to differences and commonalities cannot be identified. Only, therefore, if ideas can be found that are internally and externally rooted in China and the US in relation to national security reviews of foreign inward investment laws and practices might there be a possibility for these two countries to be oriented with great similarities and even achieve compromises, in such a way as to solve investment conflicts and design cooperative platforms.

By means of laws and practices, this book analyzes the ideas of national security in relation to foreign investment law shared by leaders and lawmakers and which determine their behavior in system formulation, and takes China and the

US as examples to prove the role of idea dominance. The term "internal idea" is employed when analyzing ideas owned by certain individuals in internal structures. It should be noted that the contents of "internal ideas" in the micro level of idea dominance and "external ideas" about the other at the macro level of process orientation refer to ideas owned by the leaders or lawmakers of a nation. The reason for focusing on ideas owned by lawmakers rather than on those held collectively by a nation, which constitute the core of constructivism in international relations, is that the aim of this book is to explore determinative factors in the evolving processes of national security reviews in Chinese and US foreign inward investment laws and practices. It is therefore the role of ideas owned by these individuals that is to be analyzed. The key difference between ideas in internal structure and external structure in this book is that internal ideas are naturally produced by both domestic and international conditions as a whole, while external ideas are specifically constituted by the interactive relationship with the other country, merely as an ideational product of bilateral relations. Chapter 2 and Chapter 3 analyze the dominant role of internal ideas in national security reviews in China and the US. Chapter 4 covers the role of external ideas owned by certain individuals either in China or the US.

1.3.2 The Effects of Ideas: Dominance

1.3.2.1 China

Historical memories of foreign phenomena, including foreign inward investment, have played a significant role in shaping China's internal ideas on national security and foreign inward investment from the earliest stage. Because of fears derived from wars and turmoil during the previous century, the newly established PRC, under the leadership of the Communist Party of China (CPC), strictly prohibited private ownership, with no exception for foreign inward investment. In the late 1970s, however, the idea that a strong modern economy was an urgent necessity if poverty was to be addressed came to the fore among the Chinese leadership, leading to the internal idea that the world market for foreign investment was of great importance to China and would enable it to increase capital and introduce advanced technology and modernized management.

Initially, there was an ideational struggle among the CPC leaders on the issue of whether allowing foreign investment would harm its national security. Two sides emerged: a moderate side favoring market reform and embracing foreign investment, and a conservative side supporting a centrally planned economy and the safeguarding of national security and perceiving foreign investment as a typical product of capitalism. As a compromise, the legal regime of foreign-invested enterprises laws (FIE laws) was established with a premise of pre-establishment approval steps for the establishment of FIEs, to avoid any potential breach of Chinese laws and regulations by foreign inward investment, which might threaten political stability and sovereignty. Despite the fact that the FIE laws failed to define national security concerning foreign inward investment, ideational concerns related to national security could be found in the conditions listed for consideration in the approval review at the market access. These included requirements to comply with Chinese laws and regulations and strictures on contractual equality, public interest, social order, and national economic development, which might be understood as the security of a socialist state with a centrally planned economy. One feature of China's foreign investment laws and practices is that the idea of national security was addressed through administrative discretion, rather than a legal approach, as the results of approval review for FIEs were determined by relevant government authorities.

In order to encourage foreign investment and protect national security in industrial fields, the emergence of the guidance system in the 1990s indicated China's new approach to governing foreign inward investment, which divided such investment into four categories: encouraged, permitted, restricted, and prohibited. At this stage, an innovative idea—socialism with Chinese characteristics—was introduced to promote socialist modernization. Also, the idea of the rule of law was gradually developed in relation to market activities. In the face of a changing external structure, especially when the Cold War ended, a paradigm shift on national security led to the introduction of a new security concept (NSC). With the NSC's assumption that war was not likely in the foreseeable future, economic security or economic modernization was closely associated with the idea of national security, in addition to those of sovereignty, independence, unity, and territorial integrity. The idea of national security reflected in the guidance system is to orient foreign investment in line with economic planning and social economic development. Despite the fact that the NSC revealed an assumption of no war in the near future, the security of national defense and its modernization remained a major strategic issue. The Catalogue for the Guidance of Industries for Foreign Investment of 1997 (Catalogue of 1997) clearly listed foreign investment that endangered the security of military facilities or their usability as prohibited. In addition, the ideological security of socialism was also stressed at this stage, in order to preserve socialist culture while continuously implementing the policy of reform and opening. On this matter, the Catalogue of 1997 elaborated to the effect that foreign investment projects which would endanger state security should be prohibited, as the idea of state security could be described as the stability of the socialist regime under the leadership of the CPC.

As the twenty-first century dawned, mergers and acquisitions (M&A) became a favorable form of foreign investment activity in China, as they avoided the strict regulatory process of approval review for both FIEs and foreign inward investment projects. The regulatory mechanism of M&A security review was established to address issues of national security with respect to foreign inward investment. Indeed, the phrase "national economic security" was expressed in M&A rules for the first time. That is to say that the idea of national security in relation to M&A security review was confined to the field of economics. The primary emphasis on national economic security was determined by the idea of national security and economic development under Hu Jintao's leadership. At that stage, national economic development was viewed as the basis for national economic security, within the ideological context of a scientific outlook on development, with the emphasis on security of strategic resources. Military security and security of scientific development were also integral to the idea of national security in M&A security review regime, as the impacts of M&A activities on national defense security and on the development capability of key technologies related to national security were matters that were considered in M&A security review.

Along with economic globalization and investment liberalization, the M&A security review has been developed into national security review for all foreign inward investments, not only those involving M&A, in experimental trials of free trade zones (FTZs) which attempted further liberalization of foreign investment by adopting pre-establishment national treatment and negative list. The Foreign Investment Law (FIL) of 2019 introduced experimental trials in FTZs nationwide. Although the FIL contains only one provision concerning national security review, the Measures for the Security Review of Foreign Investment in China ("Measures") provided detailed guidance for national security review. The idea of national security in the FIL is affected by a holistic approach to national security (HANS) in the face of the dynamic and changing internal and external structures. Within the guiding ideology of the HANS, national security is comprehensively divided into the following 11 categories: political security, homeland security, military security, economic security, cultural security, social security, science and technology security, information security, ecological security, resource security, and nuclear security. Specifically, the idea of national security involves the security of the socialist system, as security reviews will be conducted if foreign investment is deemed a potential threat to China's socialist regime. Furthermore, the security of the people has been further developed from the idea of national security in the scientific outlook on development, reflected in national security reviews in the emphasis on the basic order of social life. Homeland security and military security have always been aspects of the ideas of national security and foreign investment. As a result, the Measures require foreign investors or concerned parties to declare their investment plans if they invest in military industry, military-related supporting industry, and other fields related to national defense, or in military facilities and areas surrounding them. As the HANS stresses the significance of maintaining the basic economic system and the order of the socialist market economy, improving rules to resolve or prevent economic security risks, as well as safeguarding the security of important industries and crucial fields related to the lifeline of the national economy, the Measures highlights a number of critical sectors which require security reviews in relation to foreign investment, such as key information technology and internet products and services, key financial services, key technologies, and other key sectors. The idea of national security and foreign investment are also related to the security of resources and energy, which is developed from the idea of national security in the form of M&A security review. Consequently, under the FIL regime, particular attention must be paid in foreign inward investment national security review to critical energy and natural resources, critical transportation services and infrastructure. In addition, the HANS stresses the importance of grain security, and the Measures lists consideration of important agricultural products as regards national security review. Even though the factor of cultural security is not expressly mentioned in the Measures, the restricted and prohibited sectors reflected in the catalogues or negative lists show China's ideas on cultural security in relation to foreign investment. Because of the definition of security as regards science and technology, a foreign investor with actual control in critical technology is required to offer a declaration about security review. As emerging dimensions of national security, the cyber and information security are also taken into consideration in foreign inward investment national security review. Even though considerations of the security of the environment have been reflected in approval reviews of FIEs and foreign investment projects at the market access, moreover, the HANS reemphasizes and elaborates on them, resulting in the idea of ecological security in foreign inward investment national security review.

1.3.2.2 The US

It was not until the US participated in the First World War that it began to take national security concerns into consideration with respect to foreign inward investment, resulting in limited sectoral restrictions. In the 1970s, with the rapid growth of foreign investment in the US, the significance of analysis of the impacts of such investment on national security began to be appreciated. Against this background, the CFIUS was established, originally serving as a monitoring mechanism, but later developing into a powerful regulatory mechanism. The increasing investment from Japan raised national security concerns regarding foreign investment and led to the passage of the Exon-Florio Amendment, which authorized the US president to conduct national security review. This presidential power was later delegated to the CFIUS. Since then, the CFIUS has been a well-known interministerial agency governing national security aspects of foreign investment. There was an ideational debate on several issues, such as the role of the president and whether to incorporate economic factors into national security review. Compromises were reached and formulated in the Exon-Florio Amendment, which determined the final content of national security review. In terms of the presidential role in national security review, the president—rather than government departments as certain proposals had recommended—was eventually granted the power to veto foreign investments, and the exclusivity of that presidential power was guaranteed, as a proposal for a Congressional power of veto by means of bicameral resolution over such decisions was not adopted. These legal arrangements were designed to gain the support of the president for the enactment of the Exon-Florio Amendment in a tough ideational debate, but conditions were placed on such a determinative presidential role in order to facilitate a compromise between the president and Congress. Drafts of the Exon-Florio Amendment incorporated economic factors into national security review, but the idea of national security and foreign investment involving economic factors encountered strong oppositions from the executive branch, which consistently advocated investment liberalization and upheld the opening policy. After a fierce debate, it was widely recognized that basic economic issues arising from national security issues were hard to identify, and economic factors in national security review would inevitably result in obstacles to foreign investment. It was the abstract term "national security" in the broad sense—rather than such previous compromise suggestions as "essential commerce" or "economic welfare"—that was ultimately adopted in the Exon-Florio Amendment.

In the codification of the regulatory mechanism of national security review through the Foreign Investment and National Security Act (FINSA), the idea of national security and foreign investment in relation to critical infrastructure played a dominant role. Homeland security was highlighted and critical infrastructure began to be viewed as a vital aspect thereof. In terms of the ideas about past CFIUS practices, there were several negative comments objecting that the CFIUS's purpose of protecting national security in foreign investment had not been fully achieved. Critics of CFIUS practices argued—because of the insufficient timeframe for achieving a result in a preliminary national security review—that foreign investors or concerned parties in relation to foreign investments be encouraged to withdraw their investments and resubmit them for another national security review to extend the review process indirectly. Although the FINSA failed to make legal modifications to accommodate this ideational criticism, the fact of a growing number of national security investigations indicates a response in its enforcement. In addition, a similar ideational debate over the roles of Congress and president took place during drafting of the FINSA. It can be summarized in two parts: one is the veto power of Congress over presidential decisions; the other is congressional oversight of the process of national security review. Specifically, both Inhofe's bill and Shelby's bill involved the provision of congressional veto power, meaning that Congress could override a presidential decision of approval for foreign investments. As happened during the drafting of the Exon-Florio Amendment, these proposals for congressional veto power raised strong objections. Some critics even argued that such a legal arrangement was unconstitutional, as the president enjoys exclusive power over national security. They also argued that congressional veto power might disturb the balance between the long-held opening policy and the purpose of safeguarding national security and that the ultimate goal of establishing national security reviews would be lost, as the regulatory mechanism of national security review would be easily employed as a protectionist tool rather than an effective measure for preserving national security. In terms of ideas on the reporting requirements in national security reviews, there were some criticisms of CFIUS practices as the CFIUS did not require timely notification of the Congress about certain foreign investment deals. Because, in practice, moreover, only very few foreign investment review decisions are ultimately submitted to the president for decision, and Congress must be notified of the president's decision. Congress cannot be notified of most other investments that have not yet been submitted to the president. Responding to the inadequacy of requirements to report to Congress, which applied only during the presidential decision-making phase, the FINSA introduced regular reporting requirements to strengthen Congressional oversight of national security review.

In the reform of national security review required by the FIRRMA, ideas on national security and foreign investment led to an expanded scope of CFIUS jurisdiction. By newly incorporating foreign investment related to critical infrastructure, critical technology and sensitive personal data, ideas on national security and foreign investment, once confined to the traditional dimension, developed a broader sense. It could be anticipated that security in the field of key information and technology and the security necessary to maintaining US leadership or advantages in technology would be considered with particular concern in national security review. Ideas on national security, moreover, especially the emphasis on military security, might suggest that certain foreign investment in real estate close to military facilities and potentially threatening to military security might be subject to national security review as well. Compared to the ideational debate on congressional power and presidential action in the FINSA formulation process, the drafting of FIRRMA proceeded relatively smoothly. Despite the fact that presidential power was susceptible to constraint by increasingly robust Congressional oversight, the authority for determining the final results of national security reviews concerning foreign investments and for formulating national security policies in relation to foreign investment remained the preserve of the executive branch. It is worth noting that ideas on national security and Chinese investment played a significant role in reforming national security review through the FIRRMA, as the FIRRMA is widely regarded as a legal response to increasing Chinese investment which might threaten US national security, especially that relating to technological leadership. Although Chinese investment was not ultimately mentioned in the FIRRMA, it was listed in proposed drafts. Also, in practice, there is a growing number of Chinese investments that have been subject to national security reviews and suspended or prohibited by presidential orders since 2018 when the FIRRMA came into force.

1.4 External Structure

1.4.1 The Role of Process

Social process is always structured, and structure is always an ongoing process.[14] It is undoubtedly true that the domestic environment is also structured and instantiated by process.[15] In contrast to Waltz's deterministic view, Wendt's argument that the fact that agents are constructed by society and that structuring is a continual process might seem to suggest that society is infinitely changeable and even highly unstable.[16]

Such a constructivist approach to the ideational role in the process indicates that internal ideas of national security review seem to be changeable and even highly unstable, which also leads to changes in the legal behaviors and legal practices dominated by these concepts. This book argues that, even though a great and sudden shift in institutional reforms in the domestic environment might cause a quick change in ideas on national security and foreign investment, this ideational change still has to undergo a long and stable process in order for daily behaviors to adapt in, and transform into a real internal idea which plays a dominant role. To some degree, the adaption process by which such an external idea becomes an internal idea could also be explained as a natural process within the internal structure. Internal ideas on national security review reflect and dominate the natural evolving process in the micro structure. In other words, this natural process in the internal structure is the way in which internal ideas on national security and foreign investment finally gave rise to national security review in foreign investment laws and practices.

The process of ideas in the internal structure here is therefore not the main focus of this book, although both internal and external structures are always generated as part of a process. This part of this chapter analyzes the role of process in external structure and argues that a country's national security review in relation to foreign investment laws and practices is oriented by the process within the external structure of the other country through bilateral investment practices. Unlike the naturally changing developmental process of ideas at the micro level of internal structures, the process in external structures is quite quick and artificial. The following analysis attempts to explain how the external idea of the other nation-state in terms of national security and foreign investment is constituted by what the other nation perceives during the interaction process. It is a nation's laws and policies, that are most easily affected and oriented by the process of foreign investment practices in relation to other nations. That is to say that the evolutionary process of the regulatory mechanism of national security review of a country's foreign investment law is oriented to the other nation's corresponding mechanism through the process of interaction involving investment practices with other nations would constitute an external idea about the other and the other's investments. After a nation's legal regime is successfully oriented to those of the other nation, such an external idea reflected in the legal regime will be transformed into a nation's internal idea in the internal structure and then play a dominant role rather than an oriented role in external structure, only when such an external idea is naturally accepted within the internal structure through a long and stable internalization process.

When a nation starts to interact with another nation, its privately held ideas on the other nation may have emergent effects, which might be influenced by the shared ideas of its people in its internal structure, such as those of historical memory, culture, and tradition. No idea held by either side is either right or wrong, regardless of any basis in relevant experience.[17] A nation therefore needs to define its security situations before it chooses a course of law and practice. Wendt points out that some scholars would deny that contemporary nations share a great many beliefs about the rules of the international game, who its players are, what their interests are, what rational behavior is, and so on, while few would deny that the structure of the contemporary international system contains a lot of culture.[18] Such a culture in the international system is deeply embedded in the way in which policymakers and scholars alike understand the nature of politics, economy, and law, both in internal and external structures, considering national identities and national interests which reflect beliefs about who they are in the international social system and what the nation thinks the other nation would do.[19] When their national identities and national interests are not shared or when there is no shared knowledge of their situations in external structure, these nations are likely to be surprised by each other's behavior, and the outcomes may call their ideas into questions.[20]

In contrast to the dominant role of ideas in internal structure, the idea of a nation's security based on its national identity and national interest is also oriented by other nations' ideas, what and how the other nation believes such a nation's security to be. That is to say, the other's perceptions of the self constitute the self's idea of itself regarding security in the external structure and vice versa. Interaction also strengthens the shared knowledge between these external ideas on each other. In external structure, the other's ideas on the national security of the self in turn strengthen the self's ideas on its own national security and affect the self's behaviors in foreign investment laws and practices. If China and the US failed to enjoy a shared knowledge of each other's identities and interests in the international structure, any laws and practices concerning national security reviews in foreign investment between these two countries would surprise the other, which might exacerbate conflicts and ideational misunderstandings. To be specific, the idea of a proposition of China's non-market economy is common to the US if it believes that China's economy is socialist and not market-oriented, and China in turn believes that the US believes such a perception. The idea of a proposition of US hegemony is common to China if China believes that the US economy is aimed at maintaining a hegemonic position in the external structure, and if the US also believes that China strongly holds such a view.

Globalization has been an obvious process in the international system for several decades, which has significantly affected the politics and economy of the entire world.[21] Each nation makes great efforts to follow this mainstream trend. Opening up to foreign investment, with its purpose of promoting economic liberalization and encouraging foreign investors in host countries, is one of the major behaviors associated with globalization. Foreign investment is primarily a game created for developed nations to seek more resources and gain more economic growth in both internal and external structures. Globalization is in part a process by which nations learn how to conform to international expectations.[22] China's efforts in recent years and in accordance with international rules constitute a process of learning to conform in order to achieve other countries'—especially developed countries'—expectations of it, in external structures. After 1949, China and the US met with each other with private beliefs on the "self" and "other" which were internally constituted by their ideas on identities and interests. Because of the Chinese people's shared idea of socialism, the US regarded China as a socialist country; a country, therefore, with an ideology extremely different from its own capitalism. This shared US idea increased obstacles to US recognition of China's market economy position in international society. This situation was highly structured by each other's ideas, arising from past situations, about each other's identity. Before the establishment of the PRC, for example, the Qing Dynasty refused to welcome foreign investment and regarded foreign investors as exploiters, while at the same time the US invested vigorously overseas and encouraged the liberalization of foreign investment practices. Today, however, amid the trend for globalization, the two nations already know a lot about each other, and important elements of their ideas have been shared—not all elements, to be sure, but important elements nonetheless. They have some shared ideas, such as what the identities of "self" and the "other" are, what sovereignty implies, what international rules require, what a free trade regime or foreign investment regime is, how to be engaged in investment interactions with other nation-states and how to solve investment conflicts with other states, and so on. China began to open up and participate in investment liberalization in the external structure, and since then, investors from the US have been increasingly willing to invest in China. The relevance of common knowledge is not limited to cooperative relations, however.[23] Shared beliefs among nation-states can even constitute an economic war or a perpetual peace. Just as in game theory, shared ideas are analytically neutral between conflict and cooperation.[24] This constructivist argument could explain why a trade war occurred between China and the US with the result of further legislative reforms on national security in relation to foreign investments, even though they already have some common and shared knowledge of each other.

In this case, because of the extremely mutually conflicting identities—socialism and capitalism—it is hard for a distribution of shared ideas to institute a cooperative culture between China and the US at the macro level; in the external structure, even though US values of political democracy and economic capitalism are widespread, international politics and economics have not formed such a global democratic and capitalist culture. The achievement of free trade zones to liberalize economic activities in China cannot be regarded as the creation of a culture. As to constitutive effects, in external structure where a nation's dominant position is legitimate, such a nation will be empowered by the community of other nations to perform the functions of, and thus literally be, a hegemon.[25] In the external structure, where such a nation's intentions in a dominant position have a strictly internal basis, other nations will attribute to it the identity of a bully or an imperialist.[26] That is to say, in a constructivist view, it is the idea owned by the "other" about the "self" that decides whether the self is an economic hegemon, not the self by itself, and in that sense, the cultural constitution of identity or subjectivity is a form of power.[27] A nation may eventually be able to socialize others to accept its self-ascribed hegemonic identity in economics, but until it does so, it will be only a materially dominant state in the international economy, not a hegemon widely recognized by others.[28]

Drawing on insights upon the emphasis of constructivism on the role of the idea owned by the self and the other, which will determine and shape foreign relations and national identities, such a constructivist view is employed in the external structure to explain the oriented process between national security reviews in China and the US by means of their bilateral investment practices to constitute external idea on the other. Under the trend of globalization, China has attempted to follow the international rules of foreign investments, and its regulatory regime is directly transplanted from that of the US. It has taken a long time, however, for China to fully transplant and absorb the legal arrangements created by the ideas rooted in the internal US structure. That is why national security reviews of Chinese and US foreign investment laws and practices enjoy great similarities but retain areas of great conflict which are difficult to address.

1.4.2 The Effect of Process: Orientation

On the one hand, it is undoubtedly the case that, in a host country ideas on investment from a foreign country will affect the formulation and implementation of the host country's national security review of foreign investment laws and practices. To be specific, foreign investment practices in the US orient its national security review to be reformed. Similar to the Japanese investment of the 1980s that led to the introduction of the national security review through the Exon-Florio Amendment, for example, the transaction by which UNOCAL was acquired by China's CNOOC raised concerns about national security, which spurred the enactment of the FINSA. As Congress intervened arbitrarily in this deal on national security grounds, national security review under the Exon-Florio Amendment was viewed as a weak and unreliable instrument which needed to be improved. The FINSA therefore enhanced congressional involvement in a highly legal manner. Before the introduction of the FIRRMA, national security concerns about Chinese investment grew, resulting, in recent years, in an increased number of Chinese investments being reviewed by the CFIUS. Taking the field of telecommunications in the US as an example, Chinese investments received special scrutiny from the CFIUS. Two transactions by Huawei, for example, were eventually withdrawn as a result of national security reviews. The key reason for repeated failures of Huawei's investments in the US was the US idea about the corporate identity of Huawei, as Huawei was perceived to maintain a close relationship to the Chinese military. These Chinese investments which were regarded to threaten US national security inspired the US to strengthen the regulatory mechanism of national security review of foreign investment, especially foreign investment involving foreign governments. As a result, any investment controlled by a foreign government and related to critical technology, critical infrastructure, sensitive personal data falls within the scope of mandatory declaration in the reformed legal regime of the FIRRMA. Also, the wind farm assets from Terna Energy US Holding (Terna) close to a claimed restricted airbase acquired by Ralls Corporation (Ralls) which was an affiliate of a Chinese enterprise, were required to be divested, prompting Ralls to file a lawsuit against the CFIUS and the US president for due process claims. In order to avoid embarrassment of the sort caused by Ralls' lawsuit, the FIRRMA requires certain foreign investments in real estate close to sensitive military facilities—either airports or maritime ports—to be reviewed by the CFIUS on national security grounds. This addition means that foreign investments similar to that of Ralls might be subject to national security review under the FIRRMA.

In stark contrast to the US, China initially held a conservative attitude towards foreign investment. Since the beginning of the reform and opening up policy in 1978, foreign investment has gradually been allowed in China. Under the legal regime of FIE laws, different types of foreign investment, namely, FIEs, foreign investment projects and foreign investment M&As, have been encouraged and subject to governance. Driven by national security concerns, the approval review for the establishment of FIEs at the market access, approval review at the market access for foreign investment projects, and M&A security review have been established step by step in order to safeguard national security when attracting and encouraging foreign investment. With the advent of the twenty-first century, a dramatic surge in foreign investment M&A activities took place in China. Because the growth of foreign investment M&As significantly contributed to China's economic development, M&A became a favorable choice by which foreign investors could invest in China, in such a way as to escape strict approval reviews at the market access which had been stipulated for the establishment of FIEs and foreign investment projects in industrial sectors. Against this background, China incorporated foreign investment and mergers and acquisitions into the security review system. To be specific, in 2005, when Xugong was acquired by Carlyle Group (Carlyle), this deal was reviewed by the Ministry of Commerce (MOFCOM) in the name of M&A review, but it eventually failed because the suspension of the review process for over three years made the bid ineffective. Without an appropriate legal instrument, China's idea of preserving national security from foreign investments could only be achieved through government discretion and without transparency in practice, making the results unreliable. This acquisition raised a heated debate over the question of whether MOFCOM's response on national security grounds was justified, as the failure of Carlyle's acquisition of Xugong was viewed as a nationalistic backlash in light of the obstacles presented by US national security review to the acquisition of UNOCAL by China's CNOOC a few months earlier. In the same year that the Carlyle deal was thwarted, previous M&A rules which had not involved national security concerns were revised and introduced the regulatory mechanism of security review for foreign M&A investments to take national economic security into consideration. Another acquisition—of Chinese national champion Huiyuan by Coca-Cola—met similar obstacles. Having remained silent for three years during the review process on the Carlyle transaction, in 2009, MOFCOM took only six months to reach a decision prohibiting Coca-Cola's deal in an anti-monopoly review. Despite the fact that the reason for such a result was based on competition issues with little relation to national security, suspicions that considerations of national security played a significant role in the review process never abated. To some extent, anti-monopoly review on foreign investments at this stage could be regarded as an embryonic form of national security review, which had been established and developed in the US. This indicates that China's scrutiny over foreign investments on national security grounds had been oriented to a rather independent and legalistic approach: that of the US national security review conducted by the CFIUS. The rules of the M&A security review were eventually issued in 2011. Since then, the basis for an independent security review for foreign investment has been formed, though it has been adopted only in relation to foreign investment M&As. Under the reformed legal regime of the FIL, national security review for foreign investment has been established and adopted nationwide in the form of national law. It is worth noting that Yonghui's acquisition of Zhongbai was the first case of national security review in China, indicating that the enforcement of national security review would become the norm in practice, rather than a "paper tiger" as in the past. Even though the retail sector, in which this transaction was initiated, may appear irrelevant to national security, a national security review was still conducted and resulted in the prohibition of the transaction in April 2019. The Measures of late 2019 requires other critical sectors, in the case of foreign investments with actual control, to be subject to national security review, in addition to specifying several sectors deemed essential to national security. This arrangement could help to avoid embarrassment of Yonghui's acquisition in the retail sector, which was not listed as an essential sector in relation to national security.

On the other hand, the host country's national security review of foreign investment laws and practices is also affected by its ideas about its outbound investment to the other country and in relation to the other country's national security review. That is to say that the national security review treatment of its own investment in the other country orients its ideas on national security and foreign investment towards the other's ideas. To be specific, as China held a conservative polity towards foreign investment for a long time, the US perceived that its investments in China were treated discriminatorily, and in a manner running counter to its own friendly attitude toward Chinese investment, which it perceived as unfair to US investments. US investments in China had to encounter a variety of reviews reflecting China's national security concerns, such as approval review for the establishment of US-invested enterprises, review of US investment in industrial fields at the market access, as well as M&A security review, which, amid a lack of transparency and efficiency, caused great inconvenience to US investments. A number of US investments, especially M&As, failed in China at the stage of anti-monopoly review, while it was widely perceived by the US that China's national security concerns played a significant role in determining such unsatisfactory results. In responding to China's dramatic economic growth, moreover, the US gradually formed the perception of China as a strategic competitor or rival. As a result of perceived threats from Chinese investment in the US, especially in relation to US technological leadership in the world, a broader scope of foreign investment, including critical technology and sensitive personal data, which would fall within US national security review is covered by the FIRRMA. FIRRMA and the regulations associated with it are oriented to resemble China's all-inclusive approach to supervising foreign investment, which had been adopted at the market access within the traditional legal regime of FIE Laws. Similarly, China's ideas on its own investments in the US, especially the failures of its investment there, also orient national security review in China's foreign investment laws and practices to resemble the corresponding regulatory mechanism in the US.

Despite the fact that the majority of Chinese investments have been accepted in the US, the investments that have been prohibited or suspended by the US president all came from China or at least had a close relation to China, giving rise to the suspicion that such judgments are affected by the principle of reciprocity for unequal treatment of US investments in the corresponding sectors of the Chinese domestic market. With attempts to address increasingly hostile US ideas towards Chinese investment, China has made further great efforts to reform and open its domestic market to foreign investment, including investment from the US. The principles, for example, of pre-establishment national treatment and negative lists, advocated by the US, have been adopted in China, in order to provide an improved investment environment with fairness, transparency, and predictability. The failure of CNOOC's acquisition of UNOCAL inspired Chinese policymakers to consider the possibility of incorporating national security concerns in an independent regulatory instrument to distinguish from other instruments focusing on economic issues, which led to the introduction of M&A security review for foreign investment in the subsequent M&A rules. The challenges of US national security reviews encountered by Chinese investments, such as the repeated failures of Huawei in the US, moreover, accelerated China's path towards further reforming and opening its domestic market for foreign investment, in order to reduce or eliminate US criticisms or discriminatory ideas about the Chinese domestic market. The previous legal regime of the FIE Laws, which operated a two-track system towards domestic investment and foreign investment, has been abolished and replaced by a unified legal regime of the FIL, which, in general, grants equal treatment to both domestic investment and foreign investment, a practice which has already been adopted in the US for several decades. Chinese investment in the US also orients China's national security review to resemble the US national security review: normalized and liberalized.

1.5 The Theoretical Framework of Idea Dominance and Process Orientation in Comparing National Security Reviews

As mentioned previously, China is developing from a position of extreme restrictiveness, because of national security concerns, as regards foreign investment and towards gradual liberalization (Figure 1.1), while the US is developing from full liberalization of foreign investment towards gradual restrictions because of national security worries (Figure 1.2). When we compare China and the US, it is interesting to find that even though they are developing from extremely opposite starting points, they are oriented with each other with great similarities as regards national security reviews of investment practices (Figure 1.3). To be specific, Chapter 2 explains the dominant role of China's internal ideas on the evolving process of its national security review, which is shown in Figure 1.1. Chapter 3 analyzes the dominant role of US internal ideas on its evolving process of national security review, as shown by Figure 1.2. Chapter 4 points out the oriented role

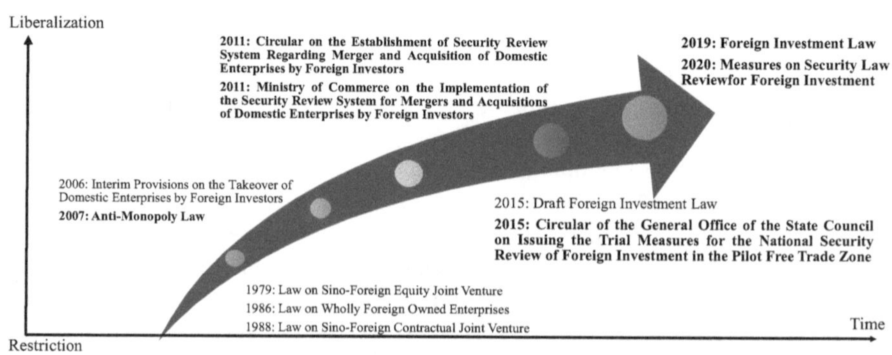

Figure 1.1 China's Evolving Process of National Security Review in Foreign Investment Law

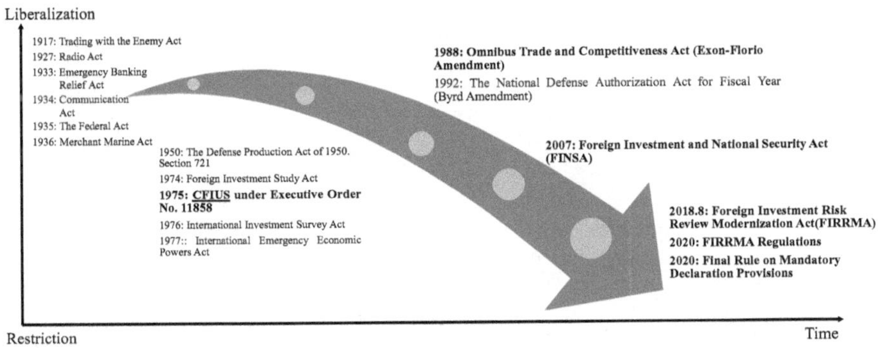

Figure 1.2 Evolving US Process of National Security Review in Foreign Investment Law

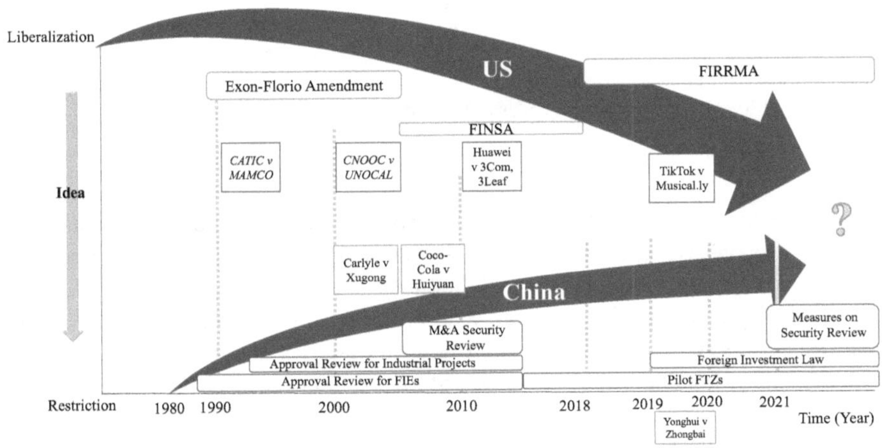

Figure 1.3 An Oriented Process of National Security Review in China and US Foreign Investment Laws and Practices

of the process of investment practices between China and the US in relation to national security review, in order to explain a mutually oriented process in national security review between them, as demonstrated in Figure 1.3.

A theoretical framework, which could be summarized as idea dominance and process orientation, as shown in Figure 1.4, could be established to explain and compare national security reviews. In terms of idea dominance, either for State A or State B, it is ideas in the internal structure, namely internal ideas, on national security and foreign investment, or on national security review, that dominate its formulation of national security reviews. Such an internal idea is owned by law-makers. Process orientation is the process whereby bilateral investment practices orient one country's national security review to resemble the other's. State A's investment in State B, for example, orients State B's national security review to

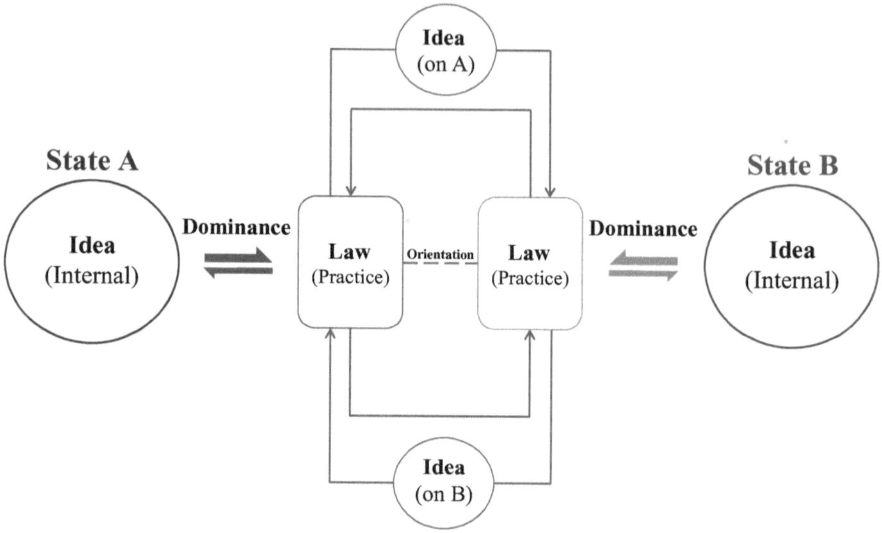

Figure 1.4 Idea Dominance and Process Orientation

resemble State A's, and such an investment practice in relation to State B's national security review also constitutes State A's external idea on State B and State B's investment, and then orients State A's national security review to resemble State B's. It is worth noting that such an external idea reflected in State A's national security review will be transformed into an internal idea and then play a dominant role only when it is naturally accepted within the internal structure through a long and stable process.

This book takes China and the US as examples, and in Figure 1.4, State A refers to China and State B refers to the US. Chinese investments in the US, for instance, orient US national security reviews to resemble China's approach in two respects. On the one hand, Chinese investment in the US directly influences US lawmakers to form an external idea on Chinese investment on national security grounds. That is why the failed investments in UNOCAL by CNOOC and Terna by Ralls led to the addition of critical infrastructure, especially from the energy industry, and certain real estate transactions to the CFIUS's jurisdiction. On the other hand, Chinese investment in the US also orients China's approach to resemble that of the US, by constituting an external idea on the US owned by China, which orients China to reform and modernize its national security review with the purpose of easing investment obstacles in the US encountered by Chinese investments, and US investment in China which also orients the US to strengthen its scrutiny, especially of Chinese investment. It is worth noting that, in this book, internal ideas and external ideas are similarly owned by leaders and lawmakers. The main difference is that internal ideas are naturally shaped by internal and external conditions as a whole, while external ideas are constituted by bilateral investment interaction with the other country. The former focuses on the law-making process internally, and the latter highlights the matter of foreign relations.

This theoretical framework will be further explained and examined in following chapters. In Chapter 2 and Chapter 3, which focuses on internal ideas in China and the US, it is worth noting that internal ideas in China and the US have slightly different meanings. In China, the internal idea mainly focuses, for several reasons, on national security and foreign investment that is owned by CPC leaders. First, an independent regulatory mechanism of national security review for foreign investment M&As was firstly formed in 2011; the internal idea on national security review did not exist in previous history. It was the internal idea on national security and foreign investment scattered in various legal forms that played a dominant role. Second, the CPC plays the leadership role in the state legislature and lawmaking.[29] In the internal structure of China, all lawmakers must abide by the party line and always conform with the CPC's policies and preferences.[30] It is, therefore, specifically the internal idea owned by CPC leaders on national security and foreign investment that dominates China's evolving legal performance of national security review in foreign investment law. On the one hand, as the CPC controls China's law-making process, the ideas of CPC leaders not only reflect the shared idea of the Chinese people on national security and foreign investment but also dominantly affect the ideas of lawmakers on this issue. On the other hand, information about the internal ideas of CPC leaders on this issue is much easier to be found and collected, from concepts, policies, systems, and other discursive means initiated by them. Slightly different from China's internal ideas, analyzed in Chapter 2, the internal ideas in the US mainly focus on national security review owned by lawmakers, as explained in Chapter 3. First, the US established the regulatory mechanism of national security review in 1988, and all the evolving phases of it have developed from this earliest stage; internal ideas on national security review have existed in the US for several decades, which could directly reflect the intentions in the internal structure. Second, because of the nature of political regimes in the US, with its separation of powers, the internal ideas consist primarily of presidential and congressional ideas. Congressional ideas are particularly easily affected by self-interested private groups who have incentives to exploit US fear of certain foreign investments, the media in promoting a public discourse of national security fear of foreign investment for the purpose of increasing ratings and viewership, and governmental officials' interests in re-election or promotion.[31] That is why Congress may well respond to ideas owned by the public and positively intervene in national security reviews conducted by the CFIUS. This brings us to the analysis of US internal ideas on national security review owned by congressmen, presidents, governmental officials, as well as businessmen in related industries, which are discussed in Chapter 3 in detail.

Interestingly, the legal performance which is reflected in the final texts of laws is dominated by internal ideas as a compromise through a process of consultation, negotiation, and bargaining among lawmakers, which means that process orientation also works in the internal structure to reach a shared idea in law from a micro perspective. Similar to the oriented role of process in the internal structure in the form of internal ideas, ideas also work in the external structure of process orientation, by constituting an external idea about the other by means of bilateral investment practices. In this way, ideas not only play a dominant role in internal structures but also dominate the oriented process. Process orientation not only exists in external structures but also works in internal structures through internal ideas. The oriented process in internal structures to reach a shared internal idea in legal behaviors and the dominated role of a country's external ideas in the oriented process in external structures, though not the main subjects of this book, are analyzed in Chapters 2 and 3's explanation of China's and the US's internal ideas, and Chapter 4's analysis of their oriented process in external structure.

Notes

1 Onuf, Nieholas. "Parsing Personal Identity: Self, Other, Agent." In Debrix, F. (Ed). *Language, Agency and Politics in a Constructed World.* New York: M.E. Sharpe, 2003, 26–49.
2 Wendt, Alexander. "Anarchy Is What States Make of It: The Social Construction of Power Politics." *International Organization* 46 (1992): 391–425; Wendt, Alexander. *Social Theory of International Politics*. New York: Cambridge University Press, 1999.
3 Weldes, Jutta. "Constructing National Interests." *European Journal of International Relations*, no. 2 (1996): 275–318; Weldes, Jutta. *Cultures of Insecurity: States, Communities, and the Production of Danger*. Minneapolis: University of Minnesota Press, 1999.
4 Theys, Sarina. "Introducing Constructivism in International Relations Theory." 2018. www.e-ir.info/2018/02/23/introducing-constructivism-in-international-relations-theory/.
5 Wendt, Alexander. *Social Theory of International Politics*. New York: Cambridge University Press, 1999, 135.
6 National Commission on Terrorist Attacks. *The 9/11 Commission Report: Final Report of the National Commission on Terrorist Attacks Upon the United States*. New York: W. W. Norton & Company, 2004.
7 Lippert, Barbara and Perthes, Volker. "Strategic Rivalry between United States and China." 2020. www.swp-berlin.org/10.18449/2020RP04/.
8 Foreign Investment Risk Review Modernization Act of 2018, H. R. 115–784, 115th Congress, 2nd Session.
9 Wendt, Alexander. "Anarchy Is What States Make of It: The Social Construction of Power Politics." *International Organization* 46 (1992): 391–425.
10 Locke, Don. "Beliefs, Desires and Reasons for Action." *American Philosophical Quarterly* 19, no. 3 (1982): 241–249; Wertz, Annie and German, Tamsin. "Belief-desire Reasoning in the Explanation of Behavior: Do Actions Speak Louder Than Words." *Cognition* 105 (2007): 184–194.
11 Wendt, Alexander. *Social Theory of International Politics*. New York: Cambridge University Press, 1999, 119.
12 Wendt, Alexander. *Social Theory of International Politics*. New York: Cambridge University Press, 1999, 163.
13 Wendt, Alexander. *Social Theory of International Politics*. New York: Cambridge University Press, 1999, 187–188.
14 Wendt, Alexander. *Social Theory of International Politics*. New York: Cambridge University Press, 1999, 186.
15 Cortell, Andrew and Davis, James. "How Do International Institutions Matter? The Domestic Impact of International Rules and Norms." *International Studies Quarterly* 40, no. 4 (1996): 458.
16 Wendt, Alexander. *Social Theory of International Politics*. New York: Cambridge University Press, 1999, 186–187.

17 Weber, Max. *Economy and Society: An Outline of Interpretive Sociology*. Berkeley, CA: University of California Press, 1978, 88.
18 Wendt, Alexander. *Social Theory of International Politics*. New York: Cambridge University Press, 1999, 190.
19 Somers, Margaret. "What's Political or Cultural about Political Culture and the Public Sphere? Toward an Historical Sociology of Concept Formation." *Sociology Theory* 13, no. 2 (1995): 113–144.
20 Kukla, Andre. "The Structure of Self-Fulfilling and Self-Negating Prophecies." *Theory & Psychology* 4, no. 1 (1994): 21.
21 Bacchetta, Marc and Jansen, Marion. *Making Globalization Socially Sustainable*. Geneva: International Labor Organization and World Trade Organization, 2011.
22 Nye, Joseph. "Nuclear Learning and U.S.-Soviet Security Regimes." *International Organization* 41, no. 3 (1987): 371–402.
23 Wendt, Alexander. *Social Theory of International Politics*. New York: Cambridge University Press, 1999, 160.
24 Wendt, Alexander. *Social Theory of International Politics*. New York: Cambridge University Press, 1999, 43.
25 Wendt, Alexander. *Social Theory of International Politics*. New York: Cambridge University Press, 1999, 177–178; Schimidt, Brain. "Hegemony: A Conceptual and Theoretical Analysis." 2018. https://doc-research.org/2018/08/hegemony-conceptual-theoretical-analysis/.
26 Wendt, Alexander. *Social Theory of International Politics*. New York: Cambridge University Press, 1999, 177–178.
27 Cho, Young. "Conventional and Critical Constructivist Approaches to National Security: An Analytical Survey." *Korean Journal of International Relations* 49, no. 3 (2009): 75–102.
28 Foucault, Michel. *Discipline and Punish*. New York: Vintage Books, 1979; Foucault, Michel. "The Subject and Power." *Critical Inquiry* 8, no. 4 (1982): 777–795; Dews, Peter. "Power and Subjectivity in Foucault." *New Left Review* 144 (1984): 72–95.
29 Wang, Jiangyu. "The Chinese Communist Party in China's Legislature and Judiciary." In Lance, Gore and Zheng Yongnian (Eds). *The Chinese Communist Party in Action: Consolidating Party Rule*. London: Routledge, 2020, 182–183.
30 Wang, Jiangyu. "The Chinese Communist Party in China's Legislature and Judiciary." In Lance, Gore and Zheng Yongnian (Eds). *The Chinese Communist Party in Action: Consolidating Party Rule*. London: Routledge, 2020, 182–183.
31 Zhang, Huyue. "Foreign Direct Investment from China: Sense and Sensibility." *Northwestern Journal of International Law & Business* 34, no. 3 (2014): 416–421.

2 Idea Dominance in National Security Review of Foreign Investment Laws in China

2.1 National Security and Foreign Investment in the FIE Legal Regime

The year 1978 witnessed a remarkable transition into a socialist market economy, when the Third Plenary Session of the Eleventh Central Committee of the CPC proclaimed the inception the Reform and Opening-up policy in China.[1] The earliest law on foreign investment was the Law on Sino-Foreign Equity Joint Ventures (EJV Law) of 1979, with its short 15 general clauses.[2] The Regulations for the Implementation of EJV Law (Regulations on the EJV Law) were issued in 1980 as a legal supplement to provide necessary guidance for foreign investors and regulators.[3] This legislative trend towards foreign investment continued to be applied for the other two types of foreign-invested enterprises, that is, wholly foreign owned enterprises and Sino-foreign contractual joint ventures, and the Law on Wholly Foreign-owned Enterprises Law (WFOE Law) and the Law on Chinese-Foreign Contractual Joint Ventures (CJV Law) were promulgated in 1986 and 1988 respectively.[4] From the late 1970s to the 1990s, these three FIE Laws and corresponding implementing regulations formed the initial basic framework for foreign investment in China, with the purpose of attracting and governing FIEs.[5] Later, between 1990 and 2000, the catalogue system for foreign investment projects in industrial sectors was gradually established, and M&A security review for foreign investment M&As emerged through M&A rules from 2003.

2.1.1 The Emergence of Approval Review for FIEs

Pursuant to the FIE Laws, FIE applicants were required to obtain administrative approval from the Ministry of Commerce (MOFCOM) before applying for business registration. Although such an approval review was not expressly identified as being for the purpose of safeguarding national security, the latter was undoubtedly one of the core considerations for this regulatory instrument at the market access, which was opaque and excessively cautious as summarized by a number of conditions for approval review listed throughout he FIE Laws

After serving their purpose for several decades, the FIE Laws were suspended in FTZs in 2013 and became ineffective nationwide in 2016, when the State Council

DOI: 10.4324/9781003543749-2

issued the Decision on Revising the Wholly Foreign-Owned Enterprises Law, the Sino-Foreign Equity Joint Venture Law, the Sino-Foreign Cooperative Joint Venture Law, and the Law on the Protection of Investment of Taiwan Compatriots (Decision on Revising the FIE Laws), which attempted to adopt filing mode for approval review at the market access.[6] Even though the impacts of the approval review at the market access, under the legal regime of the FIE Laws, had lasted 37 years—from 1979 to 2016. Chapter 2 focuses only on analyzing the dominant role of internal ideas on national security and foreign investment in the process of emergence of each regulatory instrument.

2.1.1.1 The Historical Legacy of Chinese Ideas on National Security and Foreign Investment

History plays a significant role in shaping choices.[7] The formulation of national security review in the FIE Laws was connected to long-standing Chinese ideas on national security and foreign investment. An era of extended military aggression by foreign countries began in 1839 with the first Opium War, caused by Britain's military response to the Qing Dynasty's attempt to suppress the opium trade.[8] As a result of the Opium War, the Qing government was forced to cede sovereign rights over territory to the British. A series of other unequal agreements were concluded in the form of treaties between China and other imperialist powers. Corporations established by investment from foreign countries which signed such unequal treaties with China were permitted to hold extraterritorial rights in strategic Chinese territories beyond the reach of Chinese jurisdiction.[9] In most cases, possession of enterprises in which Chinese and foreigners invested jointly was in the hands of foreigners and the Chinese had little authority over management and profits, even where the Chinese partners held majority equity.[10]

Mindful of a century of turmoil and wars throughout Chinese territory, the Chinese people perceived investment from foreign countries as a major instrument of economic encroachment, which might eventually develop into military invasions.[11] These fears derived from the past century contributed to insular policies and determined an extremely conservative policy concerning economic activity from the establishment of the PRC until 1978, when the urgent task was to maintain China's newly established independence and sovereignty. Private ownership was strictly prohibited at this stage. No commercial enterprise run by foreign investments could be found in China.[12] The policy of reform and opening up was initiated in 1978 allowing private ownership. Foreign investment took place in China when the EJV Law was promulgated in 1979.

Fears, however, that foreign investment might endanger China's hard-won sovereignty and lead to a repetition of the earlier depredations meted out by foreigners failed to subside. The regulatory approach was established of approval review for FIEs at the market access on a case-by-case basis. Ideas on national security concerning foreign investments were mainly those of a traditional context closely linked with sovereignty and independence and were among the major considerations during the approval review. The Regulations on the EJV Law in 1983, for example, clearly pointed out that, if an FIE was detrimental to China's sovereignty, approval at the market access was not to be granted. This applied also to the other two types of FIEs, contractual joint ventures and wholly owned foreign-invested enterprises, through the WFOE Law and the CJV Law, as well as the regulations governing their implementation.[13]

Because of the historical experience of foreign investments which enjoyed extraterritorial rights in the foreign concessions, the significance of obeying Chinese laws and regulations was emphatically stated in the FIE Laws. Another legal reflection on national security concerns in the FIE Laws is that foreign investment activities in the forms of EJVs, WFOEs, and CJVs should be conducted under the jurisdiction of Chinese laws and regulations.[14] To be specific, an equity joint venture would not be granted an approval license if it violated Chinese law.[15] For approval for their establishment, both a cooperative enterprise and a wholly owned foreign-invested enterprise were to comply with Chinese laws and regulations.[16] The legislative goal of the emphasis on FIE compliance with Chinese laws and regulations was to avoid any breach by foreign investors, which might threaten political stability and sovereignty.

2.1.1.2 Ideas on National Security and Foreign Investment in the Formulation of FIE Laws

Before the policy of reform and opening up in 1978, the academic world had analyzed neither national security issues nor foreign investment, but ideas on national security never disappeared in China and were understood to concern the resolute fight against imperialism for the sake of maintaining China's hard-won sovereignty and independence.[17] As the ideological emphasis on national security focused on the political and military fields, the tasks of safeguarding territorial integrity and consolidating national defense were paramount.

By 1978, if economic performance was to be improved, the need for a strong, modern economy was urgent.[18] Throughout the 1970s and 1980s, the benign influence of foreign investment in improving economic development and enhancing living standards was conspicuous in the economic miracles that occurred in Japan and Singapore and was witnessed by officials in the course of visits to developed economies and numerous collaborations with specialists from international organizations, like the World Bank. The idea that the world market, including foreign investment, would be of great importance to China as a means of bringing about modern corporate governance, advanced techniques of production and industrial know-how, and in turn fostering a higher domestic quality of life was widely recognized in China.[19] Deng Xiaoping, as the leader at that time, for example, listed three benefits of FIEs during a visit to Singapore in 1978: the government received 35 percent of FIEs' profits in taxation; employees received wages for their labor; domestic service industries were encouraged.[20] The policy of permitting foreign investment was affirmed in an amended state constitution, and foreigners were permitted to run businesses by various forms of economic cooperation with Chinese enterprises and other Chinese economic organizations, as long as they abided by Chinese laws and regulations.[21] The FIE Laws were promulgated to specify the corporation types for foreign investment, namely, EJVs, CJVs, and WFOEs.

National security worries concerning foreign investment were not immediately eliminated at this stage. Initially, there was ideological struggle in the leadership on the issue of whether embracing foreign investment would harm national security, leading to a two-way factional split throughout the 1980s: a moderate faction supported market reform and attracting foreign investment, and a conservative faction favored a central, command economy and protection of national security.[22] The moderate leaders contended that the FIEs, which would introduce modern management methods, enhance advanced machinery, and upgrade finance and industry, could resolve the problem of poor economic performance and further promote economic modernization. Li Xiannian, as the vice premier at this stage, for example, viewed foreign investment as a tool for reducing the fiscal pressure created by direct purchases of foreign technology, as advanced technology was accessible to FIEs.[23] Deng, who represented moderate leaders in rebutting the view that a market economy could exist only within a capitalist system, held the view that national economic development and socialist modernization were further important reflections of national security.[24] The Regulations on the EJV Law in 1983 and the Regulations for the Implementation of WFOE Law (Regulations on the WFOE Law) in 1990 both required a joint venture and a wholly owned foreign-invested enterprise in order to comply with the requirement to develop China's national economy.[25]

Both sets of regulations perceived foreign investment as a typical product of capitalism, which was totally incompatible with socialism at this stage when safeguarding the socialist regime was to be regarded as a prominent task. Chen Yun, for example, created the theory of the bird-cage economy to point out the inherent defects of market economies and argue that a socialist economy should be established by centralized planning and that the market should serve merely as a supplementary adjustment mechanism.[26] Such an opinion implied that all economic activities, including foreign investment, should be conducted under the guidance of government, in accordance with national economic development. In addition, the traditionalists, represented by Chen, were concerned that a market economy and foreign investment introduced from capitalist countries would negatively affect the effectiveness of central planning in maintaining economic balance and protecting the Chinese people's rights. The aim of protecting Chinese interests or rights was evinced in the approval review at the market access for FIEs by an express condition, which requires equal rights and interests between foreign investors and Chinese partners. Although, on the face of the legal text such a provision was applicable to both sides, the ultimate intention was to protect the interests of Chinese partners, and this was elaborated on. The establishment of a joint venture in whose signed agreements, contracts, and articles of associations existed inequities that might impair the rights and interests of one party, for example, was not to be approved.[27]

In practice, the corporation form of joint venture was preferred at the approval review. Among the 1,500 foreign investment contracts approved in the year 1986 at the market access review, were 870 EJVs, 560 CJVs, and 18 WFOEs.[28] These figures indicate that the establishment of FIEs in EJVs and CJVs was likely to be approved. One possible reason is that the form of joint venture would involve the participation of Chinese partners, which could, to a large extent, address China's national security concerns about controlling the socialist economic system. The reason for the tendency to protect the interests of Chinese partners was that most Chinese partners in foreign-invested joint ventures were state-owned enterprises (SOEs), the major players in the market, which were closely connected to the Chinese government. The economic interests of SOEs were naturally deemed to be national economic interests

Interestingly, neither the CJV Law nor the WFOE Law contained such a clause to protect the interests of Chinese partners. Instead, the term "public interests and social order" was introduced as a factor in the approval reviews of FIEs. The WFOE Law incorporated a clause to the effect that a foreign-invested sole should not be detrimental to social order or Chinese public interest, and this clause was similarly incorporated in the law's implementing regulations and later revisions.[29] The lack of clear definition of "public interest and social order" prompts suspicion that contractual security on which the EJV Law elaborated might involve the meanings of "public interest and social order", as "public interest and social order" was first added in the Regulations on the EJV Law in 1995, from which the requirement of "contractual equity of Chinese investors" was excluded at the same time.[30]

Another typical feature of national security in the approval review at the market access in the regime of FIE Laws is that it was addressed purely by means of administrative discretion, rather than by a legal approach. Notably, before the 1990s, a commercial legal infrastructure had not been officially established. The majority of FIE laws during this period were therefore fulfilled by administrative regulations and departmental rules promulgated by the State Council or relevant departments. Without detailed rules on approval review at the market access, such a regulatory tool with only general review criteria was a matter of great governmental discretion. The results of approval reviews of FIEs were determined by the review body, the Ministry of Commerce (MOFCOM), in its administrative role, rather than by meaningful and clear legal guidance.

2.1.2 Approval Review at the Market Access for Foreign Investment Projects

In the early years of China's reform and opening up, FIE Laws imposed strict control on foreign investment through the approval review at the market access. Because of a lack of clarity and transparency, however, such a case-by-case approval process was accompanied by cumbersome procedures and low administrative efficiency, leading to a low amount of foreign investment. To address this, a legal infrastructure, namely, a guidance system under the legal regime of the FIE Laws was established, in an attempt to provide a clear and transparent direction for foreign investment.

As early as 1983, the Regulations on the EJV Law had already regulated that the establishment of joint ventures in industrial sectors where the state encourages, permits, restricts, or prohibits should be implemented in accordance with the provisions on the EJV Law and the guidance catalogue for foreign investment industries.[31] After the Provisions on Encouraging Foreign Investment were issued in 1986 with a series of measures to attract foreign investment, the Interim Provisions on the Direction of Attracting Foreign Investment (Direction of Attracting Foreign Investment) were promulgated later by the General Office of the State Council in 1987 on national security grounds.[32] The Decision of the State Council on the Key Points of Current Industrial Policies, as well as the List of Absorbing Foreign Investment Sequences were further issued in 1989.[33] Since the Interim Provision on Guiding Foreign Investment Directions and the Guidance Catalogue for Foreign Investment Industries came into being in 1995, a basic guidance system related to industrial sectors has been formed under the legal regime of the FIE laws, providing comprehensive and detailed guidelines for foreign investment projects in industry. Under the guidance system, foreign investment projects fall into four categories: Encouraged, Permitted, Restricted, and Prohibited. Any foreign investor, including FIEs, and investors in projects for capital increase and reinvestment of FIEs, can refer to the Catalogue for the Guidance of Industries for Foreign Investment (Catalogue) for information about administrative verification conducted by the National Development and Reform Commission (NDRC) and MOFCOM.[34] A number of revisions to the Catalogue—in 1997, 2002, 2004, 2007, 2011, 2015, 2017, and 2019—have significantly improved the transparency, efficiency, and predictability of the legal regime of FIE Laws. The Catalogue for Encouraged Foreign Investment Industries (Encouraged Catalogue), specifically, underwent further revisions in 2020 and 2022.[35]

2.1.2.1 Ideas on Foreign Investment From Past Experiences

The advent of the EJV Law, the first law allowing foreign investment in 1979, was met by foreign investors with enthusiasm, as evidenced by an unprecedented and miraculous growth in economic data.[36] The period from 1978 to 1986 witnessed brilliant FIE performance, with the establishment in China of more than 2,100 joint ventures, cooperative enterprises, and businesses wholly owned by foreign investors.[37] By September 1988, 1,047 foreign representative offices had been founded in Beijing.[38] The inflows of actually realized foreign investment rose from US$916 million per year in 1983 to US$3,487 million in 1990, by then the stock of realized foreign investment had reached US$20.7 billion.[39]

The rapid growth of foreign investment in this initial stage was gradually recognized as an input-driven factor contributing to China's economic development, with the result that a set of regulations in industrial sectors was adopted with preferential measures to further encourage foreign investment in certain sectors. Concerns about national security, however, never disappeared, and the regulatory mechanism of the guidance system was established for foreign investment projects in industrial sectors.

2.1.2.2 Ideas on the Socialist Market Economy

Throughout the 1980s, national security worries concerning foreign investment featured in a heated debate on whether to continue the policy of reform and opening up, a debate ended by a series of talks in 1992 delivered by Deng during his Southern Tour.[40] The path of reform and opening up was affirmed by way of mention in the preamble of the amended Constitution of the PRC in 1993. Since then, foreign investment in China has been solidly guaranteed through a constitutional endorsement. The followers of Deng in the CPC, that is, Jiang Zemin's generation, supported Deng's public remarks and further developed the meaning of reform and opening up. During this period, an innovative idea on China's socialism was created.[41] The paradigm of the socialist market economy with Chinese characteristics was declared for the first time in 1993, allowing the market to play an essential role in allocating resources under the state's macroeconomic control and planning.[42]

2.1.2.3 Ideas on National Security

As the 1990s began, the collapse of the Soviet Union and the end of the Cold War not only weakened the ideological tension between socialism and capitalism but also altered the Chinese understanding of security. With the advent of economic globalization, foreign investment with capital exchanges and technology transfers by transnational corporations served to erode territorial borders.[43]

During the formulation stage of the guidance system, ideas on national security fells within the new security concept (NSC), which could be summarized into the following five areas. First, economic security is of great significance in national security. Jiang once claimed that China should seize the opportunity to develop and reinforce its economic strength, and that economic modernization should be the first priority.[44] Economic development was described as the cornerstone of all security factors, the fundamental driving force for national security, and an aspect of the national security concerns behind the guidance system. The phrase "protecting the security of national economic and social development", for example, was expressly stipulated in the provisions on the Direction of Attracting Foreign Investment of 1987, as foreign investment projects detrimental to national economic and social development were to be prohibited at the market access.[45] The factor of national economic development was excluded from the guidance system throughout the 1990s, however, when considering prohibited foreign investment projects. This change indicates that ideas on national security and foreign investment at this stage mainly focused on the political aspects of economic modernization, rather than the purely economic implications. In addition to the prohibited sectors which clearly revealed the national security concerns, the general principles for examining foreign investment projects in restricted industries under approval reviews at the market access implied economic development as an aspect of national security. Technology, for example, that was introduced in foreign investment projects and developed with the production capacity to meet the demands of the domestic market was to be restricted.[46] Foreign investment projects in industries designated by the state as pilot industries to absorb foreign investment or as industries in which monopoly of sales was practiced were restricted.[47] Foreign investment projects involving industries which required overall planning were restricted.[48] These rules on restricted sectors of foreign investment projects revealed that China perceived the function of overall economic planning to be an aspect of national security.

Second, national security also involves the security of science and technology. Jiang once claimed that, in addition to economic growth, China should seek major scientific and technological projects that have strategic, fundamental, and key roles in economics, science and technology, national defense and social development, and grasp the key problems and innovate independently.[49] Scientific and technological innovation was described as a leading force of economic and social development, which would play an increasingly significant role in prosperity and national security. The guidance system was designed to preserve indigenous skills, as foreign investment projects which had to use China's own special craftsmanship or indigenous skills for production were prohibited.[50] It was perceived that, although the development of science and technology would contribute to wealth increases and bring convenience and social production, it was a double-edged sword which also had a great impact on national security.

Third, national security was described as the security of national defense modernization, which was deemed a major strategic issue. Jiang issued a serious warning that neither the party nor the army should abandon the idea of national defense.[51] Accordingly, the guidance system emerged in the field of foreign investment. Foreign investment projects endangering security of military facilities or their usability were to be prohibited at the market access. Foreign investors were prohibited to invest not only in agriculture, such as when they occupied too much farmland, but also in a wide range of other fields, such as forestry, animal husbandry, light industry, mining, dressing and processing industries, energy industries and urban public facilities, the petrochemical and chemical industries, post, telecommunications and transportation, trade and finance, broadcasting, television and filmmaking, new media, military arms production, and other industrial projects that might endanger national security.[52]

Fourth, an emphasis on the ideological security of socialism was introduced. Jiang offered a seemingly convincing reason for China's sensitivity on national security and foreign investment a typical capitalist phenomenon arguing that Western countries, where capitalist ideology was intended to be maintained and advocated to the world through governments, political parties, propaganda tools, schools, churches, and other means, remained sensitive about political ideology.[53] In addition, another purpose of safeguarding socialist security was to fight against possible bourgeois liberalization, which might easily be caused by foreign investment. With the rapid growth of foreign investment in China, it was perceived by Chinese leaders that the decadent phenomena of capitalism might appear in China, that Party members and cadres might fail to withstand the temptations brought by money, and that belief in communism might be eroded, which might also lead to risks of corruption and stability within the CPC leadership. Under the guidance system, it was expressly stated that foreign investment projects which endanger state security were prohibited.[54] "State security" was defined as the stability of the socialist regime. Foreign investment which impaired social order and public interest was prohibited.[55]

Fifth, other emerging security issues featured among the national security concerns affecting approval reviews under the guidance system. Under that system, for example, foreign investment projects would be prohibited if they caused environmental pollution or brought harmful impacts to natural resources or human health.[56] Compared with the factor of environmental security described in the FIE Laws, environmental security in the guidance system paid additional attention to security of natural resources and human health. To be specific, foreign investment projects occupying too much farmland and harmful to environmental protection and development of land resources were prohibited at the market access.[57]

In the general principles for prohibiting and restricting foreign investment projects at the industrial market access, as well as the prohibited and restricted items listed in the Catalogue, as discussed previously, the great emphasis on national security considered in the approval review at the market access for foreign investment projects is to some extent apparent and still confined to traditional aspects.

2.1.3 M&A Security Review

After China's accession to the WTO, foreign investment M&A activities in China increased significantly. In order to better adapt to and accommodate the trend of globalization and effectively utilize foreign investment, laws and regulations pertaining to cross-border M&As were introduced.[58] Consequently, in 2003, the Interim Provisions on the Merger and Acquisition of Domestic Enterprises by Foreign Investors (M&A Provisions of 2003) were issued, permitting foreign investors to purchase equity in Chinese companies.[59] The M&A Provisions of 2003 provided little more than a vague outline of the process for foreign corporations to acquire controlling stakes in domestic Chinese enterprises, stipulating that any merger or acquisition of a domestic enterprise by foreign investment shall be subject to the examination of approval authorities.[60] A prototype national security review in foreign investment similar to the US national security review took place in China for the first time.

There were a number of significant factors to be taken into consideration to determine whether to report a merger or acquisition transaction by foreign investors to relevant authorities, whether a review should be launched, and whether such a transaction should be approved, which were closely linked with considerations of whether certain transactions would seriously impact market competition, the national economy, and people's livelihood.[61] It is worth noting that the phrase "national economic security" was first expressed in China's foreign investment legislation. In addition to these specific factors of impacts upon market competition, the national economy and people's livelihood outlined in M&A review, some general requirements for foreign investments were stipulated in the M&A Provisions of 2003. Such investment, for example, was to comply with laws and regulations, adhere to several principles, including fairness, reasonableness, compensation for equal value, honesty and good faith, and not create excessive concentration, eliminate or hinder competition, disturb socioeconomic order, or harm public interests.[62]

The M&A Provisions of 2003 were revised in 2006 and 2009.[63] The Interim Provisions on Mergers and Acquisitions of Domestic Enterprises by Foreign Investment of 2006 (M&A Provisions of 2006) reiterated that foreign investment should satisfy the requirements of the law and administrative rules and regulations of China concerning the qualifications of investors and comply with policies on industry, land, and environmental protection.[64] Twenty-six clauses additional to those of the M&A Provisions of 2003 attempted to smooth the way for foreign investors who would otherwise be unable to acquire ownership in Chinese companies.[65] An independent and separate regulatory mechanism of national security review for foreign investment M&As in China can be traced back to the M&A Provisions of 2006. In accordance with the M&A Provisions of 2006, where a foreign investor intends to obtain an actual controlling power in a domestic enterprise that it plans to take over, and if any important industry is concerned, or if it has an impact on or may have an impact on national economic security or will lead to the transfer of the actual controlling power of a domestic enterprise which holds a famous trademark or time-honored Chinese brand, or in any other key industries, the parties concerned shall file an application with the MOFCOM; otherwise, the MOFCOM may, jointly with the relevant departments, demand the parties concerned to terminate the transaction, transfer or divest the relevant equities and assets, or take other effective measures to eliminate the takeover's impact on national economic security.[66]

The primary reason for this independent mechanism of M&A security review was that, during this stage, neither the approval review for FIE Laws nor that for foreign investment projects at the market access within the guidance system could scrutinize foreign investment M&As. Foreign investment M&A therefore became a favorable option to avoid various strict approval reviews at the market access, and in this way, Chinese assets would be easily controlled by foreign investment through the purchase of Chinese enterprises or equity interests, which might impair national security. Because of the inadequacy of existing approval reviews, China continually brought national security factors into consideration in relation to foreign investment M&As at the market access, in line with the imperative to protect national security, which had already been considered in the approval process of FIEs and foreign investment projects. The regulatory mechanism of M&A security review was established to fill this regulatory gap and prevent national security risks which might be imposed by foreign investment M&As. The M&A Provisions of 2006, however, offered little more than a brief description and an opaque blueprint of the M&A security review, which failed to define clearly which transactions would be subject to M&A security review.[67] Even though it was created to protect national economic security, neither key factors nor a list of key economic sectors were explained in detail.[68] In addition, the lack of procedural requirements made the M&A security review nothing more than a legal text, which was hard to implement in practice. The M&A Provisions of 2006, furthermore, was a departmental regulation as it was issued by MOFCOM. Compared with national law, the status of the M&A security review within the legal hierarchy was quite low.

The problem of the low legal status of the M&A security review in the M&A Provisions of 2006 was addressed when the Anti-Monopoly Law (AML) was promulgated in 2007, containing a provision on M&A security review.[69] In addition to the review on the concentration of undertakings, the AML provided an additional security review for cases in which a foreign investor participates in the concentration of undertakings by merging and acquiring a domestic enterprise or by any other means, which seems to embody a universal concern shared by most governments for protecting national security and national economic interests amid economic globalization and investment liberalization.[70]

The content of the M&A security review in the revised M&A Provisions of 2009 remained unchanged from that of the M&A Provisions of 2006, which requires foreign investors to submit a petition of approval voluntarily to MOFCOM when national economic security is at stake, where foreign investors merge a domestic enterprise and obtain actual control over the enterprise, or such a merger involves any critical industry, affects or may affect national economic security, or causes transfer of actual control over the domestic enterprise that possesses a famous trademark or time-honored Chinese brand.[71] Where the parties fail to make an application and the merger materially affects or may materially affect the security of the national economy, the MOFCOM may, together with other competent authorities, request the parties to stop the transaction, assign relevant equity or assets, or take any other effective actions, to eliminate the effects of the merger on national economic security.[72]

Although these M&A Provisions and AML constituted the legal basis for security review of foreign investment M&As, all of them at this stage failed to give detailed instructions for implementation in practice. In 2011, the Circular of the General Office of the State Council on the Establishment of Security Review System Regarding Merger and Acquisition of Domestic Enterprises by Foreign Investors (State Council Circular 6) was promulgated, with long-awaited but detailed stipulations on the scope, content, working mechanism, procedures, and other provisions for security review in foreign investment M&As.[73] It contained four criteria for evaluating an M&A security review: (i) national defense security, including the ability for producing domestic products and providing domestic services required for national defense and the relevant equipment and facilities; (ii) the stable operation of the national economy; (iii) basic order of social life; and (iv) the capacity for research and development of key technologies involving national security.[74] Then, the Announcement of MOFCOM concerning the Provisions of the Ministry of Commerce for the Implementation of the Security Review System for Merger and Acquisition of Domestic Enterprises by Foreign Investors promulgated by MOFCOM (MOFCOM Announcement 53) formulized procedures for security review and set different thresholds to trigger national security review when necessary.[75]

As a result of these developments, a basic, workable regulatory mechanism for M&A security review of foreign investment M&As was established in the form of legal text. State Council Circular 6 and MOFCOM Announcement 53 enjoy a lower status within the legal hierarchy than national laws promulgated by the National People's Congress (NPC) and its Standing Committee. Arguably, the security review system for foreign investment M&As was categorized in the administrative system at the market access, in which approval or denial of an administrative license is expected. Under the Administrative Licensing Law, however, administrative regulations and departmental rules generally do not possess the authority to deal with the issuance of administrative licenses, with an exception of issuing temporary administrative licenses.[76] The legitimacy of detailed rules on security review for foreign investment M&As through State Council Circular 6 and MOFCOM Announcement 53 which would make administrative approval licenses as results was therefore challenged.[77]

2.1.3.1 Ideas on Foreign Investment through M&A Practices

In the early stages of reform and opening up, most foreign investment in China was made through the establishment of FIEs, and M&As accounted for only a small fraction of total inward foreign direct investment, in part because foreign investment M&As had been and continued to be largely prohibited in China. The value of foreign investment M&As flowing into China in 1990 totaled US$8 billion, representing only 0.22 percent of the total amount of foreign investment in China.[78] With the advent of the twenty-first century, however, foreign investment activities through M&As developed significantly. The total number of M&A deals announced, including domestic and cross-border M&As, grew from 250 in 2000 to 2,409 in 2010, almost a tenfold increase, and the value of M&As jumped to US$193 billion in 2010 from US$47 billion in 2000, a fourfold increase.[79]

Although foreign investment M&As exert some positive effects, such as the liquidation of remnant assets of SOEs, promotion of innovative technology, and introduction of advanced managerial expertise to Chinese companies, fears emerged in China that these unregulated foreign investment M&As would result in the loss of Chinese national brands and time-honored Chinese brands, unemployment of Chinese workers, environmental destruction, the sale of state assets and monopolies on foreign capital in key sectors.[80] Also, several world-renowned MNEs had successfully acquired Chinese corporate champions, large-scale enterprises or state-owned listed companies. These acquisitions included, for example, French-based Alcatel-Lucent acquiring a Chinese SOE, Shanghai Beier; US-based Emerson Electric Company acquiring a well-known Chinese private company, Ansheng Electric Company; US-based American Aviation LDC acquiring a well-known Chinese private company, Hainan Airlines; US-based Coca-Cola acquiring Huiyuan Juice, which was not only a private Chinese company but also considered a national corporate champion and a well-known brand. The takeovers of Chinese companies accounted for 23 percent of all M&A transactions in China between 2000 and 2010.[81] As the FIE Laws and guidance system considered only national security implications posed by FIE or foreign investment projects at the market access, the increasing M&A investments on Chinese national brands raised China's sensitivities about national security. It was as a result of this that the government policy on establishing M&A security review and regulating M&A investment for national security concerns was introduced.[82]

2.1.3.2 Ideas on National Economic Security

Under Hu Jintao's leadership, economic development was continually stressed as the first priority. Although it was necessary for further expansion of the breadth and depth of opening to the outside world, economic development through opening up was closely linked with security. Hu warned that China was entering an era of insecurity without development, in a dynamic and changing global economy.[83] The report of the Fifth Plenary Session of the Sixteenth CPC Central Committee in November 2003 comprehensively emphasized the need to cope with the issue of national economic security, on the basis of analysis of external political and economic conditions.

First, under the ideological context of the scientific outlook on development proposed by Hu, national economic development was described as both a starting point and a destination for national economic security.[84] The idea of national economic security refers to the stable, sustained, and healthy development of the national economy, enhanced and comprehensive national strength and international competitiveness. Without economic development, the ability to survive, resist, and adapt to internal and external threats would be greatly reduced, disturbing economic stability.[85] The security of sustainable economic development was one of the considerations of M&A security review, because of the factor of the impact of M&As on the stable operation of the national economy, as elaborated in State Council Circular 6.[86]

Second, the importance of security of strategic resources was implied in the notion of national economic security. Hu held the view that strategic resources were an essential factor related not only to a country's economic lifeline and its people's livelihood, but also to world peace and common interests in international cooperation with other countries. In order to secure national strategic resources, it is necessary to adhere to the basic principle of mutual benefit under the ideological meaning of the NSC: harmonious development to pursue national economic security. Pursuant to State Council Circular 6, foreign investment M&A transactions related to important agricultural products, important energy and resources, important infrastructure, important transportation services, key technologies, and major equipment manufacturing enterprises for national security would be subject to M&A security review.[87]

Third, military security was a consideration in M&A security review because of the scientific outlook on development in the field of national defense. Hu proclaimed that China must implement the strategic military principles, accelerate military reform with Chinese characteristics, and fully prepare for potential military threats.[88] This resulted in impacts of foreign investment M&As on the security of the national defense field being considered among the evaluation criteria in M&A security review, including production capacity of domestic goods, domestic service provision capacity and equipment and facilities required for national defense.[89] The impact of foreign investment M&As on research and development (R&D) capability in key technologies related to national security was also included.[90]

Fourth, the ideology of the scientific outlook on development under Hu's leadership also required the active building of a harmonious socialist society. On the one hand, in terms of sustainable economic development, it required an increase in the material wealth of society and constant improvement of living standards. On the other hand, social justice was stressed to be necessary to the securing of a harmonious society. This idea puts people first and takes the people's interests into consideration as the starting point and ultimate purpose of security and development, to ensure that development is for the people, by the people, and with the people sharing its fruits and striving to advance the all-round development of security strategies.[91] It can be seen that the people-oriented value of security was officially recognized in China for the first time. It was for these purposes that the impact of foreign investment M&As on basic order of social life was dimedone of the factors to be considered in the M&A security review.[92]

2.2 National Security Review in the Foreign Investment Law

2.2.1 Pilot Experiments in Free Trade Zones

Experimental trials in free trade zones (FTZs) were initiated to further liberalize foreign investment and create an investor-friendly regulatory environment. On September 30, 2013, the first Pilot Free Trade Zone (PFTZ) was established in Shanghai.[93] The Measures for Administration of the China (Shanghai) PFTZ were issued, with radical changes to legal rules long accepted under the legal regime of FIE laws, adopting approval reviews at the market access for foreign investment.[94] The pre-establishment national treatment principle for foreign investment, together with negative lists, among the core tenets of international investment rules, was introduced in the SPFTZ to test the possibility of their nationwide adoption in the coming FIL.[95] The FIE laws were suspended on a trial basis and the regulatory tool of approval review at the market access for different foreign investment types were, in SPFTZ, replaced by the filing system. On the same day, the high-profile Special Management Measures of Foreign Investment Access in China (Shanghai) Pilot Free Zone containing 190 items came into effect (SPFTZ Negative List). These were revised in 2014 and reduced to 139.[96]

Other regions were also subject to this legal experiment. On April 20, 2015, for example, the State Council approved the establishment of another three free trade zones: Guangdong, Fujian, and Tianjin. On the same day, the Special Administrative Measures for Foreign Investment Access in Pilot Free Trade Zones (FTZ Negative List) was accordingly promulgated.[97] There were 122 items on the FTZ Negative List, with a reduction of 17 items from the SPFTZ Negative List of 2014. The same year, the CPC Central Committee and the State Council issued the Several Opinions on Developing a New System of Open Economy, which required a comprehensive and innovative plan for foreign investment management.[98] Since then, in 2017 free trade zones were officially launched in another seven provinces—Liaoning, Zhejiang, Henan, Hubei, Sichuan, Shanxi, Hainan provinces—and, in

2018, Chongqing. The legal practices in these pilot FTZs were aimed at offering an initial testing platform to examine whether a more liberalized approach in line with international principles of pre-establishment national treatment and negative lists could be implemented effectively nationwide. A few months after the introduction of the FIL, free trade zones were established in Shandong, Jiangsu, Guangxi, Hebei, Yunnan, and Heilongjiang provinces. In 2020, Hunan and Anhui provinces and Beijing witnessed the launch of free trade zones too. Development of China's FTZs has persisted for a decade, and there are now 21 FTZs.

The items on the negative list in the FTZs have been gradually reduced. As Figure 2.1 illustrates, the FTZ negative list has been revised and the number of items reduced several times; there were 190 items in 2013 and only 27 in 2021, after eight rounds of streamlining in the past 12 years.[99] The NDRC clearly stated in early 2024 that it will revise the national version of the negative list for foreign investment at the market access, and policies will be issued to lift restrictions on foreign investment access fully in relation to manufacturing industry.[100]

Before a nationwide negative list came into being in 2018, the revised Catalogue served as an alternative outside FTZs from 2013 to 2017. Foreign investment could enjoy the same treatment as domestic investment and directly begin filing procedures in areas not restricted or prohibited in the Catalogue. On July 28, 2018, when the Special Administrative Measures for Foreign Investment Access (National Negative List 2018 Version) came into force, the negative list for FTZs, which had been promoted nationwide, replaced the revised Catalogue of 2017 within the context of the guidance system issued by the MOFCOM and NDRC, while the encouraged items in the Catalogue continued to be implemented.[101] The FTZ Negative List and National Negative List both served as a supplementary basis for implementing the international principle of pre-establishment national treatment in China. Foreign investment outside the negative list was to be managed in accordance with the principle of consistency between domestic and foreign investment, which is given national treatment. All regions and departments were prohibited to set restrictions at the market access on foreign investment in areas other than the negative list.

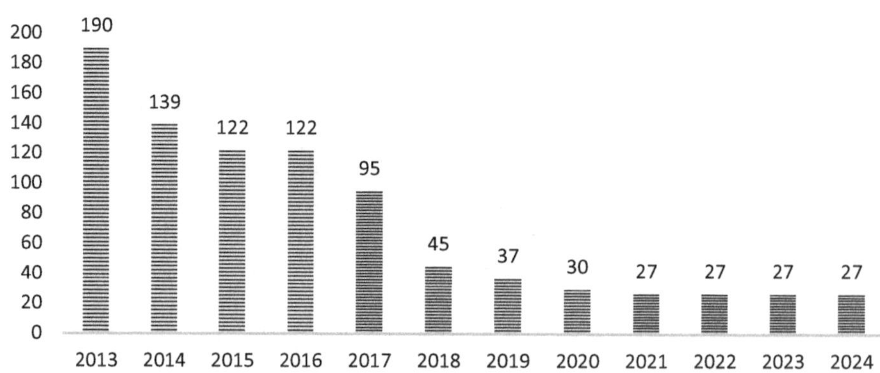

Figure 2.1 Number of Items in the FTZ Negative List from 2013 to 2024

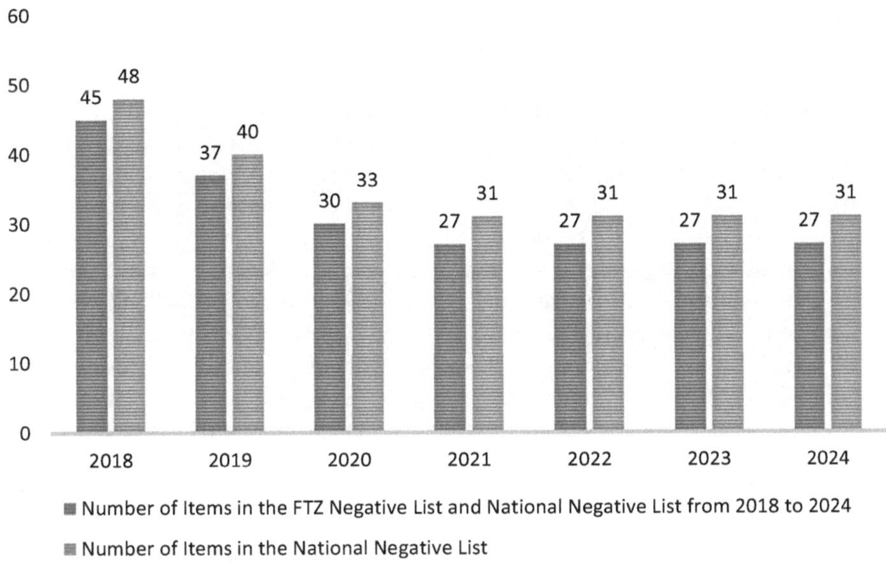

Figure 2.2 Number of Items in the FTZ Negative List and National Negative List from 2018 to 2024

As shown in Figure 2.2, the FTZ Negative List and National Negative List updated in 2021 were reduced by 27 items and 31 items respectively, indicating that the experimental role of FTZs was fully utilized in further opening to the outside world, as foreign investment enjoyed a greater degree of openness within the FTZs and more areas had been opened at the market access for foreign investment.[102] When horizontally comparing these two negative lists from 2018 to 2020, the FTZ Negative List is three items shorter than the National Negative List. The three deleted items in FTZ Negative List refer to the fields of Chinese herbal pieces, fishing, and publication printing. Agriculture, water transportation, telecommunications, education, culture, and ten other fields are much more open to foreign investment. In the FTZ Negative List, for example, the proportion of Chinese investment in the breeding of new wheat and corn varieties and seed production was relaxed to no less than 34 percent, while in the National Negative List, only the proportion of Chinese shares in the breeding of new wheat and seed production was relaxed to no less than 34 percent, and the breeding of new corn and seed production still needs to be controlled by the Chinese parties.[103] The FTZ Negative List allows art performing groups to be established if they are controlled by the Chinese parties, while this sector is prohibited in the National Negative List.[104] The FTZ Negative List allows foreign-funded vocational education institutions, while this sector is not open for foreign investment in the National Negative List.[105]

Even though the items on the FTZ Negative List have always been fewer than those on the National Negative List, their adoption in China in parallel reflects the characteristic of substantial downsizing. The substantial reduction in items on the negative lists eligible for foreign investment reflects significant progress in China's further opening up. The contents of both negative lists, however, also reflect national security concerns relating to foreign investment.

There are four factors which determine prohibited and restricted sectors in the negative lists. The first of these is whether such industrial fields are related to national security. In the ideological context of the holistic approach to national security (HANS), "national security" refers to the security of people's life and property, political security, homeland security, military security, economic security, financial security, cultural security, social security, scientific and technological security, information security, ecological security, resource security, nuclear security, and other emerging forms of security. The second factor is whether the sector is related to the national distribution of major productive forces, strategic resource development or major public interests. The third is whether it is able to issue administrative licenses in accordance with laws and related to the investment and operational behaviors of market players. The fourth is other circumstances stipulated by laws, administrative regulations, and decisions of the State Council.[106] These considerations revealed national security concerns in the negative list to some extent. The main focus is on security in key industries and security of economic development.

In addition, the regulatory mechanism of national security review was further developed, on the basis of M&A security review, for much more liberalized experiments in the FTZs, as almost all types of foreign investment would no longer be reviewed at the market access unless categorized as prohibited or restricted sectors specified in the negative list. Where the requirement for approval review at the market access was replaced by a record-filing system, security review is applicable to a larger scope of foreign investment, which is no longer limited to foreign investment M&As, but also involving FIEs and foreign investment projects. In this case, other factors in the approval process at the market access under the FIE Laws have been eliminated and only the issue of national security is preferentially focused. The regulatory mechanism of security review in FTZs could also be regarded, therefore, as reflecting significant progress in liberalizing foreign investment, as *ex ante* review of most foreign investment is no longer adopted, and instead, security review serves as the sole layer of supervision.[107] This demonstrates that the focus of administrative management procedures on national security and foreign investment is gradually shifting from prior approval to subsequent supervision.

2.2.2 The Foreign Investment Law

The earliest draft version of FIL (MOFCOM Draft FIL) was issued for public comment in 2015. As the name indicates, it was drafted by the MOFCOM. Unfortunately, the MOFCOM Draft FIL with over-detailed provisions on high-impact contentious issues failed to become effective immediately, and the drafting process of the FIL was postponed for almost three years.[108] In late 2018, another draft version of FIL was submitted for deliberation.[109] In March 2019, the FIL was officially approved, as a big step in China's legislative process in foreign investment, to further open the domestic market and liberalize foreign investment, protect the rights of foreign investors, and serve a stable, transparent, and predictable environment for foreign investment. The FIL demonstrates China's renewed commitment to substantially unifying the legal regime governing foreign investment, by covering all types of foreign investment and consolidating laws and regulations, such as FIE laws, regulations on green-field investments, and M&A rules governing foreign investment M&As.[110] The two-track legal system for foreign investment and domestic investment was ended.

Unlike the MOFCOM Draft FIL of 2015, which was organized into 11 chapters with a total of 170 articles, the enacted FIL contains only 42 articles, making it one-fifth shorter than the MOFCOM Draft FIL. The latter had contained detailed rules on various issues, such as the definitions of key terms, market access administration, national security review, information reporting, investment promotion, investment protection, coordination and handling of complaints, supervision and inspection, legal liability and supplementary provisions, each of which occupied a single chapter. In contrast to the MOFCOM Draft FIL, the FIL gives prominence only to guiding principles, without detailing specific forms of implementation. It contains only one provision mentioning security review, requiring the establishment of security review for foreign investment, to be conducted in the case of investments that affect or may affect national security, and stipulating that the decisions of security review made in accordance with the rule of law are final.[111] This opaque provision for security review indicates China's prudent idea on national security and foreign investment even during the quick process of formulation and passage of the FIL and might result in suspicion of arbitrary abuse of power.[112] In order to address the doubts and uncertainty about security review in the FIL, the Measures, which took effect on January 18, 2021, provides detailed guidelines for a unified security review for all kinds of foreign investments under the new FIL regime.[113] These positive rules on the implementation of national security review are expected to address important issues of national security and foreign investment.

2.2.3 Ideas on Foreign Investment

On November 8, 2012, the Eighteenth CPC Central Committee under Xi Jinping's leadership called for vigorous development of reform and opening up and adoption of innovative measures to further utilize and attract foreign investment.[114] The following year, the Resolution of the Central Committee of the CPC on Some Major Issues Concerning Comprehensively Deepening Reform (Resolution on Reform) issued at the Third Plenary Session of the Eighteenth CPC Central Committee indicated the problem of excessive governmental intervention in the field of foreign investment by highlighting the several regulatory layers for approval review at the market access, such as that for FIEs, that for foreign investment projects at the market access and M&A security review for foreign investment M&As, and acknowledged the necessity of striking a balance between government and market.[115] It stipulated that the market should be emphasized as playing the dominant role in economic activities, and governmental responsibilities should be redefined and confined clearly to the following roles: promoting sustainable economic development, maintaining macroeconomic stability and market order, intervening in situations of market failure, improving the service capabilities of public goods, safeguarding fair competition, and strengthening the oversight of the market.[116]

On October 23, 2014, the Fourth Plenary Session of the Eighteenth CPC Central Committee adopted the Resolution concerning CPC Central Committee Decision Concerning Some Major Questions in Comprehensively Moving Governing the Country According to the Law Forward, which held that the lack of transparency and predictability in legal rules always resulted in the tendency to place the political interests of governmental authorities ahead of the legislative purposes of the law, or even lead to corruption, and required radical reform to avoid problems which might further cause violation of the principles of the socialist rule of law or harm the interests of the people.[117] This demonstrates that, during this stage, it was widely acknowledged that the necessity for and significance of addressing the issues of a dualist legal system, such as excessive governmental intervention, discriminatory treatment at the market access, and the unpredictable and non-transparent investment environment for foreign investment activities. The introduction of a unified FIL for foreign investment was viewed as the realization of a commitment to relax foreign investment restrictions and create a level playing investment field.[118] As Figure 2.3 shows, the actual amount of utilized foreign investment in China has been growing for a decade, with a rapid increase since the implementation of the FIL in 2019.[119] The Implementation Plan for Comprehensive Reform Pilot in Pudong New Area (2023–2027) was released in January 2024, with the purpose of improving the high standard of market rules for foreign investment.[120] On the basis of a unified national negative list of market access, more relaxed measures are necessary at the market access in Pudong New Area.[121] To be specific, restrictions at the market access for foreign investment will be relaxed, in an orderly manner in the consumer markets for telecommunications services, health care, and other services.[122]

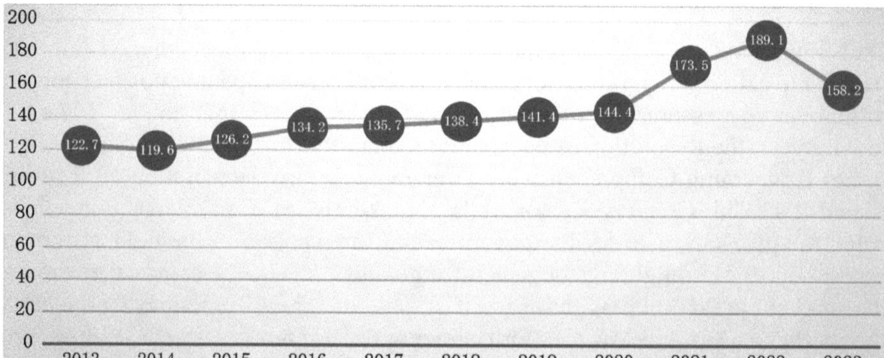

Figure 2.3 Actual Amount of Utilized Foreign Investment (US$ Billion)

2.2.4 The Holistic Approach to National Security

In the face of the dynamic and changing security conditions, the National Security Council of the CPC (NSCCPC) was set up in early 2014. After collectively absorbing the essence of national security thoughts in the past decades, HANS with the purpose of carrying out the national security work well in the new era was established on April 15, 2014, at the 1st Plenary Session of the NSCCPC, to serve as the theoretical basis and guiding ideology of China's national security strategies and behaviors during 2010s. Within the HANS, national security is comprehensively classified into the following 11 categories: political security, homeland security, military security, economic security, cultural security, social security, science and technology security, information security, ecological security, resource security, and nuclear security.

In July 2015, the revised National Security Law (NSL) was promulgated, establishing the multifaceted nature of national security-HANS-in the form of national law.[123] According to the NSL, "national security" refers to a state in which national power, sovereignty, unity and territorial integrity, the people's well-being, sustainable economic and social development, and other major national interests are relatively free from danger and free from internal and external threats, as well as the ability to ensure continued security.[124] National security work should adhere to a holistic approach, with people's security as its purpose, political and economic security as its foundation, military, cultural, and social security as its guarantees, and the promotion of international security. In order to rely on promoting international security, safeguarding national security in various field, building a national security system, and following the path of national security with Chinese characteristics.[125]

The NSL contains an explicit reference to address national security concerns in relation to foreign investment. It elaborates that the state establishes national security review and supervision structures and mechanisms to conduct the national security review of foreign investments, specific goods or core technologies, online information technology products and services, construction projects involving national security affairs, as well as other major affairs and activities that influence or may influence national security, in order to prevent national security risks.[126] This provision offers, for the first time in the form of national law, a basis for security review of foreign investments that affect or may affect national security as the AML only legalized security review for foreign investment M&As. It can be seen that, although the Chinese government had not yet taken formal actions concerning foreign investments through security review in 2015, when a similar regulatory mechanism was established in relation to FTZs through State Council Circular 24 and MOFCOM Announcement 53, efforts had been made before the enactment of the FIL in 2020 to reinvigorate the security review.

Under the reformed FIL regime, a unified mechanism of security review for foreign investments is established, with detailed instructions in the Measures. It is worth noting that such a regulatory review of foreign investment on national security grounds has been termed "security review", rather than "national security review", as in the US, despite the fact that both are employed to assess national security implications. Unlike the objective term "security", "national security" is generally associated with foreign affairs, giving an impression that it is always determined subjectively with political or retributive concerns. To some extent, the term "security review" reveals the Chinese government's intention to make it an objective and neutral legal phenomenon, unlike a political instrument, and reduce criticisms about governmental intervention in foreign investment, or at least make it sound justifiable and rational. In accordance with the text of the FIL, however, it is national security that is taken into consideration.

Ten points explain the Chinese idea of national security. First, national security is the security of the socialist system, that is, the stability of the CPC leadership, as the state is required to adhere to the leadership of the CPC, maintain the socialist system with Chinese characteristics, develop socialist democratic politics, improve the socialist rule of law, reinforce the mechanism for checks and oversight of power, and protect the people's rights when governing the country.[127] Security review is required if foreign investment might threaten China's socialist regime, and such an investment might be prohibited.

Second, the people's security has been further developed from the definition of national security in the scientific outlook on development, as one of the typical features of China's internal ideas on national security within the CPC. In addition to the people's physical well-being, property, and other lawful rights, the fundamental interests of the overwhelming majority of people should be protected.[128] That is why the notion of "basic order of social life" has been continually emphasized in regulatory reviews of foreign investments.

Third, in order to safeguard homeland security and military security, it is necessary to strengthen border defense, maritime defense, and air defense and take all measures to protect the security of territory, inland waters, territorial seas, territorial airspace, territorial sovereignty, and maritime rights and interests.[129] Pursuant to the Measures, foreign investors or relevant parties should voluntarily declare their investment plans if they wish to invest in military industry, military-related supporting industry, and other fields related to national defense security, or if their investment is located in military facilities or in areas surrounding military facilities.[130] This reflects the idea that national security foreign investment in facilities close to places of homeland security or military security sensitivity might endanger national security and are therefore subject to security review.

Fourth, in terms of economic system, the HANS stresses the significance of maintaining the basic economic system and the order of the socialist market economy, improving the rules and mechanisms for preventing and resolving economic security risks, safeguarding the security of important industries and crucial fields related to the lifeline of the national economy, key sectors, major infrastructure, major construction projects, and other major economic interests. The Measures highlights a number of critical sectors which require security review for foreign investment, such as those involving important information technology and internet products and services, important financial services, critical technologies, and other important industries.[131]

Fifth, national security in foreign investment involves the security of resources and energy, a concept which has continued to develop from national security thinking during the period of emergence of the M&A security review. To be specific, the NSL requires the state to utilize and protect resources and energy rationally, enhance the preservation of strategic resources and energy, improve the construction of transport channels for strategic resources and security protection measures, and comprehensively enhance emergency safeguarding capability, to ensure the sustainable, reliable, and effective supply of resources and energy for economic and social development.[132] It expressly elaborates to the effect that a special concern of security review regarding foreign investments is critical energy and resources, critical transportation services and infrastructure.[133]

Sixth, in addition to strategic energy resources, the HANS perceives grain as an essential agricultural resource and attaches importance to grain security, in order to protect and improve the comprehensive capacity of grain production. The Measures states that important agricultural products might be paid special attention. Foreign investment in critical agricultural products related to national security must be declared in the course of security review if it has obtained actual control.[134] The implications of the COVID-19 pandemic for food supplies, furthermore, such as the fact that major food exporting nations decided to stop selling agricultural produce in anticipation of possible repercussions for their own food supplies, raise concerns about food security and stability of food supplies.[135] Indeed, the Fourteenth Five-Year Plan (2021–2025) for National Economic and Social Development and the Long-Range Objectives Through the Year 2035 (Fourteenth Five Year Plan) released and ratified by the NPC on March 11, 2021, appear to be much more focused than past plans on food stability and security, particularly with regard to local grain security.[136] The concern in the agricultural field is to avoid possible risks caused by foreign investment which would affect food supply and social stability.

Seventh, cultural security is expressly integral to national security review considerations in the FIL. The NSL requires adherence to the direction of an advanced socialist culture, the inheritance and development of traditional Chinese culture, the cultivation and practice of the core values of socialism, the maintenance of the ideological domination, and the enhancement of overall cultural strength and competitiveness.[137] The catalogues or existing negative lists restrict or prohibit foreign investment in the fields of mass media and education, and foreign investors in critical cultural products and services must make a voluntary declaration if they obtain actual control in the investment transaction.[138]

Eighth, ideas of national security regarding foreign investment include the security of science and technology, referring to the intrinsic capacity for innovation and the development of self-controllable strategic technologies and critical technologies in important fields, guaranteeing the security of major technologies and projects.[139] Xi pointed out that security in the field of science and technology is an important aspect of national security, noting that the overall efficiency of the innovation system should be improved.[140] The Decision of the CPC Central Committee on Major Issues Concerning How to Uphold and Improve the System of Socialism with Chinese Characteristics and Advance the Modernization of China's System and Capacity for Governance, which was reviewed and adopted at the Fourth Plenary Session of the Nineteenth Central Committee of the CPC in 2019, further enhanced the position of security in science and technology in the context of national security, placing it at the same level as military security as an important guarantee of national security.[141] The report of the Twentieth National Congress of the Communist Party of China uses a special chapter to make strategic arrangements for maintaining national security and social stability, and for the first time proposes to "use the new security architecture to safeguard the new development pattern",[142] coordinating domestic security and international security, traditional security and nontraditional security.[143] Scientific and technological self-reliance and self-improvement has been emphasized as functions fundamental to China's survival and development.[144] Foreign investment in critical technology with actual control is subject to national security review, with the purposes of strengthening the supervision and technological protection of foreign investment.[145] In response to the potential issues of information leakage and technology transfer caused by foreign investment, scientific and technological security are necessary to strengthen the supervision of foreign investment, preventing technology transfers resulting from foreign investment from posing a threat to China's interests and security.

Ninth, the security of cyberspace and information is a crucial consideration, as an emerging dimension of national security aspects of foreign investment.[146] Xi noted that, without cybersecurity, there would be no national security, and without informatization, there would be no modernization.[147] The stability of economic and social operations and the interests of the general public would be difficult to safeguard.[148] China has made great efforts to safeguard the security of cyberspace and information by improving system construction and implementing laws and regulations.[149] The Office of the Central Leading Group for Cyberspace Affairs, which was replaced by the Office of the Central Cyberspace Affairs Commission and Cyberspace Administration of China in 2018, was set up in 2014, designed to lead and coordinate cyber-security and informatization work among different sectors, as well as to draft national strategies, development plans and major policies in this field.[150] China's first Cyber Security Law (CSL) was passed in 2016, allowing regulators to take action against individuals and organizations that harm national interests and cyber-security.[151] In order to improve the internet environment, a notice on soliciting public opinions on the Decision on Amending the Cyber-Security Law (Draft for Comments) was issued in 2022 by the Cyberspace Administration of China. The Data Security Law, which expressly outlined the data security regulatory framework, and the Personal Information Protection Law, which provided a localized approach for personal privacy protection in accordance with important principles of internationally prevailing regulations, were adopted in 2021. Since then, China has formed a sound legal framework for safeguarding national cyber-security and information security.[152] Cases in which a foreign investor acquiring actual control of the investee company in industries relevant to national security, such as important information technology and internet product and services industries, will be subject to national security review.[153]

Tenth, as ecological deterioration directly threatens the sustainable development of China, ecological security is taken into consideration in security review. The Opinions of the CPC and the State Council on Comprehensively Promoting the

Development of a Beautiful China were released in December 2023, calling for an improved national ecological security regime which strengthens cooperation in areas of economic security, resource security and other fields.[154] One might expect that foreign investment which is not in line with the building of a beautiful China may fall within the purview of security review, from the perspective of ecological considerations.

Notes

1 Liu, Ziyu. "Security Review in the Evolution of Foreign Investment Law with Chinese Characteristics: Part I." *Business Law Review* 41, no. 5 (2020): 172–179; Beijing Review. "The Third Plenary Session of the 11th Central Committee of the Communist Party of China." 2009. www.bjreview.com/nation/txt/2009-05/26/content_197538.htm

2 Law of the PRC on Chinese-Foreign Equity Joint Ventures (1979).

3 Regulations for the Implementation of the Law on Sino-foreign Equity Joint Ventures (1980).

4 Law of the PRC on Wholly Owned Enterprises (1986).

5 Liu, Ziyu. "Security Review in the Evolution of Foreign Investment Law with Chinese Characteristics: Part I." *Business Law Review* 41, no. 5 (2020): 172–173.

6 Decision on Revising Wholly Foreign-owned Enterprise Law, the Sino-Foreign Equity Joint Venture Enterprise Law, the Sino-Foreign Cooperative Joint Venture Enterprise Law, and the Law on the Protection of Investment of Taiwan Compatriots (2016) (Decision on Revising FIE Laws).

7 North, Douglass. *Institutions, Institutional Change and Economic Performance*. Cambridge: Cambridge University Press, 1990, vii.

8 Wang, Yan. *Chinese Legal Reform: The Case of Foreign Investment Law*. London: Routledge, 2002.

9 Lovell, Julia. *The Opium War: Drugs, Dreams and the Making of China*. London: Picador, 2011.

10 Beeching, Jack. *The Chinese Opium Wars*. Boston: Mariner Books, 1977.

11 Wang, Yan. *Chinese Legal Reform: The Case of Foreign Investment Law*. London: Routledge, 2002.

12 Graham, Edward and Marchick, David Matthew. *US National Security and Foreign Investment*. Washington, DC: Institute for International Economics, 2006, 97.

13 Regulations on EJV Law, Article 4; Regulations on WFOE Law, Article 5; Regulations on CJV Law, Article 5.

14 Regulations on EJV Law, Article 2; WFOE Law, Article 4; CJV Law, Article 3.

15 Regulations on EJV Law, Article 4.

16 CJV Law, Article 3; WFOE Law, Article 4; Regulations on WFOE Law, Articles 4.

17 Hu, Hongbin. "China's National Security Studies: History, Evolution and Trends." *Journal of Renmin University of China*, no. 4 (2014): 149.

18 Cai, Dingjian and Wang, Chengguang. *China's Journey towards the Rule of Law: Legal Reform, 1978–2008*. Leiden: Brill Publishers, 2010, 36.

19 Su, Huimin. "China's Relations with West European Countries." In Su, Huimin, Wang, Yi, Wu, Chuntai and Han, Lu (Eds). *New China in the New International Setting*. Brussels: Egmont Institute, 1996, 149–193; Zoellick, Robert. *Op-ed: A Constructive Role with China*, 2010, https://www.worldbank.org/en/news/opinion/2010/09/13/op-ed-constructive-role-china; Fujita, Natsuki and James, William. "Growth Patterns of the Japanese Economy in the 1980s: Before and after the Appreciation of the Yen." *Economic Systems Research* 3, no. 4 (1991); Siok Hwa, Cheng. "Economic Change in Singapore, 1945–1977." *Southeast Asian Journal of Social Science* 7, no. 1/2 (1979): 81–113.

20 Deng, Xiaoping. *Selected Works of Deng Xiaoping, 1975–1982*. Beijing: Foreign Languages Press, 1984.
21 Constitution of PRC (1982 revision), Article 18; Kim, Chin and Kearley, Timothy. "The 1978 Constitution of the People's Republic of China." *Hastings International and Comparative Law Review* 2, no. 2 (1979).
22 Peerenboom, Randall. "Globalization, Path Dependency and the Limits of Law: Administrative Law Reform and Rule of Law in the People's Republic of China." *Berkeley Journal of International Law* 19, no. 2 (2001): 161–163.
23 Wen, Tiejun, Dong Xiaodan and Cui, Xue. "Evolution of Chinese Reform and Open Up Policy and Logic behind It." *Researches in Chinese Economic History*, no. 2 (2012): 148.
24 Deng, Xiaoping. "Hold High the Banner of Mao Zedong Thought and Adhere to the Principle of Seeking Truth from Facts." In Deng, Xiaoping (Ed). *Selected Works of Deng Xiaoping, 1975–1982*. Beijing: Foreign Languages Press, 1984, 141–143; Deng, Xiaoping. "We Can Develop a Market Economy under Socialism." 1979. www.china.org.cn/english/features/dengxiaoping/103388.htm; Vogol, Eraz. *Deng Xiaoping and the Transformation of China*. Cambridge: Harvard University Press, 2011, 717–722; Huang, Yasheng. *Capitalism with Chinese Characteristics*. Cambridge: Cambridge University Press, 2008, 50–108.
25 Regulations on EJV Law, Article 4; Regulations on WFOE Law, Article 5.
26 Gao, Shan. "The Evolution of China's Foreign Investment Policy and Law (1978–2016)." Doctoral thesis of the Pennsylvania State University, 2017, 31–32.
27 Regulations on EJV Law, Article 4.
28 CIA Office of East Asia Analysis. "Directorate of Intelligence: Foreign Investment in China in 1986, and Prospects for 1987." www.cia.gov/library/readingroom/docs/CIA-RDP90T00114R000200110001-4.pdf: 28.
29 Regulations on WFOE Law, Articles 4, 5; CJV Law, Article 3.
30 Regulations on EJV Law, Article 9(1).
31 Regulations on WFOE Law, Article 4.
32 Interim Provisions on the Direction of Attracting Foreign Investment (1987).
33 Decision of the State Council on the Key Points of Current Industrial Policies (1989); List of Absorbing Foreign Investment Sequences (1989).
34 Interim Measures of the National Development and Reform Commission for the Examination and Approval of Foreign Investment Projects, Article 1; Catalogue for the Guidance of Industries for Foreign Investment.
35 State Council of PRC. "Catalogue for Encouraged Foreign Investment Industries. 2020." www.gov.cn/gongbao/content/2021/content_5587654.htm; State Council of PRC. "Catalogue for Encouraged Foreign Investment Industries." 2020. www.gov.cn/gongbao/content/2022/content_5730682.htm.
36 World Bank. "China 2020: China Engaged." 1997. http://documents.worldbank.org/curated/en/656981468743976946/pdf/multi0page.pdf.
37 Gao, Shan. "The Evolution of China's Foreign Investment Policy and Law (1978–2016)." Doctoral thesis of the Pennsylvania State University, 2017, 26.
38 Shen, Jiaming. "Investment in the People's Republic of China: The Basic Legal Framework." *University of Pennsylvania Journal of International Law* 10, no. 3 (1988): 409.
39 OECD. *The Role of FDI in China's Economic Development*. Paris: OECD Publishing, 2003: 33.
40 Vogel, Ezra. *Deng Xiaoping and the Transformation of China*. Cambridge: Harvard University Press, 2011, 876.
41 Beijing Review. "Full Text of Jiang Zemin's Report at 14th Party Congress." 1992. www.bjreview.com.cn/document/txt/2011-03/29/content_363504.htm.
42 Decision of the Central Committee of the Communist Party of China on Some Issues concerning the Establishment of a Socialist Market Economic Structure (1993); Jones, Carol. "Capitalism, Globalization and Rule of Law: An Alternative Trajectory of Legal

Change in China." *Social & Legal Studies* 3, no. 2 (1994): 195–221; Karsten, Siegfried. "China's Approach to Social Market Economics: The Chinese Variant of Market Socialism Seeks to Escape from the Difficulties of Central Command Planning." *The American Journal of Economics and Sociology* 47, no. 2 (1988): 129–148; Guo, Jian'an, Zha, Qingjiu and Han, Xiutao. "The Rule of Law and Economic Development in China." *China Law* 1 (2008).

43 Edelman, Marc and Haugerud, Angelique. *The Anthropology of Development and Globalization: From Classical Political Economy to Contemporary Neoliberalism*. Oxford: Blackwell Publishing, 2005.

44 Jiang, Zemin. *Selected Works of Jiang Zemin (Volume II)*. Beijing: People's Publishing House, 2006, 423.

45 Interim Provisions on the Direction of Attracting Foreign Investment (1987), Article 7(1).

46 Interim Provisions on Guiding the Orientation of Foreign Investment (1995), Article 6(1).

47 Interim Provisions on Guiding the Orientation of Foreign Investment (1995), Article 6(2).

48 Interim Provisions on Guiding the Orientation of Foreign Investment (1995), Article 6(4).

49 Jiang, Zemin. *Selected Works of Jiang Zemin (Volume III)*. Beijing: People's Publishing House, 2006, 36.

50 Interim Provisions on Guiding the Orientation of Foreign Investment (1995), Article 7(4).

51 Jiang, Zemin. *Selected Works of Jiang Zemin (Volume III)*. Beijing: People's Publishing House, 2006, 586.

52 Catalogue of Industries for Guiding foreign investment (1995).

53 Cui, Zhiyuan. "Making Sense of the Chinese Socialist Market Economy: A Note." *Modern China* 38, no. 6 (2012): 665–676; Ou, Chen. "The Characteristics of China's National Security." *Journal of Politics and Law* (2011): 84–93.

54 Interim Provisions on the Direction of Attracting Foreign Investment (1987), Article 7(1); Interim Provisions on Guiding the Orientation of Foreign Investment (1995), Article 7(1).

55 Interim Provisions on Guiding the Orientation of Foreign Investment (1995), Article 7(1).

56 Interim Provisions on Guiding the Orientation of Foreign Investment (1995), Article 7(2).

57 Provisions on Guiding the Orientation of Foreign Investment (2002), Article 7(3).

58 Wen, Xiantao. "Discussion about the No. 10 Decree: Views on the End and Renascence of a Regime." *China Law Review* 9, no. 1 (2016): 223.

59 Interim Provisions on the Merger and Acquisition of Domestic Enterprises by Foreign Investors (2003).

60 Interim Provisions on the Merger and Acquisition of Domestic Enterprises by Foreign Investors (2003), Article 20; Li, Yuwen and Bian, Cheng. "A New Dimension of Foreign Investment Law in China: Evolution and Impacts of the National Security Review System." *Asia Pacific Law Review* 24, no. 2 (2016): 156.

61 Interim Provisions on the Merger and Acquisition of Domestic Enterprises by Foreign Investors (2003), Article 19.

62 Interim Provisions on the Merger and Acquisition of Domestic Enterprises by Foreign Investors (2003), Article 19.

63 Interim Provisions on Mergers and Acquisitions of Domestic Enterprises by Foreign Investment (2006); Provisions of the Ministry of Commerce on M&A of a Domestic Enterprise by Foreign Investor (2009).

64 Interim Provisions on Mergers and Acquisitions of Domestic Enterprises by Foreign Investment (2006), Article 10.

65 Jensen, Eric. "Balancing Security and Growth: Defining National Security Review of Foreign Investment in China." *Pacific Rim Law & Policy Journal Association* 19, no. 1 (2010): 168.

66 Interim Provisions on Mergers and Acquisitions of Domestic Enterprises by Foreign Investment (2006), Article 12; Qingxiu Bu. "China's National Security Review: A Tit-for-Tat Response?" *Law and Financial Markets Review* 6, no. 5 (2012): 347.

67 Jensen, Eric. "Balancing Security and Growth: Defining National Security Review of Foreign Investment in China." *Pacific Rim Law & Policy Journal Association* 19, no. 1 (2010): 169.

68 Interim Provisions on Mergers and Acquisitions of Domestic Enterprises by Foreign Investment (2006), Article 12.

69 Anti-Monopoly Law (2007), Article 31; Fox, Eleanor. "An Anti-Monopoly Law for China: Scaling the Walls of Government Restraints." *Antitrust Law Journal* 75, no. 1 (2008): 174.

70 Bu, Qingxiu. "China's National Security Review: A Tit-for-Tat Response?" *Law and Financial Markets Review* 6, no. 5 (2012): 347. Howell, Thomas, Wolff, Alan, Howe Rachel and Oh, Diane. "China's New Anti-Monopoly Law: A Perspective from the United States." *Pacific Rim Law & Policy Journal* 18, no. 1 (2009): 92; Sothmann, Stephen. "Let He Who Is Without Sin Cast the First Stone: Foreign Direct Investment and National Security Regulations in China." *Indiana International & Comparative Law Review* 19 (2009): 219.

71 Provisions of the Ministry of Commerce on M&A of a Domestic Enterprise by Foreign Investor (2009), Article 12; Li, Yuwen and Bian, Cheng. "A New Dimension of Foreign Investment Law in China: Evolution and Impacts of the National Security Review System." *Asia Pacific Law Review* 24, no. 2 (2016): 160.

72 Provisions of the Ministry of Commerce on M&A of a Domestic Enterprise by Foreign Investor (2009), Article 12.

73 Circular of the General Office of the State Council on the Establishment of Security Review System Regarding Merger and Acquisition of Domestic Enterprises by Foreign Investors (State Council Circular 6, 2011); Mahony, Tarrant. *Foreign Investment Law in China: Regulation, Practice and Context*. Beijing: Tsinghua University Press, 2015, 74.

74 State Council Circular 6, Article 2; Li, Yuwen and Bian, Cheng. "A New Dimension of Foreign Investment Law in China: Evolution and Impacts of the National Security Review System." *Asia Pacific Law Review* 24, no. 2 (2016): 160–161.

75 MOFCOM Announcement of Provisions on the Implementation of the Security Review System for Mergers and Acquisitions of Domestic Enterprises by Foreign Investors (MOFCOM Announcement 53, 2011)

76 Law of the PRC on Administrative Licensing (2003), Article 14.

77 Qi, Tong. "Several Important Issues Concerning the Legislation on National Security Review on Foreign Investment." *China Law Review* 5, no. 3 (2015): 79.

78 Zhou, Huan and Simpson, Paul. "Cross-Border Mergers and Acquisitions in China: An Industry Panel Study, 1991–2005." *Asia Pacific Business Review* 14, no. 4 (2008): 492.

79 Li, Yuwen and Bian, Cheng. "A New Dimension of Foreign Investment Law in China: Evolution and Impacts of the National Security Review System." *Asia Pacific Law Review* 24, no. 2 (2016): 153.

80 Li, Ningshun. "Discussion on Issues Pertaining to the Acquisitions of State-Owned-Enterprises by Foreign Investment." *Commercial Times* 29, no. 3 (2010): 108–109.

81 Li, Ningshun. "Discussion on Issues Pertaining to the Acquisitions of State-Owned-Enterprises by Foreign Investment." *Commercial Times* 29, no. 3 (2010): 108–109; Li, Yuwen and Bian, Cheng. "A New Dimension of Foreign Investment Law in China: Evolution and Impacts of the National Security Review System." *Asia Pacific Law Review* 24, no. 2 (2016): 153.

82 Hartge, Cathleen. "China's National Security Review: Motivations and the Implications for Investors." *Stanford Journal of International Law* 49, no. 1 (2013): 245.

83 Wang, Houshuang. "On the Characteristics of National Economic Integrity in the Era of Economic Globalization." *Pacific Journal*, no. 1 (2001): 41.
84 Zhao, Suisheng. "Chinese Foreign Policy under Hu Jintao: The Struggle between Low-Profile Policy and Diplomatic Activism." *Hague Journal of Diplomacy* 5, no. 4 (2010): 357–378.
85 Tanner, Murray. "Hu Jintao as China's Emerging National Security Leader." In Scobell, Andrew and Wortzel, Larry (Eds). *Civil-Military Change in China: Elites, Institutes, and Ideas after the 16th Party Congress*. Pennsylvania: Strategic Studies Institute-US Army War College, 2004, 49–76.
86 State Council Circular 6, Article 2(2).
87 State Council Circular 6, Article 1(1).
88 Mulvenon, James. "Chairman Hu and the PLA's New Historic Missions." *China Leadership Monitor*, no. 27 (2009): 1–11.
89 State Council Circular 6, Article 2(1).
90 State Council Circular 6, Article 2(4).
91 Information Office of the State Council. "White Paper China's Peaceful Development Was Issued." 2011. www.fmcoprc.gov.hk/eng/xwfw/gszxxw/t856249.htm.
92 State Council Circular 6, Article 2(3).
93 General Plan for the China (Shanghai) Free Trade Zone (2013).
94 Measures for Administration of the China (Shanghai) Pilot Free Trade Zone (2013); Mahony, Tarrant. *Foreign Investment Law in China: Regulation, Practice and Context*. Beijing: Tsinghua University Press, 2015, 81–82.
95 Announcement of the Shanghai Municipal People's Government on Issuing the Special Management Measures (Negative List) for foreign investment in China (Shanghai) Pilot Free Trade Zone (2013).
96 Special Management Measures of Foreign Investment Access in China (Shanghai) Pilot Free Zone (2013).
97 Special Administrative Measures for Foreign Investment Access in Pilot Free Trade Zone (FTZ Negative List) (2015).
98 Several Opinions of the CPC Central Committee and the State Council on Developing a New System of Open Economy (2015).
99 Special Administrative Measures for Foreign Investment Access in Pilot Free Trade Zones (Negative List) (2013); Special Administrative Measures for Foreign Investment Access in Pilot Free Trade Zones (Negative List) (2014); Special Administrative Measures for Foreign Investment Access in Pilot Free Trade Zones (Negative List) (2015); Special Administrative Measures for Foreign Investment Access in Pilot Free Trade Zones (Negative List) (2017); Special Administrative Measures for Foreign Investment Access in Pilot Free Trade Zones (Negative List) (2018); Special Administrative Measures for Foreign Investment Access in Pilot Free Trade Zones (Negative List) (2019); Special Administrative Measures for Foreign Investment Access in Pilot Free Trade Zones (Negative List) (2020); Special Administrative Measures for Foreign Investment Access in Pilot Free Trade Zones (Negative List) (2021).
100 "Comrade in Charge of the National Development and Reform Commission Attended the Press Conference of the State Council Information Office to Interpret the Macroeconomic Situation and Policies, and Answered Questions from Reporters." 2024. www.ndrc.gov.cn/fzggw/wld/yd/zyhd/202401/t20240119_1363542.html.
101 Special Administrative Measures for Foreign Investment Access (Negative List) (2018).
102 Special Administrative Measures for Foreign Investment Access (Negative List) (2021); Special Administrative Measures for Foreign Investment Access in Pilot Free Trade Zones (Negative List) (2021); Special Administrative Measures for Foreign Investment Access (Negative List) (2020); Special Administrative Measures for Foreign Investment Access in Pilot Free Trade Zones (Negative List) (2020); Special Administrative Measures for Foreign Investment Access (Negative List) (2019); Special Administrative Measures for Foreign Investment Access in Pilot Free Trade

Zones (Negative List) (2019); Special Administrative Measures for Foreign Investment Access (Negative List) (2018); Special Administrative Measures for Foreign Investment Access in Pilot Free Trade Zones (Negative List) (2018).

103 Tang, David and Wei, Serina. "Brief Comments on China's Commitments on the Foreign Investment Access under the RCEP." 2020. www.hankunlaw.com/downloadfile/newsAndInsights/4cbeea5e53234067290b7aaafc7963b0.pdf, 2; Special Administrative Measures (Negative List) for Market Access of Foreign Investment (2020 Edition).

104 Special Administrative Measures (Negative List) for Market Access of Foreign Investment (2020 Edition); Webre, Edwarde and Wang, Sean. "Foreign Investment Restrictions to be Further Relaxed: A Brief Analysis on the Negative Lists." 2018. www.deacons.com/news-and-insights/publications/foreign-investment-restrictions-to-be-further-relaxed-a-brief-analysis-on-the-negative-lists-2018.html.

105 Special Administrative Measures (Negative List) for Market Access of Foreign Investment (2020 Edition); Seto, Myles and Wang, Sean. "China Announced the 2020 Negative Lists for Foreign Investment Access." 2020. www.deacons.com/news-and-insights/publications/china-announced-the-2020-negative-lists-for-foreign-investment-access.html.

106 Opinions of the State Council on the Implementation of the Negative list for Market Access (2015), Article 2(7).

107 China Law & Practice. "National Security Review Creates FDI Hurdle." 2015. www.cov.com/~/media/files/corporate/publications/2015/07/national_security_review_creates_fdi_hurdle.pdf.

108 Dong, Lyong and Stone, Charles. "China Passes New Foreign Investment Law." 2021. http://hk-lawyer.org/content/china-passes-new-foreign-investment-law.

109 Foreign Investment Law of the PRC (2019) (FIL).

110 Li, Qiang, Wang, Stewart and Huang, Michael. "China Passes Foreign Investment Law." 2019. www.dlapiper.com/en/hongkong/insights/publications/2019/04/china-passes-foreign-investment-law/.

111 FIL, Article 35.

112 Li, Yuwen and Bian, Cheng. "A New Dimension of Foreign Investment Law in China: Evolution and Impacts of the National Security Review System." *Asia Pacific Law Review* 24, no. 2 (2016): 151; Oster, Shai. "China Fuels Concern for Planning Tougher Security Reviews." 2015. www.bloomberg.com/news/articles/2015-02-10/china-s-plan-to-toughen-national-security-review-fuels-concerns. Russell, Chris. "Rules of the Game, Changes in China's Foreign Investment Law." 2015. http://knowledge.ckgsb.edu.cn/2015/06/25/finance-and-investment/rules-of-the-game-changes-in-chinas-foreign-investment-law/.

113 Measures on Security Review for Foreign Investment (2020) (Measures).

114 BBC News. "Full Text: China's New Party Chief Xi Jinping's Speech." www.bbc.com/news/world-asia-china-20338586.

115 Resolution of the Central Committee of the Communist Party of China on Some Major Issues Concerning Comprehensive Deepening the Reform (2013).

116 Resolution of the Central Committee of the Communist Party of China on Some Major Issues Concerning Comprehensive Deepening the Reform (2013).

117 Resolution concerning Some Major Issues in Comprehensively Moving Ruling the Country According to the Law Forward (2014); Chua, Eu Jin. "The Laws of the People's Republic of China: An Introduction for International Investors." *Chicago Journal of International Law* 7, no. 1 (2006): 133–140; Horsley, Jamie. "The Rule of Law: Pushing the Limits of Party Rule." In Fewsmith, Joseph (Ed). *China Today, China Tomorrow: Domestic Politics, Economy and Society*. Lanham: Rowman & Littlefield Publishers, 2010.

118 Fewsmith, Joseph. *China Today, China Tomorrow: Domestic Politics, Economy and Society*. Lanham: Rowman & Littlefield Publishers, 2010.

119 Data from MOFCOM website.
120 Implementation Plan for Comprehensive Reform Pilot in Pudong New Area (2023–2027), Article 1. www.gov.cn/govweb/zhengce/202401/content_6927505.htm.
121 Implementation Plan for Comprehensive Reform Pilot in Pudong New Area (2023–2027), Article 1. www.gov.cn/govweb/zhengce/202401/content_6927505.htm.
122 Implementation Plan for Comprehensive Reform Pilot in Pudong New Area (2023–2027), Article 1. www.gov.cn/govweb/zhengce/202401/content_6927505.htm.
123 National Security Law (2015) (NSL).
124 NSL, Article 2.
125 NSL, Article 3.
126 NSL, Article 59.
127 NSL, Article 15.
128 NSL, Article 16.
129 NSL, Article 17.
130 Measures, Article 4(1).
131 Measures, Article 4(1).
132 NSL, Article 21.
133 Measures, Article 4(2).
134 Measures, Article 4(2).
135 Marchisio, Matteo. "The Potential Impact of COVID-19 on China's Food Security: Prospects for FOOD Imports." 2020. www.ifad.org/en/web/latest/blog/asset/41937713.
136 Compilation and Translation Bureau. *The 13th Five-Year Plan for Economic and Social Development of PRC (2016–2020)*. Beijing: Central Compilation & Translation Press, 2020. https://en.ndrc.gov.cn/newsrelease_8232/201612/P020191101481868235378.pdf; Xinhua Net. "Resolutions of the Fourth Session of the Thirteenth National People's Congress on the Fourteenth Five-Year Plan for National Economic and Social Development and the Outline of Vision Goals for 2035." 2021. www.xinhuanet.com/politics/2021-03/11/c_1127200766.htm; Zhang, Zoe. "What Is China's Dual Circulation Strategy and Why Should Foreign Investors Take Note." 2020. www.china-briefing.com/news/what-is-chinas-dual-circulation-strategy-and-why-should-foreign-investors-take-note/.
137 NSL, Article 23.
138 Measures, Article 4(2).
139 NSL, Article 24.
140 "Xi Jinping Addresses the Opening Ceremony of a Study Session at the Party School of the CPC Central Committee Attended by Senior Provincial and Ministerial Officials to Adhere to the Bottom Line and Focusing on Preventing and Defusing Major Risks." 2019. www.gov.cn/xinwen/2019-01/21/content_5359898.htm?eqid=9b9b02fb000371dc0000000664905a68; Social Stability. "Xi Urges Major Risk Prevention to Ensure Healthy Economy." https://english.www.gov.cn/news/top_news/2019/01/22/content_281476489537858.htm.
141 "DecisionofCPCCentralCommitteeonMajorIssuesConcerningHowtoUpholdandImprove the System of Socialism with Chinese Characteristics and Advance the Modernization of China's System and Capacity for Governance." 2019. www.gov.cn/zhengce/2019-11/05/content_5449023.htm?eqid=fe205c30002083660000000264636647; Liu, Fengyi. "Taking the Significant Advantages of the Basic Economic System to Advance the Modernization of China's System and Capacity for Governance." *China Economic Transition* 3, no. 4 (2020): 41–49.
142 "Report to the 20th National Congress of the CPC. Hold High the Great Banner of Socialism with Chinese Characteristics and Strive in Unity to Build a Modern Socialist Country in All Respects." https://english.news.cn/20221025/8eb6f5239f984f01a2bc45b5b5db0c51/c.html.
143 Center for Studies on a Holistic Approach to National Security Taskforce. "Implement Guiding Principles of the 20th CPC National Congress and Safeguard National Security on the New Journey." *China Security Studies*, no. 5 (2022): 14.

144 Xinhua Net. "Grasp the New Stage of Development, Implement the New Development Concept, and Construct a New Development Pattern." 2021. www.xinhuanet.com/politics/2021-04/30/c_1127397175.htm.
145 Measures, Article 4(2).
146 Measures, Article 4(2).
147 Guangming Net. "Without Cybersecurity, There Can Be No National Security." 2022. https://m.gmw.cn/baijia/2022-09/06/36007431.html.
148 Guangming Net. "Without Cybersecurity, There Can Be No National Security." 2022. https://m.gmw.cn/baijia/2022-09/06/36007431.html.
149 Li, Yan. "China's Cyber Governance Undergoes Revamp." *Global Times*. 2017. www.ecns.cn/m/2017/10-17/277272.shtml.
150 Li, Yan. "China's Cyber Governance Undergoes Revamp." *Global Times*. 2017. www.ecns.cn/m/2017/10-17/277272.shtml.
151 Li, Yan. "China's Cyber Governance Undergoes Revamp." *Global Times*. 2017. www.ecns.cn/m/2017/10-17/277272.shtml.
152 Chen, Jihong and Sun, Jiabin. "China's Data Security Law: Analysis and Compliance Guidance." 2021. www.sohu.com/a/474133961_121123759; Data Security Law (2021); Personal Information Protection Law (2021).
153 Measures, Article 4(2).
154 Opinions of the CPC and the State Council on Comprehensively Promoting the Development of a Beautiful China (2024).

3 Idea Dominance in National Security Review of Foreign Investment Laws in the US

3.1 The Embryonic Period of the National Security Review

3.1.1 Sectoral Restrictions

The earliest national security concerns regarding foreign investment can be traced back to the Trading with the Enemy Act (TWEA) of 1917, when the US officially entered World War I.[1] The TWEA bestowed on the president, in times of war or national emergency, the power to take a number of measures in relation to foreign investment transactions which might carry national security implications.[2] In response to US Navy concerns about national security during the war, the Congress passed a number of sectoral restrictions in the fields of oil, mineral resources, radio, and telecommunications. To be specific, the Merchant Marine Act of 1920 closed the seaborne sector to foreign investment and forbade foreign investors to register their vessels in US territory.[3] The Mineral Lands Leasing Act, passed in the same year, explicitly prohibited foreign investment from leasing mineral lands in the US for the purpose of refining or transporting oil, unless the countries from which the foreign investment originated allowed reciprocal treatment.[4] Similarly, under the Mineral Leasing Act of 1920, foreign investment was not permitted for the exploitation of coal, petroleum, phosphate, or sodium in the US, unless the right to exploitation of such resources was reciprocal to US citizens in the home country of the investor.[5] These sectoral restrictions were not purely designed to protect energy security in the US. The principle of reciprocity reflected in the rules revealed a hidden intention: to guarantee mineral resources to the US Navy worldwide by providing US enterprises with investment opportunities in foreign countries. Because of the US Navy's worries about espionage activities involving radio in times of war, the Radio Act of 1927 prohibited foreign investment in the radio sector. The Communication Act of 1934, which incorporated the Radio Act of 1927, expanded the scope of prohibited sectors, involving both radio and mass media.[6]

3.1.2 The Emerging CFIUS

With increasing investments from the Organization of Petroleum Exporting Countries throughout the 1970s, the US began to realize the necessity for sufficient data

DOI: 10.4324/9781003543749-3

on foreign investments to enable identification of their impacts on national security, and the Foreign Investment Study Act of 1974 was passed as a result, to authorize the Department of Commerce and the Department of the Treasury to investigate and evaluate foreign investments.[7]

Later, in 1975, an interministerial agency—the CFIUS—was created through Executive Order 11858 signed by President Gerald Ford.[8] The CFIUS originally functioned as a research and monitoring mechanism for investigating and evaluating the impacts of foreign investment on industry and the economy, providing adjustments for foreign investment laws and policies, considering legal proposals when they appeared necessary, and requesting foreign investors to submit preliminary reports regarding their activities.[9]

In contrast to the TWEA, which authorized the president to seize and nationalize foreign assets following declarations of war or in international emergencies, the Congress attempted to regulate the president's power by amending the TWEA. The International Emergency Economic Powers Act (IEEPA) was enacted to limit the president's power in emergency situations. The IEEPA also affirmed foreign investors' ownership of their assets by requiring the president not to take title to foreign-owned assets and to return them when the emergency ended, which was quite different from the practice during World War I, when the US government expropriated foreign assets in the US and never returned them, especially those from Germany.[10] There were several obstacles to implementation of the IEEPA, however. On the one hand, it was difficult in practice to prove that certain foreign investment transactions would pose a significant threat to US national security. On the other hand, and more importantly, the IEEPA applies only in emergency situations which are always hard to be declared in practice.

3.2 The Period of Establishment of the National Security Review

3.2.1 The Exon-Florio Amendment and Following Amendments

In the wave of M&A activities sweeping over US business sectors, especially by Japanese investors, growing US concerns about national security in relation to foreign investment led, with the Omnibus Trade and Competitiveness Act of 1988, to the passage of the Exon-Florio Amendment to Section 721 of the Defense Production Act (DPA) of 1950.[11] The Exon-Florio Amendment explicitly authorized the president to investigate any foreign acquisition, merger, or takeover of US enterprises on national security grounds and suspend or prohibit such a transaction if it met two conditions: (i) credible evidence that the controlling transactions proposed by the foreign investor would or might threaten to impair US national security,[12] and (ii) the inadequacy and inappropriateness of laws other than the IEEPA in regard to measures to mitigate potential risks to national security.[13] The Exon-Florio Amendment contains eight provisions: definitions of essential terms, national security reviews and investigations, confidentiality of information, action by the president, actions and findings non-reviewable, factors to be considered; additional information to Congress and confidentiality, and other regulations.[14]

President Ronald Reagan, upon assuming office, delegated his Exon-Florio Amendment authority to the CFIUS through Executive Order 12661.[15] The CFIUS could therefore conduct the national security review, declare national security threats in certain transactions, and even make recommendations to the president regarding prohibiting or suspending transactions.[16] This change transformed the CFIUS role from that of a toothless tiger focusing on fact-finder and reporter, to the much powerful one of gatekeeper. That is why the national security review of foreign investments in the US is often referred to as "the CFIUS review". Although the DPA expired in 1990, the Exon-Florio Amendment was given permanent force by the Defense Production Act Extension and Amendments of 1991.[17] In addition, the presidential power to make implementing regulations for national security review was transferred to the chair of the CFIUS, the Department of Treasury, in coordination with other CFIUS members. The Regulations Pertaining to Mergers, Acquisitions, and Takeovers by Foreign Persons were promulgated by the Department of the Treasury in 1991, providing guidelines about enforcing the national security review in accordance with the Exon-Florio Amendment.

Another regulation supplementary to the Exon-Florio Amendment proposed by Senator Robert Byrd was the Byrd Amendment in Section 837(a) of the National Defense Authorization Act for Fiscal Year 1993. The Byrd Amendment provided an additional phase in which the CFIUS was to carry out a mandatory investigation when, upon completion of initial review, it was held that an acquiring party was controlled by or acting on behalf of a foreign government and such a transaction would threaten US national security.[18] In terms of factors to be taken into account, the potential effects of proposed transactions on sales of military goods, equipment, or technology to any country with terrorist links or the capacity to build weapons of mass destruction, and on US international technological leadership, were added to the considerations of national security review conducted by the CFIUS.[19] Also, the president was required to submit a written report explaining national security considerations to the Congress, no matter what kinds of decisions were made, indicating a potential for congressional involvement in national security review.[20]

In the same year, another amendment, proposed by Senator Donald Riegle, was formally incorporated in the Defense Production Act Amendments of 1993, with the specific purpose of attracting congressional attention to foreign investment in certain sectors and enhancing congressional monitoring power over the enforcement of national security review by the CFIUS.[21] The Riegle Amendment required the CFIUS to report to the Congress every four years on foreign investment M&As in the US. This was aimed at answering the questions of whether there was credible evidence showing foreign strategic intentions to acquire American companies in research and development or critical technology fields, and whether there was any industrial espionage targeting the US and aimed at seizing critical technological secrets.[22]

3.2.2 Ideas on National Security

Throughout the 1980s, much of the debate over formulating the Exon-Florio Amendment focused on how to conduct the national security review and whether economic factors would be taken into consideration in the national security review.[23] Another bill was proposed by Representative Bryant (Bryant's Bill) which provided detailed procedural requirements to enhance the transparency of national security review,[24] indicating suspicions that previous rules on foreign investment failed to provide early warning functions when foreign investments occurred in industrial fields related to national security. As the transparency of national security review would in turn negatively influence the interests of US multinational enterprises investing abroad, Bryant's Bill failed, and the revised Exon bill was suggested as a compromise within the Congress.

Several revisions were made to Exon's bill. First, in order to secure presidential support during the legislative process, the president, rather than the Department of Commerce as earlier proposed, was granted veto power to block foreign investments.[25] Such a presidential veto—enabling prohibition or suspension of foreign investments from the highest administrative level—also reflected US prudence on halting foreign investment, amid its general commitment to attracting and utilizing foreign investment. Second, a clause from an earlier proposal, stating that Congress could veto the president's actions through a joint resolution, was deleted as a compromise to obtain government support for the bill.[26] Two restrictions on regulating presidential actions were retained, however, on the insistence of Congress. One was that the presidential action should be statutorily conditioned, meaning that there must be credible evidence that foreigners may act to damage US national security, and that no law other than the IEEPA can provide adequate and appropriate relief powers. The other was that the president must report his decision to the Congress with detailed explanations of his judgments. Third, the president was empowered to take any appropriate mitigating measures, including suspension of the investment, application for a ban, or other equitable measures,[27] demonstrating that prohibition would be a last resort, adopted only if other alternatives could not adequately safeguard US national security or mitigate national security risks.

In addition, the question was raised of whether economic factors would constitute criteria for use in the national security review. Other than national security, the considerations of essential commerce and economic welfare were deemed equivalent factors to national security for evaluating whether to block certain transactions.[28] To be specific, Exon's bill listed five aspects to elaborate on such essential commerce and economic welfare: (i) whether the foreign investment involved domestic production essential for national defense; (ii) whether it related to the growth of national defense industries; (iii) the extent of the control of such industries by foreign investment; (iv) the impact of foreign control on the economic welfare of individual domestic industries, including its potential to cause substantial unemployment; (v) possible results of revenue decrease, loss of skills or investment, or other serious effects.[29] Similarly, Florio's bill proposed expanding the scope of national security from the field of national defense and incorporating concerns related to economic health and economic conditions.

Regarding Florio's bill, which attempted to expand the scope of military security, some governmental departments expressed their opposition, arguing that national security had already been well covered through the existing legislation for foreign investment and further legislation was not necessarily needed. David Mulford, for example, the assistant secretary in the International Affairs Bureau of the Department of the Treasury, pointed out that, although several mergers and acquisitions of American companies by Japanese investors would raise national security issues to some extent, their potential threats involving advanced technology and national defense had already been solved by prompt action by the DOD.[30] The export control law, provisions on confidential DOD contracts, departmental exceptions in the provisions on national treatment, and the IEEPA were all, moreover intended to address national security issues in the military.[31]

Ideas on national security that included essential commerce or economic welfare received strong criticism from the executive branch. Malcolm Baldrige, for example, when serving as the Secretary of Commerce, argued that the criteria in the Exon bill were purely economic and unrelated to national security for four reasons. First, there were no clear clues to the impact of foreign investment on the economy. The criteria of economic welfare in CFIUS reviews would make US regulators pay inappropriate attention to market competition. This might lead to the CFIUS being abused in disguised attacks on foreign investors' enthusiasm.[32] Second, the adverse economic implications of CFIUS reviews demonstrate a regression of US opening policy on the national treatment principle and liberalizing foreign investment as advocated in the global context.[33] Third, he held the view that it was quite difficult to judge the impact of foreign investment on the issue of unemployment.[34] Fourth, he contended that there was no clear and direct relation between foreign investment and governmental revenue. Other objections were that the application of economic factors in national security review would create an unfriendly atmosphere and give rise to bureaucratic obstacles to foreign investment, and that the CFIUS could not be defined as a special mechanism, as each government agency already had the responsibility of safeguarding national security and the national interest.[35] As a result, President Reagan even threatened to veto any bill in which economic factors were established as criteria for CFIUS reviews.

In addition to objections from the executive branch, some practitioners from industry groups also opposed the expansion of the scope of national security, supporting its confinement within the scope of pure national security.[36] Robert McNeill, executive vice chairman of the Emergency Committee for American Trade, for example, argued that the objective of preserving national security as generally acceptable but that the industrial groups perceived essential commerce and economic welfare goals with great concern as they were enormously broad and vague standards that were of great significance to business activities in the US.[37] They argued that it was hard to distinguish basic economic issues from national security issues in CFIUS review enforcement, and such an expansion of the scope of the review would inevitably constitute an undue obstacle for foreign investment, contradicting the nation's long-held open policy.[38]

Interestingly, a rather general concept in the name of "national security" seemed much easier to agree than an ideational consensus within the Congress in which each side had various sometimes controversial concerns and interests. From the perspective of legislative technique, a consensus was hard to achieve on a specific issue but could be achieved in a broad sense.[39] It is apparent that the term "national security" is much more abstract than "essential commerce and economic welfare" and can be interpreted broadly. Although the question of whether the national security review should involve economic aspects is controversial in the internal US structure, the significance of national security is undoubted. The necessity of safeguarding national security is not denied by any party. Neither governmental departments nor industrial representatives would oppose the presidential veto power over foreign investment in industries that are vital to national security.[40]

In the passage of the Exon-Florio Amendment, it was much easier to achieve a consensus on the term "national security". An ideational consensus reached within the Congress was that the review criteria ought to be limited to pure national security. The review standards of "essential commerce" and economic welfare were excluded from the final text of the Exon-Florio Amendment, and economic interests, such as market competitiveness, governmental revenue and employment, were not to be taken into consideration in CFIUS reviews. Instead, pure national security was affirmed as the sole statutory reason for prohibiting and blocking foreign investment, in line with the traditional open policy.[41] As a result, the executive branch and the Congress reached an ideational consensus on the definition of national security and foreign investment by answering the question of whether to involve economic considerations, and the revised Exon bill, different in several respects from its original version, eventually became law.[42]

3.3 The Codification Period of the National Security Review: FINSA

On October 24, 2007, the FINSA was adopted as a landmark for codifying the regulatory mechanism of the national security review.[43] The Regulations Pertaining to Mergers, Acquisitions, and Takeovers by Foreign Persons, FINSA promulgated as its implementing regulations by the Department of the Treasury on November 21, 2008.[44] The FINSA made several prudent but significant changes to the national security review established in the Exon-Florio Amendment.

3.3.1 Legal Rules

First, the FINSA broadened the definition of what is considered "national security" by listing a number of factors that CFIUS may consider when evaluating national security implications of proposed transactions.[45] The terms "critical infrastructure" and "critical technologies" were first introduced to evaluate national security.

If the CFIUS determines that the proposed transaction would result in control of any critical infrastructure or critical technologies which threatens to impair US national security, and such a threat has not been mitigated during the preliminary national security review, a 45-day investigation is triggered.[46] Accordingly, in addition to five factors listed in the Exon-Florio Amendment, the FINSA enumerated another five for consideration: (i) potential national security-related effects on US critical infrastructure, including major assets; (ii) potential national security-related effects on US critical technologies; (iii) whether the transaction in question was a foreign government-controlled transaction covered by the Byrd Amendment; (iv) whether it could meet long-term US requirements for energy and other critical resources and material; (v) other factors that would be determined appropriate by the president or the CFIUS, generally or in connection with a specific review or investigation.[47] It can therefore be concluded that, in the FINSA, critical infrastructure, critical technology, foreign governmental control, key resources and materials were additional aspects for evaluating national security impacts regarding foreign investment. The term "critical infrastructure" was employed as a new condition for the first time, to determine whether to undertake investigation, indicating an expansion of the scope of national security review in the US at this period. The emphasis on critical infrastructure as another key aspect of national security was heavily influenced by the 911 incident.[48]

Second, in addition to the Department of the Treasury as the chair of the CFIUS with liaison functions in each reviewed transaction, the FINSA empowered the CFIUS to designate another agency or other agencies to take the lead on its behalf on a case-by-case basis.[49] Generally, it is the CFIUS member or CFIUS members with the greatest interest or who is most affected by or connected to a specific reviewed foreign investment transaction that will often take the lead in serving substantive functions of the review process. This dualist institutional arrangement is designed to avoid unreasonable and unprofessional judgments made by a sole lead lacking expertise in connection with specific transactions.[50] In addition to reviewing in the process of preliminary national security review and national security investigation, the designated lead agency acts as the lead position as it is empowered to undertake the negotiations on mitigation with the parties and monitor mitigation compliance.[51] Tasks relating to mitigation measures, however, are not conducted arbitrarily by the lead agency as they were under the oversight of the CFIUS. The lead agency has to provide periodic reports to the CFIUS, for example, concerning any material modifications to mitigation measures imposed with respect to the transaction, and it needs to ensure that such material modifications are reported to the Director of National Intelligence (DNI), the Attorney General of the US, and any federal departments or agencies that might have a material interest in such modifications.[52]

Third, the FINSA mandates a 45-day mandatory investigation beyond the preliminary national security review on any transaction which is controlled by or conducted on behalf of a foreign government or which would result in the control of any critical infrastructure by default, unless both the Department of the Treasury and the lead agency determine that such a foreign investment does not affect national security. Although the requirement of foreign government-controlled transaction was originally created in the Byrd Amendment, the key difference lies in the approaches to making such a judgement. Pursuant to the Byrd Amendment, an additional 45-day investigation is required only when the CFIUS as a whole collectively determines that such a foreign government-controlled transaction would trigger or has already triggered any national security-related impact. This arrangement was criticized as a loophole, because the decisions were still made by the CFIUS with little modification offered by the Exon-Florio Amendment. The FINSA addressed the matter, however, by transferring the decision on national security investigations from all CFIUS members to the chair and the lead agency. As the chair and the lead agency are more likely to reach a consensus on whether a foreign government controlled transaction would pose national security risks, national security investigations are expected to increase in practice to facilitate better scrutiny of foreign investment and safeguard national security.[53]

Fourth, the FINSA attempted to enhance congressional oversight. It requires the CFIUS, for example, to transmit certified notice to the Congress after the completion of a preliminary national security review or national security investigation, and must, on request from specific members of Congress, provide prompt briefings on a covered transaction for which all action has concluded or on compliance with a mitigation agreement or condition imposed with respect to such transaction, on a classified basis, if deemed necessary by the sensitivity of the information.[54] In addition, the CFIUS is required to transmit an annual report to the chair and the ranking member of the committee of jurisdiction in the Senate and the House of Representatives, before July 31 of each year on all of the national security reviews and investigations of covered transactions reviewed and completed by the CFIUS during the 12-month period.[55] Although a similar requirement in the Exon-Florio Amendment had already required quadrennial CFIUS reporting to the Congress, it was almost neglected in practice, except for an initial report in 1993.[56] This annual reporting obligation implies that the Congress intended to strengthen its involvement in supervision of national security review *ex post*.

Fifth, the FINSA created an evergreen provision that the CFIUS is able to relaunch any covered or completed transaction which has previously been reviewed or investigated, in cases where any party to the transaction submitted false or misleading material information to the CFIUS in connection with the review or investigation or where any party omitted material information, as well as in cases in which any party to the transaction or the entity resulting from consummation of the transaction intentionally and materially breaches the conditions of a mitigation agreement, and there are no other remedies or enforcement tools available to address the impacts caused by such breaches.[57]

3.3.2 Ideas on National Security

Prior to 2001, national security in the context of CFIUS review mainly focused on the impacts on military power caused by state actors, which is a rather traditional perspective shaped by thinking from the world wars and Cold War. The 911 terrorist incident demonstrated that globalization could be used to destroy the international order and threaten national security, challenging traditional ideas on national security.[58] The US began to realize that boundaries of national security were becoming blurred, which led to the transition of national security concerns towards threats triggered by non-state actors, as well as the protection of critical infrastructure, such as ports, chemical factories, and airports, from foreign control.[59]

In this case, the Patriot Act was adopted immediately—within a month after 911—and attaching great emphasis to the security of critical infrastructure.[60] Critical infrastructure was defined as the physical and cyber systems and assets that are so vital to the US that their incapacity or destruction would have a debilitating impact on its physical security, economic prosperity, public health or safety, the living standards of American citizens, such as telecommunications, energy, finance, water supply, transportation network, and so on.[61] A new integrated governmental agency, the Department of Homeland Security (DHS), was established. The Homeland Security Act provided a number of critical resources to secure the basic operation of the US economy and government.[62] Critical infrastructure was viewed as a vital aspect of the maintenance of homeland security in the broad sense of the term. Ever since President George W Bush added the DHS as a statutory CFIUS member in national security review of foreign investments by in February 2003, it has played an active, conservative role in such reviews, especially those of foreign investment transactions in connection with critical infrastructure and national defense technology.[63] As we can see, therefore, ideas on national security and foreign investment in the US have evolved and are no longer limited to traditional military security, but also embrace homeland security, including, among other things, security of critical infrastructure.

3.3.3 Ideas on CFIUS Practices

Given the facts, which were underscored by the Congress, of a small number of foreign investments under national security investigation and a large number of withdrawn transactions under the review process, critics alleged that the CFIUS failed to protect national security fully when formulating the FINSA. Among more than 1,500 foreign investment filings between 1988 and 2005, only 24 transactions underwent investigation, and only one transaction was blocked by the president.[64] The CFIUS received criticisms that it failed to mandate investigations over foreign investment transactions controlled by foreign governments, such as the well-known CNOOC and DPW transactions.[65]

There are two main reasons for the poor performance of the CFIUS in relation to national security investigations. First, the CFIUS was seriously worried about its negative impacts on US open investment policy and reluctant to initiate additional investigations of foreign investments which might lead to stricter and longer reviews and become obstacles to foreign investment.[66] Second, there was a large number of withdrawals prior to national security investigation.[67] Because of the complexity of analyzing whether foreign investment activities harm national security, the process required extensive review time. The Defense Trade: Enhancements to the Implementation of Exon-Florio Could Strengthen the Law's Effectiveness was issued by the Government Accountability Office (GAO Report) in 2005 revealed that the Department of the Treasury often encouraged foreign investment parties to withdraw their notices and resubmit their applications after supplementing the materials, in order for additional time to be available to restart the preliminary national security review process rather than directly proceed to the next phase of investigation.[68] In this way, the time calculated by the withdrawals and resubmissions would provide a longer time for preliminary review, and at the same time, the investigation procedure could be avoided. Critics pointed out, however, that in practice, even though more transaction parties decided to withdraw their notices, fewer of them reapplied for national security review, eliminating the need for investigation. Because foreign investment parties who were encouraged to withdraw a preliminary national security review application in favor of a later resubmitted preliminary national security review application were unwilling to file again voluntarily as the CFIUS wished, it was hard to determine and eliminate potential threats to national security caused by these transactions. As a result, the GAO Report made several specific suggestions. First, temporary measures should be created for the withdrawal of transactions, such as a time limit for reapplication after the withdrawal notice, and tracking and monitoring the behaviors of withdrawn foreign investments prior to reapplication.[69] Second, the GAO Report proposed integrating the processes of preliminary national security review and investigation into a unified, 75-day process.[70]

The Department of the Treasury, however, rejected these proposals. In relation to small number of investigated transactions, it argued that the situation indicated that all CFIUS members had already reached a consensus at the preliminary national security review, as investigation procedures would be launched only if any CFIUS member believed that there was a national security issue related to a specific foreign investment transaction. With respect to the criticisms about encouraging withdrawals related in the GAO report, the Department of the Treasury claimed that any decision which permitted foreign investment parties to withdraw their notice was made on adequate and reasonable grounds, without any subjective intentions on the part of CFIUS members.[71] The Department of the Treasury therefore declined to carry out the temporary measures suggested in the GAO Report, because of the difficulties of implementation after the withdrawal of notice and likely negative impacts on the efficiency of national security review.[72]

Interestingly, even though the CFIUS refused to make statutory modifications on addressing the small number of investigations and large number of withdrawals, there were 12 foreign investment transactions, including withdrawals, under investigation in 2006, significantly more than the total for the previous decade.[73] This indicates the tendency for frequent national security investigations into foreign investment activities. In responding to the suggestion of integrating the initial review and investigation phases, the Department of the Treasury emphasized the significance of an independent layer of preliminary national security review which would serve as an efficient gatekeeper for scrutinizing foreign investment on complicated national security grounds.

3.3.4 Ideas on Presidential Independence and Congressional Oversight

The debate on governmental independence and congressional involvement in the formulation of FINSA involved two main areas of contention: the issue of congressional veto power over decisions made by the president and the issue of normalization of congressional oversight of the review process.

On the former issue, some claimed that the existing reporting requirement failed to provide the Congress with enough information about the enforcement by the CFIUS actions and the presidential actions.[74] As a result, two bills, proposed by James Inhofe and Richard Shelby, which contained the provision of congressional veto authority to override a presidential decision to approve a transaction. To be specific, Inhofe's bill required the president to notify the Congress of all investigated transactions with approvals, and the Congress was empowered to prohibit, within 10 days after the president reported the notice to Congress, transactions which were subject to an investigation and had been approved by the president.[75] Inhofe's bill also stipulated a 30-day delay in blocking such a foreign investment if either chairman of the relevant congressional committee introduced a resolution to do so, and when such a resolution was jointly adopted by the two parties of the Congress, the transaction would not be consummated.[76] Similarly, Shelby's bill, which was aimed at revising Inhofe's bill, sought to challenge the independence of the executive branch in CFIUS reviews, by means of an additional provision authorizing the congressional committees to force the CFIUS to investigate or carry out an extended review of certain transactions.[77]

The rules of congressional veto power over national security review mirrored a provision on congressional veto power drafted in the original Exon bill and accepted in the Exon-Florio Amendment because governmental independence was deemed to take priority.[78] Similarly, in the drafting of the FINSA, the suggestion of congressional veto power encountered strong opposition. Some critics argued that congressional veto power of presidential decisions was unconstitutional for several reasons, as judicial precedents offered the highest judicial preference for presidential independence over congressional veto power on national security issues, with no exception in the field of foreign investment.

First, the US Supreme Court ruled on the power struggle between the government and the Congress in *US INS v. Chadha* and held that a veto resolution passed by only one house of Congress was constitutionally invalid, unenforceable, and nonbinding, and that, out of consistency with the bicameral spirit, Congress may not promulgate a statute granting itself a legislative veto over actions of the executive branch. Legislative acts must be approved by both houses and submitted to the president for signature unless this would violate the US Constitution.[79] In order to make congressional involvement constitutional and valid, procedures must be strictly followed which have been jointly decided by both houses of Congress and signed by the president before coming into force. This indicates that a joint resolution by the Congress on blocking certain transactions by seeking to override a presidential decision would violate the constitutional principle of the separation of powers.

Second, in *Sibbach v. Wilson*, the Federal Supreme Court acknowledged that it was constitutional to require the newly announced federal civil settlement procedure to take effect only after being submitted to the Congress after a set time period.[80] Even though the provision of congressional veto power in Inhofe's bill, a rule of substantive rather than procedural law, seems to be constitutional, it still cannot completely veto decisions made by the president over foreign investment.[81]

Third, the Federal Supreme Court provides solid judicial support for exclusive presidential power over national security issues. In the *US v. Curtiss-Wright Export Corp.*, on the basis of the evaluation of the legality of a provision which authorized the president to prohibit the sale of weapons to certain countries if necessary for the sake of peace and granted the president full decision-making power over national security, the court held that the president, as the nation's sole organ in international relations, is intrinsically vested with significant powers over foreign affairs that far exceed those permitted in domestic affairs or accorded to the Congress.[82] Thus was established the rule of presidential power that is independent from congressional involvement, and the judgment is credited with providing legal precedent for further expanding the president's exclusive power over foreign affairs. What is more, it is the president, rather than the Congress, that has the greatest access to confidential information on foreign affairs, especially in war situations, with the assistance of diplomatic officials and the intelligence community.[83] The Supreme Court has ruled that the president has the discretion in law-making on international relations issues to ensure that he may fully implement his constitutional duties in handling international relations issues. As the national security review focuses on national security related to international relations, it is appropriate for the president alone, rather than the Congress, to take final action.

Fourth, in *Youngstown Sheet & Tube Co. v. Sawyer*, the majority held the view that the president had no power to act except in those cases that are expressly or implicitly authorized by the Constitution or an Act of Congress, that the president cannot usurp Congress's role to create new laws, and his role in law-making is solely to recommend or veto laws.[84] To some extent, this ruling indicates that the president's power could be maximized once it is authorized by the Congress. The presidential role in national security review was established in line with the same legal logic. It is the president that should obtain and maximize his power over national security review, as this exclusive and complete presidential power has been authorized by the Congress through either the Exon-Florio Amendment or the IEEPA.

On the latter issue, given the fact that the CFIUS failed to notify Congress in a timely manner about certain foreign investment transactions, especially the CNOOC and DPW deals, where many members learned of them as a result of media uproars, and a formal requirement to report to Congress applied only when a recommendation had gone to the president from the CFIUS after completion of national security investigation—during which presidential judgments are rare—prompting Congress's complaints about denial of transparency.[85] Also, the chair of the CFIUS—the Department of the Treasury—failed to provide the compulsory report to Congress on foreign investment activities involving the national security review on a regular four-year basis, as required by the Exon-Florio Amendment. A proposal was therefore made to enhance congressional oversight by requiring the CFIUS to report to the Congress on a regular basis.[86] The CFIUS expressed its willingness to negotiate further with the Congress on the periodic reporting mechanism, notify the Congress upon the completion of its actions on a particular transaction, and provide quarterly briefings to relevant committees. The detailed monthly reporting required by the Inhofe Amendment, and the quarterly reporting required by the Shelby Amendment, both indicate ideas on strengthening congressional oversight on national security review conducted by the CFIUS and the president.[87]

As a compromise on the ideational debate about the independent presidential role and Congressional oversight, provisions for supervision of specific reviewed transactions and annual reporting obligations were finally reached in the FINSA.

3.4 The Reformed Period: FIRRMA

One decade after the 2007 enactment of the FINSA, the Congress resumed the debate regarding the need for reforming the national security review. In November 2017, a proposed bill titled FIRRMA, offering comprehensive modifications of the national security review, was introduced by Senator John Cornyn.[88] This draft bill was incorporated in the Senate version of the National Defense Authorization Act for Fiscal Year 2019, and it came into law with President Trump's signature in August 2018.[89] Notably, it took only ten months before FIRRMA became law, with unanimous support from both parties in Congress, as well as the executive branch. The majority of important provisions of the FIRRMA did not come into force immediately as the period of 18 months was to commence with the date on which the FIRRMA came into effect, or 30 days after the promulgation of the Department of Treasury's FIRRMA Implementing Regulations, whichever came first.[90] The FIRRMA Implementing Regulations were issued by the Department of the Treasury in January 2020, and the major changes introduced by FIRMMA accordingly came into force on February 13, 2020. Like previous reforms, the FIRRMA is designed to strike a balance between the twin goals of preserving the open policy for foreign investment and enabling the CFIUS to safeguard aspects of national security threatened by foreign investment in the current era.[91]

3.4.1 Significant Modifications

First, in order to expand the scope of transactions covered by the FIRRMA and its implementing regulations, the jurisdiction of the CFIUS was broadened so that it was no longer limited to controlling mergers, acquisitions, or takeovers by foreign persons.[92] Another five types of foreign investment were added within the context of the CFIUS review. The first were purchases, leases, or concessions by or real estate transactions of private or public real estate located in close proximity to a military installation, a US government facility, or property of national security sensitivities.[93] Foreign investment transactions related to sensitive real estate had already been prohibited on national security grounds in CFIUS practice, as for example, in the DPW and Ralls cases, and the FIRRMA codifies this kind of practice by providing a statutory reference. The second expansion includes any non-controlling foreign investment which is engaged in critical technology, critical infrastructure, or sensitive personal data of Terminal Identification number US business (TID US business).[94] In other words, foreign investment involving TID US business would be subject to national security review, no matter whether it would result in foreign control. The third involves any change in foreign investor rights with respect to a US business if that change results in foreign control of a US business.[95] The fourth expansion involves transactions prompting concerns as to whether a foreign government has a direct or indirect substantive interest.[96] The fifth type includes any other form of transaction, transfer, agreement, or arrangement intended to evade scrutiny of a national security review conducted by the CFIUS.[97]

Second, in terms of the initiation of national security review, a new format known as "declaration" was introduced as an alternative to written notice to facilitate review efficiency. Any party to a covered transaction was allowed to submit short-form filings, in which the CFIUS must act within 30 days to declarations. instead of filing a written notice that would officially initiate a CFIUS review process.[98] The initiation of light filing through the FIRRMA would substantially shorten the timeline for the review process, resulting in a more efficient and expedited clearance of benign transactions involving foreign acquirers with a strong track record.[99] In addition, in certain cases, the FIRRMA replaces the voluntary filing process for foreign investment with mandatory declaration granting the CFIUS discretion to require parties to file mandatory declarations before closing such a transaction.[100] The FIRRMA Implementing Regulations on Mandatory Declaration provide detailed guidelines on mandatory declarations for investments in TID US business by investors with foreign government ownership.

Third, the FIRRMA expands the timeline for national security reviews. The preliminary national security review is expanded from 30 to 45 days and the previous 45-day national security investigation is extended for an additional 15 days in extraordinary circumstances, while the 15-day period of presidential decision remains unchanged.[101] If a complicated foreign investment transaction is not withdrawn and refiled, the maximum national security review period is 120 days, instead of 90 days as previously.

Fourth, the FIRRMA is designed to strengthen requirements on mitigation measures. The compliance plans are accordingly employed to inform and update the implementation of mitigation agreements, so that mitigation implementation can be strengthened.[102]

Fifth, the FIRRMA granted the CFIUS special hiring authority and established the CFIUS Fund. The long-standing challenge was addressed of the timely replacement and recruitment of CFIUS staff requiring specialized experiences and clearances, as the heads of the departments and agencies may, on behalf of the CFIUS, appoint candidates to important positions through the FIRRMA.[103] The FIRRMA also authorizes the funding of CFIUS, which amounts to US$20 million per fiscal year.[104] The act introduced a filing fee for transacting parties who wish to submit a voluntary notification to the CFIUS, at an amount equal to either 1 percent of the value of the transaction, or $300,000, whichever is the lesser, to be adjusted annually for inflation.[105]

3.4.2 Ideas on National Security

Ideas on an expanded context of national security for foreign investment led to a broader CFIUS jurisdiction in several respects, such as transactions related to critical technology, critical infrastructure, sensitive personal data, and certain sensitive real estate transactions. Ideas on national security which had been confined to traditional dimensions, such as pure defense security, are to be developed more broadly, to include security in the fields of key information and technology with the prioritized purpose of maintaining US leadership or advantages in technology.

The expansion of national security underwent heated debate during the formulation of FIRRMA. First, the CFIUS was recommended to review American outbound investment and prohibit inbound investment from foreign companies which were found to have stolen or expected to receive US intellectual property, in order to cover a broader range of technology transfers, but this encountered a number of objections.[106] Opponents believed there was no adequate reason to extend CFIUS jurisdiction to outbound investment, as it would lead to regulatory gaps and overlaps between the regulatory mechanisms of national security review and export control review, disadvantaging US multinational enterprises in relation to foreign companies that manufacture and distribute similar technology.[107] Instead, the regulatory mechanism of export control review was reformed as a legal companion of FIRRMA.

Second, the ideas on national security in FIRRMA highlight the importance of critical technology. The FIRRMA offers a list of sensitive technologies which, in relation to covered transactions, trigger national security review by the CFIUS.[108] Even though this might strengthen CFIUS competence in tracking foreign investments in sensitive technologies, and foreign investment related to multiple sensitive technologies might encounter greater reservations in CFIUS review, there are worries that it might form unexpected obstacles to dampen the innovative potential of technological development.[109]

Third, ideas on national security through the expanded category of certain real estate transactions under national security review are a reflection of strengthening military security, as the purchase or lease of, or concessions related to, real estate under the CFIUS review are described as activities occurring in close proximity to military installations or air or maritime ports, reflected in a consensus reached during the formulation of both the Senate and House bills. The key difference is that the Senate version provides a much broader jurisdiction in cases of proximity to land border crossings and US government facilities that are sensitive as regards national security.

3.4.2 Ideas on the Roles of President and Congress

Compared with the contentious ideological debate on congressional power and presidential action during the formulation period of the FINSA, the FIRRMA experienced a relatively peaceful legislative process on this issue, as is mainly reflected in the additional amendments respectively introduced by Senators Patrick Toomey and Chris Van Hollen.[110] Toomey's amendment, for example, authorized the Congress to review and approve major rulings of national security review conducted by the CFIUS, as a safeguard to ensure legislative oversight of national security and foreign investment issues.[111] This amendment was ultimately withdrawn for several reasons, however. First, such a congressional preapproval in the rulemaking process might cause unexpected delays. Second, the existing legislation, such as the Congressional Review Act, already provided adequate congressional oversight of the rulings.

In contrast to Toomey's amendment, which was designed to expand congressional oversight, Hollen's was made to restrict presidential action. To be specific, it elaborated to the effect that sanctions against companies that violate US laws cannot be arbitrarily withdrawn by the president.[112] The president is prohibited, for example, from modifying sanctions against a Chinese telecommunications company until he or she certifies to the Congress that the company (i) has not violated US law for 365 days and (ii) is cooperating with all US government investigations, if any, into its activities.[113] It is worth noting that Hollen's amendment was passed by a 23–2 vote, indicating that the perception within the Congress about constraining presidential power over national security review was in line with the relatively enhanced congressional oversight shaped in the FINSA.[114]

Although presidential power might be limited through enhanced congressional oversight, the power of determining national security policy in foreign investment remains with the government. Section 1069 of the National Defense Authorization Act of 2018, for example, which authorizes annual US defense expenditures, directs the secretaries of defense, state, and treasury, as well as the director of national intelligence, to make recommendations to Congress to improve the effectiveness of the inter-agency vetting of foreign investments which could pose threats to US national security, reflecting an attempt by Congress to involve US governmental stakeholders other than the Department of Defense, in order to further safeguard national security, especially that related to industry and technology.[115] This section, however, met with strong objection from President Trump, who claimed that it might dictate the position of the US in external military and foreign affairs and provide insights into how the administration viewed the interplay of foreign investment and national security issues as Congress deliberated CFIUS reform.[116]

The executive branch offered great support in the passage of FIRRMA. The Department of Treasury, as the chair of the CFIUS, publicly stated that the FIRRMA would provide the necessary tools to protect national security. President Trump also expressed his support for FIRRMA, despite the fact that the executive branch continued to insist on an open investment policy.[117] This underscored close collaboration on the legislation between the Congress and the President, as well as the strength of administrative support for the passage of FIRRMA within the US internal structure.[118]

3.4.4 Ideas on Chinese Investment

Even though a section titled "Countries of special concern" was removed from the final version of the FIRRMA to avoid criticisms of discriminatory treatment of foreign investments of particular origins, this issue was considered during the FIRRMA legislative process and took effect in an indirect manner in FIRRMA and its implementing regulations, if a country causes concerns that have a declared strategic goal of acquiring a type of critical infrastructure or critical technology and would affect US leadership in areas related to national security.[119]

With respect to Chinese investment, there is a bipartisan agreement in relation to emerging technologies that the acquisitions of US companies by Chinese investments which might not trigger national security reviews by the CFIUS are characterized to be potentially detrimental to US national security, as they might help China to obtain US technology and "know-how". This applies, for example, to investments with defense or military applications, or intelligence impacts, robotics, artificial intelligence, automation, quantum computing, biotechnology advancements, and semiconductors.[120] It is widely believed in the US that China is pursuing alternative investment strategies with the purpose of establishing technological superiority.[121] Senator Cornyn, for example, claimed that the Chinese government's Made in China 2025 strategic plan might pose a great threat to US national security, possibly one even more severe than those caused by Russia or Iran.[122] Similarly, Mr. Chewning, chief of staff to the Acting Secretary of Defense, expressed his concern that China obtains US advanced technology through joint ventures, and then enhances it, but forbids the export of any intellectual property concerning these enhancements to persons outside of China.[123]

In spite of sensitivity, on national security grounds, about Chinese investment, the long-lasting policy of encouraging an open market and maintaining a friendly investment climate is continually stressed, with no exception made for Chinese investments. Foreign investment has continued to be widely recognized as a crucial force in relation to American technological innovation and economic prosperity and might in turn become a cornerstone of the safeguarding of US national security. Technological security is closely related to national political, military, economic, social, and cultural security. Breakthroughs in science and technology can effectively enhance national competitiveness and maintain national security. As a result, China and Chinese investment are not explicitly mentioned anywhere in the final text of the FIRRMA. Admittedly, one of the indirect purposes of the FIRRMA is to address the national security risks posed by Chinese investment in the development of critical technology.[124]

With the ever-changing technological competition between China and the US, it is possible for national security reviews in practice to be employed frequently for restricting or even prohibiting Chinese investment. The focus of the strategic game between China and the US has shifted from the trade sector to the technology sector, and the ways in which the US places restrictions on China continue to increase. During the Trump administration, the friction between China and the US mainly focused on the trade sector, with restrictions on technological exchanges in the field of technology, including export controls, investment controls, and talent blockades. During the Biden administration, the US has continued to escalate its technology blockade against China, with increasing restrictions and a greater emphasis on external alliances and system building. The US government is reshaping its leadership position in global semiconductor manufacturing. Since 2018, there have been frequent recruitment campaigns targeting China's semiconductor industry. The introduction of the 2022 Chip and Science Act is a further escalation of the US technology blockade of China.[125] In this situation, Chinese investors need to remain cautious and carefully discern where there might be room for mitigation and whether their transactions may realistically be completed, given the CFIUS analysis of national security threats and vulnerabilities.

Notes

1 Trading with the Enemy Act, Pub. L. 65–91, 40 Stat. 411 (1917); Berg, Manfred and Jansen, Axel. "Americans in World War I-World War I in America." *The Journal of the Gilded Age and Progressive Era* 17, no. 4 (2018): 599–607.
2 50 U.S.C. § 4301 et seq. App. 5(b)(1)(B).
3 Merchant Marine Act, Pub. L. No. 66–261, 41 Stat. 988 (1920), codified at 46 U.S.C. § 50101; Bian, Cheng. *National Security Review of Foreign Investment: A Comparative Legal Analysis of China, the United States and the European Union*. London: Routledge, 2020, 96.
4 Mineral Lands Leasing Act, Pub. L. No. 66–146, 41 Stat. 437 (1920).
5 Mineral Leasing Act, Pub. L. No. 66–146, 41 Stat. 437 (1920), codified at 30 U.S.C. § 181.
6 Communication Act, Pub. L. No. 73–416, 48 Stat. 1064 (1934); Radio Act, Pub. L. No. 69–632, 44 Stat. 1162 (127).
7 Foreign Investment Study Act, Pub. L. No. 93–479, 88 Stat. 1450 (1974); Mundheim, Robert and Heleniak, David. "American Attitudes Toward Foreign Direct Investment in the United States." *Journal of Comparative Corporate Law and Securities Regulation* 2, no. 4 (1979): 223.
8 Executive Order No. 11858 (1975), 40 FR 20263, 3 C.F.R., 1971–1975 Comp., 990.
9 Executive Order No. 11858 (1975), 40 FR 20263, 3 C.F.R., 1971–1975 Comp., 990; Travalini, Joanna Rubin. "Foreign Direct Investment in the United States: Achieving a Balance between National Economy Benefits and National Security Interests." *Northwestern Journal of International Law & Business* 29, no. 3 (2009): 783–784; Li, Xingxing. "National Security Review in Foreign Investments: A Comparative and Critical Assessment on China and US Laws and Practices." *Berkeley Business Law Journal* 13, no. 1 (2015): 261.
10 Graham, Edward M. and Marchick, David Matthew. *US National Security and Foreign Investment*. Washington, DC: Institute for International Economics, 2006, 20; International Economic and Emergency Act, Pub. L. No. 94–223, 91 Stat. 1626 (1977), codified at 50 U.S.C ch. 35 § 1701 et seq).
11 The Exon-Florio Amendment was set out in the Omnibus Trade and Competitiveness Act, Pub. L. No. 100–418, 102 Stat. 1107 (1988), titled as "Authority to Review Certain Mergers, Acquisitions, and Takeovers." Pub. L. No. 100–418, § 5021, 102 Stat. 1107, 1425–1426 (50 U.S.C. § 2170). The original authorization was scheduled to expire in 1991 but was made permanent by Section 8 of Defense Production Act Extension and Amendments of 1991, Pub. L. No. 102–99, 105 Stat. 487 (1991); Djuristic, Paul L. "The Exon-Florio Amendment: National Security Legislation Hampered by Political and Economic Forces." *DePaul Business Law Journal* 3, no. 1 (1990): 179–212.
12 Omnibus Trade and Competitiveness Act, Pub. L. No. 100–418, 102 Stat. 1107 (1988).
13 50 U.S.C. § 1701.
14 50 U.S.C. § 2170 (1988), a-h.
15 Executive Order No. 12661 (1988), 54 FR 779, 3 C.F.R., Comp., p. 618 (1988).
16 Weimer, Christopher M. "Foreign Direct Investment and National Security Post-FINSA 2007." *Texas Law Review* 87, no. 3 (2009): 664–666.

17 Defense Production Act Extension and Amendments, Pub. L. No. 102–99, 105 Stat. 487 (1991).
18 Section 837 of the National Defense Authorization Act for Fiscal Year 1993, Pub. L. No. 102–484, 106 Stat. 2315, 2463.
19 Section 837 of the National Defense Authorization Act for Fiscal Year 1993, Pub. L. No. 102–484, 106 Stat. 2315, 2463, with the reference of the Export Administration Act of 1979 and the Nuclear Non-proliferation Act of 1978.
20 50 U.S.C.A. § 2170(g) (1993).
21 50 U.S.C. § 2170(j) (1993).
22 50 U.S.C. § 2170(k) (1993).
23 Graham, Edward M. and Marchick, David Matthew. *US National Security and Foreign Investment*. Washington, DC: Institute for International Economics, 2006, 40–42.
24 Kang, C. S. Eliot. "US Politics and Greater Regulation of Inward Foreign Direct Investment." *International Organization* 51, no. 2 (1997): 322; Foreign Investment Disclosure and Reciprocity Act; Tolchin, Martin and Tolchin, Susan. *Buying into America: How Foreign Money Is Changing the Face of Our Nation*. New York: Times Books, 1988, 223–246.
25 Statement of Senator Exon, Foreign Investment, National Security and Essential Commerce Act of 1987, H. R. 3, 100th Congress, 1st Session, 134 Cong.Rec. S4833 (1987).
26 Statement of Senator Exon, Foreign Investment, National Security and Essential Commerce Act of 1987, H. R. 3, 100th Congress, 1st Session, 134 Cong.Rec. S4833 (1987).
27 Statement of Senator Exon, Foreign Investment, National Security and Essential Commerce Act of 1987, H. R. 3, 100th Congress, 1st Session, 134 Cong.Rec. S4833 (1987).
28 Foreign Investment, National Security and Essential Commerce Act of 1987, § 905(a); Mostaghel, Deborah M. "Dubai Ports World Under Exon-Florio: A Threat to National Security or a Tempest in a Seaport?" *Albany Law Review* 70 (2007): 591.
29 Foreign Investment, National Security and Essential Commerce Act of 1987, § 905(a). Foreign Investment, National Security and Essential Commerce Act of 1987, H. R. 3, 100th Congress, § 905(a) (1987); Feng, Yiheng. "We Wouldn't Transfer Title to the Devil: Consequences of the Congressional Politicization of Foreign Direct Investment on National Security Grounds." *International Law and Politics* 42, no. 1 (2009): 262.
30 Foreign Takeovers and National Security: Hearings on § 905 of H.R. 3 Before the Subcommittee on Commerce, Consumer Protection, and Competitiveness of the House Committee on 20 October 1987 (Hearing on 20 October 1987); Comments of D. Mulford, The Association for Foreign Investment in America and Bureau of National Affairs, Conference on Foreign Investment: The Economic Perspective, Fed. News Serv. on 6 October 1988; Foreign Takeovers and National Security: Hearing on § 905 of H.R. 3 Before the Subcommittee on Commerce, Consumer Protection, and Competitiveness of the House Committee on Energy and Commerce, 100th Congress, 1st Session, 17–18 (1988); Greidinger, Marc. "The Exon-Florio Amendment: A Solution in Search of a Problem." *American University International Law Review* 6, no. 2 (1991): 111–177.
31 Lorell, Mark A., Lowell, Julia, Moore, Richard M., Greenfield Victoria and Vlachos, Katia. "The Legal, Regulatory, and Policy Framework for Aerospace Industry Globalization." In *Going Global: US Government Policy and the Defense Aerospace Industry*. Santa Monica: Rand Corporation, 2002, 85–134; Schmidt, Patrick L. "The Exon-Florio Statue: How It Affects Foreign Investors and Lenders in the United States." *The International Lawyer* 27, no. 3 (1993): 797; Acquisitions by Foreign Companies: Hearing Before the Senate Committee on Commerce, Science and Transportation, 100th Congress, 1st Session, 17 (1987) (Acquisitions Hearing); Greidinger, Marc. "The Exon-Florio Amendment: A Solution in Search of a Problem." *American University International Law Review* 6, no. 2 (1991): 168.
32 Acquisitions by Foreign Companies: Hearing Before the Senate Committee on Commerce, Science, and Transportation, 100th Congress, 1st Session, 15 (1987).

33 Acquisitions by Foreign Companies: Hearing Before the Senate Committee on Commerce, Science, and Transportation, 100th Congress, 1st Session, 15 (1987).
34 Acquisitions by Foreign Companies: Hearing Before the Senate Committee on Commerce, Science, and Transportation, 100th Congress, 1st Session, 15 (1987).
35 Hearing on 20 October 1987.
36 Hearing on 20 October 1987; Byrne, Matthew R. "Protecting National Security and Promoting Foreign Investment: Maintaining the Exon-Florio Balance." *Ohio State Law Journal* 67, no. 4 (2006): 862.
37 Acquisitions Hearing, 21; Byrne, Matthew R. "Protecting National Security and Promoting Foreign Investment: Maintaining the Exon-Florio Balance." *Ohio State Law Journal* 67, no. 4 (2006): 862.
38 Hearing on 20 October 1987.
39 Sunstein, Cass. R. *Legal Reasoning and Political Conflict*. London: Oxford University Press, 1998; Congressional Research Service. Statutory Interpretation: Theories, Tools, and Trends." www.everycrsreport.com/reports/R45153.html, 12; Breyer, Stephen. "On the Uses of Legislative History in Interpreting Statutes." *Southern California Law Review* 65 (1992): 860.
40 Testimony of Robert McNeill, Executive Vice Chairman, Emergency Committee for American Trade, Hearings on 10 June 1987.
41 Testimony of Robert McNeill, Executive Vice Chairman, Emergency Committee for American Trade, Hearings on 10 June 1987.
42 Feng, Yicheng. "We Wouldn't Transfer Title to the Devil: Consequences of the Congressional Politicization of Foreign Direct Investment on National Security Grounds." *International Law and Politics* 42 (2012): 262.
43 Section 721 of the Defense Production Act of 1950, as amended by the Foreign Investment and National Security Act of 2007, Pub. L. No. 110–49, 121 Stat. 246, 50 U.S.C. § 2170.
44 31 C.F.R. Part 800, Regulations Pertaining to Mergers, Acquisitions, and Takeovers by Foreign Persons; Final Rule, Fed. Register, Vol. 73, No. 226, on 21 November 2008.
45 50 U.S.C. § 2170 (a)(5), (f); George, Stephanov Georgiev. "The Reformed CFIUS Regulatory Framework: Mediating between Continued Openness to Foreign Investment and National Security." *Yale Journal on Regulation* 25 (2008): 130; Saha, Souvik. "CFIUS Now Made in China: Dueling National Security Review Frameworks as a Countermeasure to Economic Espionage in the Age of Globalization." *Northwestern Journal of International Law & Business* 33, no. 1 (2012): 211.
46 50 U.S.C. § 2170 (b)(2)(B).
47 50 U.S.C. § 2170 (f).
48 White House. "The National Strategy for the Physical Protection of Critical Infrastructures and Key Assets." 2003. https://rosap.ntl.bts.gov/view/dot/33977; David, Lois M. (Ed). *Long-Term Effects of Law Enforcement's Post-9/11 Focus on Counterterrorism and Homeland Security*. Santa Monica: Rand Corporation, 2010.
49 Thomas, Peter C. and Dave, Brijesh P. "Reform of the CFIUS Process in the Wake of Dubai Ports World." www.stblaw.com/docs/default-source/cold-fusion-existing-content/publications/pub624.pdf, 2.
50 Bian, Cheng. *National Security Review of Foreign Investment: A Comparative Legal Analysis of China, the United States and the European Union*. London: Routledge, 2020, 102–103.
51 Thomas, Peter C. and Dave, Brijesh P. "Reform of the CFIUS Process in the Wake of Dubai Ports World." www.stblaw.com/docs/default-source/cold-fusion-existing-content/publications/pub624.pdf, 2.
52 Foreign Investment and National Security Act (2007), 50 U.S.C. app. 2061, Section 721(B)(i)(I)-(II).
53 Cox, Jason. "Regulation of Foreign Direct Investment after the Dubai Ports Controversy: Has the US Government Finally Figured Out How to Balance Foreign Threats to

National Security Without Alienating Foreign Companies?" *The Journal of Corporation Law* 34, no. 1 (2008): 306–307.

54 50 U.S.C. § 2061, Section 2 (3)(A)(B); 50 U.S.C. § 2061, Section 7 (g) (i).

55 50 U.S.C. § 2170 (m).

56 Sullivan, Matthew C. "CFIUS and Congress Reconsidered: Fire Alarms, Police Patrols, and a New Oversight Regime." *Willamette Journal of International Law and Dispute Resolution* 17, no. 2 (2009): 234.

57 50 U.S.C. § 2061, Section 2 (D); Thomas, Peter C. and Dave, Brijesh P. "Reform of the CFIUS Process in the Wake of Dubai Ports World." www.stblaw.com/docs/default-source/cold-fusion-existing-content/publications/pub624.pdf, 3.

58 Carroll, James F. F. "Back to The Future: Redefining the Foreign Investment and National Security Act's Conception of National Security." *Emory International Law Review* 23 (2009): 179.

59 Miller, Steven E. "After the 9/11 Disaster: Washington's Struggle to Improve Homeland Security." www.belfercenter.org/publication/after-911-disaster-washingtons-struggle-improve-homeland-security.

60 US Patriot Act, Pub. L. 107–56, 115 Stat. 272 (2001).

61 Dunn, Myriam Anna and Kristensen, Kristian Soby. *Securing "the Homeland": Critical Infrastructure, Risk and (In) Security*. London: Routledge, 2008.

62 6 U.S.C., 116 Stat. 2135, Sec. 101(9).

63 Travalini, Joanna Rubin. "Foreign Direct Investment in the United States: Achieving a Balance between National Economy Benefits and National Security Interests." *Northwestern Journal of International Law & Business* 29, no. 3 (2009): 783; Li, Xingxing. "National Security Review in Foreign Investments: A Comparative and Critical Assessment on China and US Laws and Practices." *Berkeley Business Law Journal* 13, no. 1 (2015): 261;

64 H.R. Rep. No. 110–24, at 12 (2007); National Defense Authorization Act for Fiscal Year 1993, Pub. L. No. 102–484, § 837, 106 Stat. 2315, 2464 (1992) (prior to 2007 amendment); Young, Kristy E. "The Committee on Foreign Investment in the United States and the Foreign Investment and National Securities Act of 2007: A Delicate Balancing Act That Needs Revision." *U.C. Davis Journal of International Law & Policy* 15, no. 1 (2009): 55.

65 H.R. Rep. No. 110–24, at 12 (2007); National Defense Authorization Act for Fiscal Year 1993, Pub. L. No. 102–484, § 837, 106 Stat. 2315, 2464 (1992) (prior to 2007 amendment); Young, Kristy E. "The Committee on Foreign Investment in the United States and the Foreign Investment and National Securities Act of 2007: A Delicate Balancing Act That Needs Revision." *U.C. Davis Journal of International Law & Policy* 15, no. 1 (2009): 55.

66 US Government Accountability Office. "Defense Trade: Enhancements to the Implementation of Exon-Florio Could Strengthen the Law's Effectiveness." 2005. www.gao.gov/products/gao-05-686 (GAO Report).

67 GAO Report.

68 GAO Report; Young, Kristy E. "The Committee on Foreign Investment in the United States and the Foreign Investment and National Securities Act of 2007: A Delicate Balancing Act That Needs Revision." *U.C. Davis Journal of International Law & Policy* 15, no. 1 (2009): 51; Press Release. U.S. Senator Evan Bayh, Bayh Calls for Increased Oversight of Foreign Takeovers with National Security Concerns; Casselman, Joshua W. "China's Latest 'Threat' to the United States: The Failed CNOOC-UNOCAL Merger and Its Implications for Exon-Florio and CFIUS." *Indiana International & Comparative Law Review* 17, no. 1 (2007): 170.

69 GAO Report.

70 GAO Report.

71 GAO Report; Young, Kristy E. "The Committee on Foreign Investment in the United States and the Foreign Investment and National Securities Act of 2007: A Delicate

Balancing Act That Needs Revision." *U.C. Davis Journal of International Law & Policy* 15, no. 1 (2009): 12–15.

72 GAO Report; Young, Kristy E. "The Committee on Foreign Investment in the United States and the Foreign Investment and National Securities Act of 2007: A Delicate Balancing Act That Needs Revision." *U.C. Davis Journal of International Law & Policy* 15, no. 1 (2009): 12–15.

73 H.R. Rep. No. 110–24, p. 13; Young, Kristy E. "The Committee on Foreign Investment in the United States and the Foreign Investment and National Securities Act of 2007: A Delicate Balancing Act That Needs Revision." *U.C. Davis Journal of International Law & Policy* 15, no. 1 (2009): 55.

74 "Exon-Florio Foreign Investment Provision: Overview of H.R. 556." 2007. www.everycrsreport.com/reports/RL33856.html.

75 Graham, Edward M. and Marchick, David Matthew. *US National Security and Foreign Investment.* Washington, DC: Institute for International Economics, 2006, 51; Inhofe, James. Foreign Investment Security Act of 2005, S. 1797, 109th Congress (2005).

76 151 Cong. Rec. S5874–76 (on 20 July 2005), proposed Senate 1311 by Senator Inhofe to S. 1042, 109th Congress, 1st Session).

77 Senator Richard Shelby, Foreign Investment and National Security Act of 2006, S. Rep. No. 109–264, 2nd Session, p. 3 (2006); Shelby Amendment, SA 1467 to 1042, 109th Congress (2005).

78 151 Cong. Rec. S8, 845–46 (on 25 July 2005), proposed Senate 1467 by Senator Shelby to S. 1042, 109th Congress.

79 Immigration & Naturalization Serv. v. Chadha, 462 US 919 (1983), No. 80–1832. https://supreme.justia.com/cases/federal/us/462/919/.

80 Sibbach vs. Wilson & Co., Inc., 312 US 1 (1941), no. 28. https://supreme.justia.com/cases/federal/us/312/1/; Sen. Richard Shelby, Foreign Investment and National Security Act of 2006, S. Rep. No. 109–264, 2nd Session, p. 3 (2006); Shelby Amendment, SA 1467 to 1042, 109th Congress (2005).

81 Sibbach vs. Wilson & Co., Inc., 312 US 1 (1941), no. 28. https://supreme.justia.com/cases/federal/us/312/1/.

82 United States vs. Curtiss-Wright Exp. Corp., 299 US 304 (1936), no. 98. https://supreme.justia.com/cases/federal/us/299/304/.

83 Tower, John G. "Congress Versus the President: The Formulation and Implementation of American Foreign Policy." www.foreignaffairs.com/articles/united-states/1981-12-01/congress-versus-president-formulation-and-implementation-american; Powell, H. Jefferson. "President's Authority over Foreign Affairs: An Executive Branch Perspective." *George Washington Law Review* 67 (1999): 527–576.

84 Urofsky, Melvin I. and Finkelman, Paul. "Youngstown Sheet & Tube Co. vs. Sawyer." In Urofsky, Melvin I. and Finkelman, Paul (Eds). *Documents of American Constitutional and Legal History* (2008). New York: Oxford University Press, 1952, 723–725.

85 H.R. Rep. No. 110–24, p. 12; Young, Kristy E. "The Committee on Foreign Investment in the United States and the Foreign Investment and National Securities Act of 2007: A Delicate Balancing Act That Needs Revision." *U.C. Davis Journal of International Law & Policy* 15, no. 1 (2009): 55.

86 GAO Report.

87 Graham, Edward M. and Marchick, David Matthew. *US National Security and Foreign Investment.* Washington, DC: Institute for International Economics, 2006, 52; Shelby Amendment, SA 1467 to S 1042, 109th Congress (2005); Senator Inhofe's Foreign Investment Security Act of 2005 (S.1797) was later converted into a Senate Amendment to the Defense Authorization bill; National Defense Authorization Act for Fiscal Year 2006, Pub. L. No. 109–163, § 1234(c)(8), 119 Stat. 3136, 3472 (2006).

88 Foreign Investment Risk Review Modernization Act, S. 2098, 115th Congress (2017–2018); Jackson, James K. "The Committee on Foreign Investment in the United States (CFIUS)." *Political Science, Business, Economics* (2016). https://fas.org/sgp/crs/natsec/RL33388.pdf.

89 John S. McCain National Defense Authorization Act for Fiscal Year 2019, S. 2098. H. R. 5515, 115th Congress (2017–2018), Title XVII, Review of Foreign Investment and Export Controls. www.congress.gov/115/bills/hr5515/BILLS-115hr5515enr.pdf.
90 Bian, Cheng. *National Security Review of Foreign Investment: A Comparative Legal Analysis of China, the United States and the European Union*. London: Routledge, 2020, 108–111.
91 Covington & Burling LLP. "The New CFIUS: Final Regulations Implementing Expanded Authorities Issued." 2020. www.cov.com/-/media/files/corporate/publications/2020/01/the-new-cfius-final-regulations-implementing-expanded-authorities-issued.pdf.
92 50 U.S.C. § 4565 (a)(4).
93 50 U.S.C. § 4565 (a)(4)(B)(ii).
94 50 U.S.C. § 4565 (a)(4)(B)(iii).
95 50 U.S.C. § 4565 (a)(4)(B)(iv).
96 50 U.S.C. § 4565 (b)(1)(B); Jackson, James K. "The Committee on Foreign Investment in the United States (CFIUS)." *Political Science, Business, Economics* (2016). https://fas.org/sgp/crs/natsec/RL33388.pdf, 11–12.
97 50 U.S.C. § 4565 (a)(4)(B)(v).
98 50 U.S.C. § 4565 (b)(1)(C)(v)(II).
99 Covington & Burling LLP. "The New CFIUS: Final Regulations Implementing Expanded Authorities Issued." 2020. www.cov.com/-/media/files/corporate/publications/2020/01/the-new-cfius-final-regulations-implementing-expanded-authorities-issued.pdf, 1.
100 50 U.S.C. § 4565 (b)(1)(C)(v)(IV).
101 50 U.S.C. § 4565 (b)(1)(F); 50 U.S.C. § 4565 (b)(2)(C).
102 50 U.S.C. § 4565 (l)(6)(C).
103 50 U.S.C. § 4565 (k)(4).
104 50 U.S.C. § 4565 (p)(1); 50 U.S.C. § 4565 (p)(2).
105 50 U.S.C. § 4565 (p)(3).
106 Covington & Burling LLP. "CFIUS Developments: House of Representatives Hearings to Evaluate CFIUS Reform." 2018. www.cov.com/-/media/files/corporate/publications/2018/01/cfius_developments_house_of_representatives_hearings_to_evaluate_cfius_reform.pdf, 2.
107 Covington & Burling LLP. "CFIUS Developments: House of Representatives Hearings to Evaluate CFIUS Reform." 2018. www.cov.com/-/media/files/corporate/publications/2018/01/cfius_developments_house_of_representatives_hearings_to_evaluate_cfius_reform.pdf, 2.
108 Covington & Burling LLP. "CFIUS Developments: House of Representatives Hearings to Evaluate CFIUS Reform." 2018. www.cov.com/-/media/files/corporate/publications/2018/01/cfius_developments_house_of_representatives_hearings_to_evaluate_cfius_reform.pdf, 3.
109 Covington & Burling LLP. "CFIUS Developments: Senate Committee on Banking, Housing, and Urban Affairs Hearing to Examine CFIUS Reform." 2018. www.cov.com/-/media/files/corporate/publications/2018/01/cfius_developments_senate_committee_on_banking_housing_and_urban_affairs_hearing_to_examine_cfius_reform.pdf, 2–3; Covington & Burling LLP. "House Committee on Financial Services Considers Updates to CFIUS Reform Language." 2018. www.cov.com/-/media/files/corporate/publications/2018/04/house_committee_on_financial_services_considers_updates_to_cfius_reform_language.pdf, 2.
110 Covington & Burling LLP. "CFIUS Developments: House and Senate Committees Hold Markup of CFIUS Reform Legislation." 2018. www.cov.com/-/media/files/corporate/publications/2018/05/cfius_developments_house_and_senate_committees_hold_markup_of_cfius_reform_legislation.pdf; S.Amdt.999 to H.R.2810, 115th Congress. www.congress.gov/amendment/115th-congress/senate-amendment/999?q=%7B%22search%22%3A%5B%22Pat+Toomey%22%5D%7D&s=6&r=55;

S.Amdt.764 to H.R.2810, 115th Congress, H.R. 2810, National Defense Authorization Act for Fiscal Year 2018. www.congress.gov/amendment/115th-congress/senate-amendment/764?s=7&r=44 (S.Amdt.764).

111 S.Amdt.999toH.R.2810,115thCongress.www.congress.gov/amendment/115th-congress/senate-amendment/999?q=%7B%22search%22%3A%5B%22Pat+Toomey%22%5D%7D&s=6&r=55.

112 Varas, Jacqueline. "The Current Status of Reforms to the Foreign Investment Review Process." 2018. www.americanactionforum.org/insight/the-current-status-of-reforms-to-the-foreign-investment-review-process/ (visited 10 April 2021); S.Amdt.764.

113 Covington & Burling LLP. "CFIUS Developments: House and Senate Committees Hold Markup of CFIUS Reform Legislation." 2018. www.cov.com/-/media/files/corporate/publications/2018/05/cfius_developments_house_and_senate_committees_hold_markup_of_cfius_reform_legislation.pdf, 3; S.Amdt.764.

114 Meyer, Ben. "Senate Panel Aims to Block Easing of ZTE Sanctions." 2018. www.freightwaves.com/news/senate-panel-aims-to-block-easing-of-zte-sanctions.

115 H.R.2810, National Defense Authorization Act for Fiscal Year 2018.

116 Covington & Burling LLP. "CFIUS Developments: House of Representatives Hearing and Presidential Signing Statement on Defense Authorization Act." 2017. www.cov.com/-/media/files/corporate/publications/2017/12/cfius_developments_house_of_representatives_hearing_and_presidential_signing_statement_on_defense_authorization_act.pdf, 2.

117 Covington & Burling LLP. "CFIUS Developments: House of Representatives Hearing and Presidential Signing Statement on Defense Authorization Act." www.cov.com/-/media/files/corporate/publications/2017/12/cfius_developments_house_of_representatives_hearing_and_presidential_signing_statement_on_defense_authorization_act.pdf, 2–3.

118 Covington & Burling LLP. "White House Support for CFIUS Reform and Affirmation of U.S. Open Investment Policy/Senate Committee on Banking, Housing, and Urban Affairs Hearing on CFIUS Reform." 2018. www.cov.com/-/media/files/corporate/publications/2018/01/white_house_support_for_cfius_reform_and_affirmation_of_us_open_investment_policy.pdf, 2.

119 Covington & Burling LLP. "Export Control Reform Act Introduced in Congress." 2018. www.cov.com/-/media/files/corporate/publications/2018/03/export_control_reform_act_introduced_in_congress.pdf, 12; 50 U.S.C. § 4565 (f)(5);

120 Covington & Burling LLP. Update on CFIUS Developments: Proposed Legislation and Reflections on CFIUS Under the Trump Administration." 2017. www.cov.com/-/media/files/corporate/publications/2017/06/update_on_cfius_developments_proposed_legislation_and_reflections_on_cfius_under_the_trump_administration.pdf, 2.

121 S.Hrg. 115–160. "CFIUS Reform: Administrative Perspectives on the Essential Elements." 2018. www.congress.gov/event/115th-congress/senate-event/LC56101/text.

122 S.Hrg. 112–741. "Current and Future Worldwide Threats to the National Security of the United States." 2012. www.govinfo.gov/content/pkg/CHRG-112shrg79855/html/CHRG-112shrg79855.htm.

123 Covington & Burling LLP. "CFIUS Developments: House Committee on Foreign Affairs Considers CFIUS Reform and Related Export Control Regimes." www.cov.com/-/media/files/corporate/publications/2018/03/cfius_developments_house_committee_on_foreign_affairs_considers_cfius_reform_and_related_export_control_regimes.pdf (visited 10 April 2021), p. 4.

124 Covington & Burling LLP. "CFIUS Developments: House of Representatives Hearings to Evaluate CFIUS Reform." 2018. www.cov.com/-/media/files/corporate/publications/2018/01/cfius_developments_house_of_representatives_hearings_to_evaluate_cfius_reform.pdf, 2.

125 Zhao, Jianya, Chen, Meihua, Chen, Feng and Yang, Lei. "Analysis of the Impact on Science and Technology Security for China by United States CHIPS and Science Act of 2022." *Journal of Intelligence* 42, no. 11 (2023).

4 The Process Orientation of National Security Reviews in China and US Foreign Investment Laws and Practices

4.1 Foreign Investment Practices and National Security Reviews in the US

4.1.1 Foreign Investment Practices in the Exon-Florio Amendment

Foreign investment had traditionally been viewed as a rather valuable auxiliary, and American policy with respect to foreign investment as one of general openness, partly because of US beliefs in the free market system free of governmental involvement.[1] From the late nineteenth and early twentieth centuries, most foreign investment flowing into the US originated from Europe, in particular Germany, contributing a substantial portion of US productive labor and useful enterprises.[2] The fact that a vast amount of foreign investment had provided vital support for US prosperity by promoting industrial development and economic growth in the earlier stage in the US strengthened the nation's belief in encouraging foreign investment.[3] With its quick economic recovery following World War I, the outward investment of the US grew rapidly, transforming it from a debtor country to an emerging creditor country.[4] As early as the 1920s, American firms began to expand their international presences and conducted overseas investment activities.[5] The stock value of US outward investments increased to around US$8 billion at the end of 1930, more than three times greater than the US$2.6 billion of 1914.[6] By 1930 outward investments were almost six times larger than inward investments.[7] US investments abroad rose sharply, especially after World War II, far exceeding the rate and scale of foreign inward investment in the US. Since the US had a clear interest in foreign investment, it continued to support the policy of general openness and advocate the liberalization of foreign investment worldwide, with the ultimate purpose of making US enterprises seek maximum interests in other countries.[8]

4.1.1.1 Increasing Takeovers in the Exon-Florio Amendment

Since the late 1970s, foreign inward investment had been advocated in the US. It was officially announced that foreign investors should be able to make the same kinds of investment, under the same conditions, as nationals of the host country, with limited exceptions where there were legitimate national security or

DOI: 10.4324/9781003543749-4

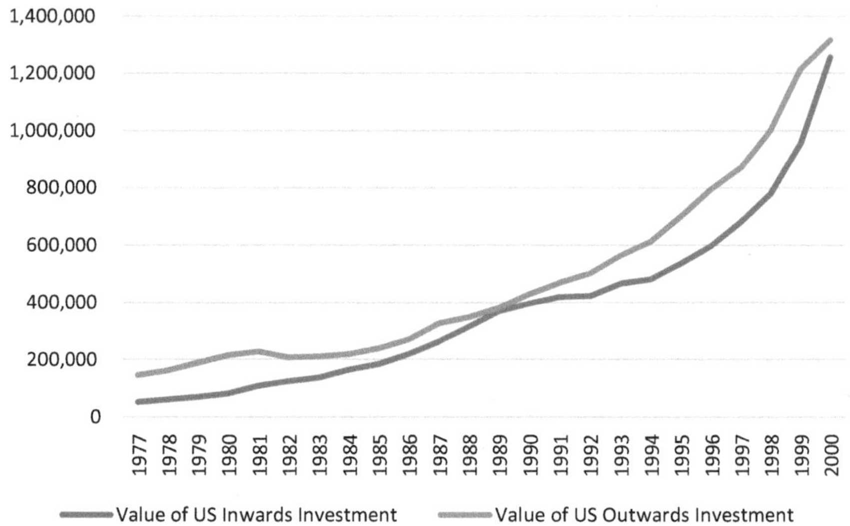

Figure 4.1 Value of US Inwards and Outward Investment from 1977 to 2000

related interests.[9] During the two decades prior to 1977, US outward investment far exceeded its inward investment, while inward investment began to increase more rapidly than outward investment. As Figure 4.1 shows, the value of outward investment reached US$215 billion by 1980, almost three times greater than that of inward investment, at around US$83 billion. By the end of 1989, outward investment had climbed by about 76 percent, to US$381.7 billion, while inward investment had soared by 345 percent, to almost US$369 billion.[10] It can be seen that between 1980 and 2000, the flow of foreign investment into the US saw massive—more than fifteenfold—growth, from about US$83 billion in 1980 to slightly under US$1.3 trillion in 2000 (See Figure 4.2).[11]

4.1.1.2 Ideas on Japanese Investment and the Ineffectiveness of the CFIUS

The CFIUS, at this initial stage, failed to play an effective role in protecting national security, meet only ten times in the first five years since its establishment in 1975.[12] With the wave of increasing investments from Japan acquiring large brands in the US in the 1980s, anxieties on national security were stoked both among the public and in the Congress, raising the questions of whether the CFIUS could respond to national security worries and eliminate the potential risks of foreign investment in the US. These worries prompted the Congress to enact the Exon-Florio Amendment, transforming the CFIUS from a toothless tiger to a gatekeeper with substantial power.

In particular, one of the salient transactions attracting US attention to national security of foreign investments was that of Fujitsu Ltd. (Fujitsu), a computer manufacturing company based in Japan, which sought to make a merger offer and

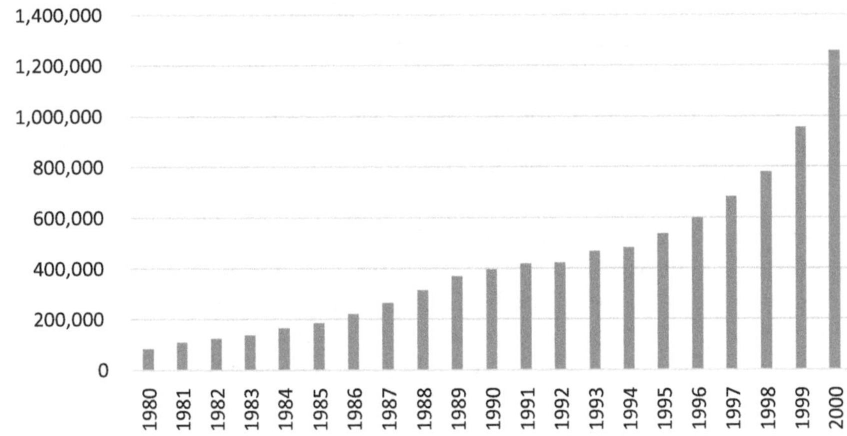

Figure 4.2 Value of US Inward Investment from 1980 to 2000

announced its bid of US$200 million to Fairchild Semiconductor Corp. (Fairchild), acknowledged as the "mother company of Silicon Valley", in October 1986. Fairchild was a major supplier of microchips critical to the manufacturing of advanced weaponry and held contracts with the DOD.[13] Although the transaction was carried out in a friendly atmosphere and with negotiations between the two sides, it provoked heightened sensitivity, public outcry, and opposition from the semiconductor industry.[14]

The opponents in industry regarded this proposed deal as a highly aggressive for several reasons. First, there was a competitive relationship between Fujitsu and Fairchild over overlapping products, which would make US enterprises heavily reliant on Fujitsu.[15] Second, the transaction might lead to further acquisitions by Japanese enterprises in the chip industry, weaken the competition or even result in the disastrous extinction of the US semiconductor industry, which was at the heart of production of cutting-edge high-tech weapons.[16]

The executive branch divided into two groups. The "techno hawks", who were recognized as protectionists, were determined to block the deal, while the "free traders" supported the deal and opposed government intervention.[17] The supporters argued that obstructing Japanese enterprises at home defeated the purpose of letting Japan open its market and would obviously reduce enthusiasm for foreign investment in the US.[18] They also pointed out potential complementary advantages to both of the parties, as the success of this transaction would save Fairchild, and enhance US competitiveness in this industry.[19] In responding to concerns about sensitive technologies associated with the DOD being acquired by foreign investors, they explained that the existing DOD national security review procedures could largely avoid the possible appropriation of these technologies.[20] Officials from the DOD and the Department of Commerce were the main forces opposing this transaction. Stephen D. Bryen, the deputy secretary of the DOD, warned that the US would eventually lose its control over the semiconductor industry or even lose its advantage in the field of science and technology as a whole, if the influential semiconductor company was acquired by the Japanese enterprise.[21] As a result, lawyers were required by the Department of Commerce to provide opinions within 24 hours as to whether there was any legal channel to prevent this acquisition, but concluded that there was insufficient legal basis to prevent such a deal either from an anti-monopoly or a national emergency perspective.[22]

Similar intense pressure and opposition also came from Congress, some of whose members wrote to the president and the Department of Justice (DOJ) to express their concerns. Senator Exon, for example, wrote to President Reagan, pointing out that Fairchild was one of the DOD's major suppliers of components and the acquisition of such a company would lead to a dangerous sign that defense-related industries were permitted to be controlled by foreign investors.[23] Despite the fact that Japan was a US ally, he argued that the president should carefully consider the consequences of such a transaction and take measures to safeguard the security of the US defense industry at least at a minimum and prudent level.[24]

Prior to any conclusive decision by the CFIUS, Fujitsu voluntarily withdrew its offer in March 1987, amidst increasing national security concerns about Japanese transactions. While the CFIUS was able to review transactions on national security grounds, it had absolutely no substantial power to block such transactions. Inspired by this failed deal, Senator Exon introduced a bill to the Senate Commerce Committee in June 1987, which eventually came into effect as the Exon-Florio Amendment after going through several revisions.[25] It was basically through this amendment that the regulatory mechanism of national security review was established.

4.1.2 Foreign Investment Practices in the FINSA

4.1.2.1 Increasing Investment in the US

In the late 1990s, foreign investment in the US grew rapidly. Inbound foreign investment in the US was worth US$1.63 trillion in 2005, three times more than in 1980 (see Figure 4.3).[26]

Despite the fact that the CFIUS was given discretion to assess on a transaction-by-transaction basis, it operated prudently in practice.[27] While the number of notices of national security review, including those for withdrawals, reached a peak of 295 in 1990 after the passage of the Exon-Florio Amendment, this remained low in the following decades, hovering around 50 annually (Figure 4.4).[28]

From 1988 to 2005, only 25 transactions entered the additional phase of national security investigation, accounting for 1.5 percent of the total filings (Figure 4.5). In the three years from 2003 to 2005, there were six investigations, more than the total number (four) for the previous decade. This indicates heightened scrutiny of foreign investment on national security grounds.[29]

From 1988 to 2005, during the nearly 20 years after the promulgation of the Exon-Florio Amendment and before the enactment of the FINSA, there were 12 decisions made by the president, with one rejected deal (Figure 4.6).[30] The deal to acquire Mamco Manufacturing Company (MAMCO) with Chinese investment,

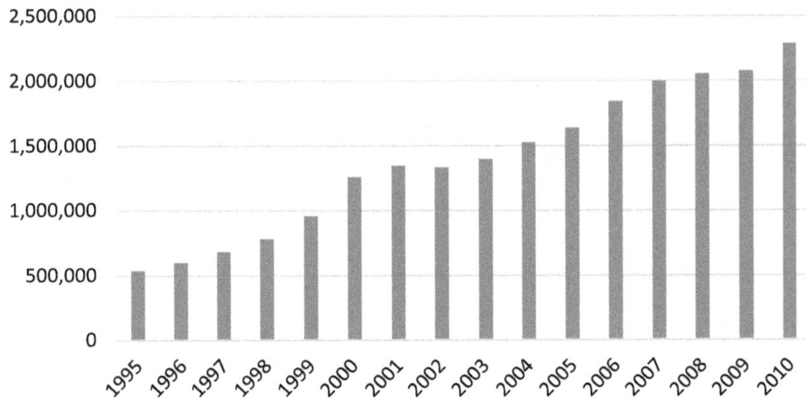

Figure 4.3 Inward Investment in the US from 1995 to 2010

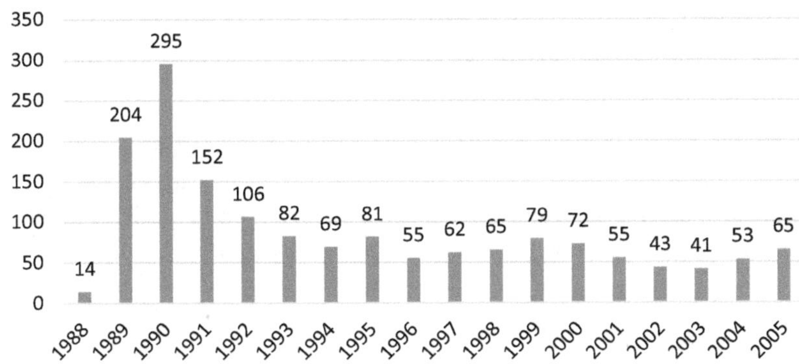

Figure 4.4 Number of Notices for National Security Review from 1988 to 2005 (Including Withdrawals)

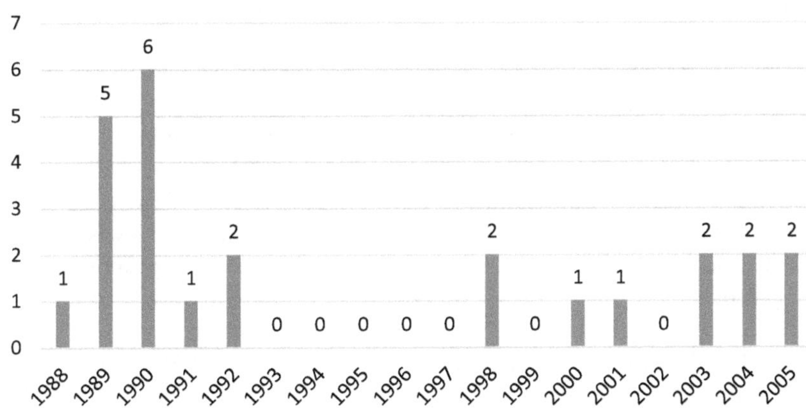

Figure 4.5 Number of National Security Investigations from 1988 to 2005

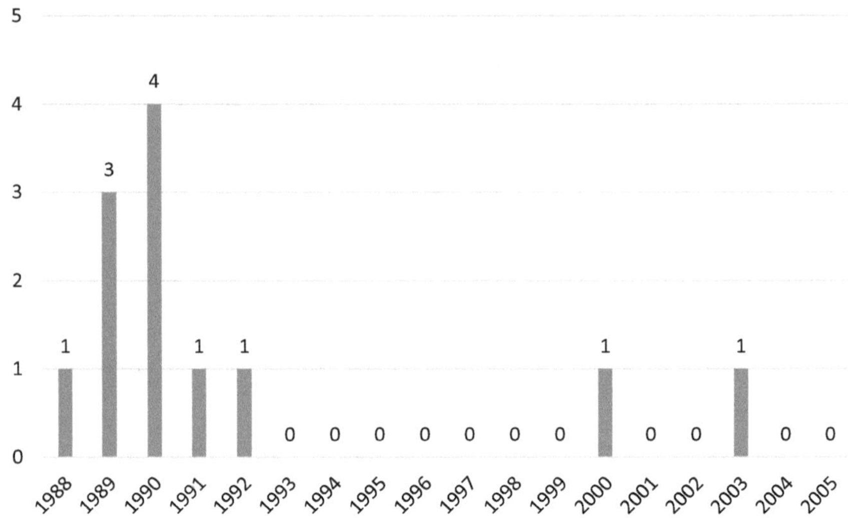

Figure 4.6 Presidential Decisions on National Security Reviews from 1988 to 2005

that is, China National Aero-Technology Import & Export Corporation (CATIC), was the only one which was rejected by President Reagan. This shows a presidential effort to insist on the traditional opening policy for foreign investment while exercising a prudent attitude towards prohibiting foreign investment.

4.1.2.2 Ideas on CNOOC v. UNOCAL

Similar to the Japanese investment in the 1980s that spurred the passage of the Exon-Florio Amendment, Chinese investment began to fall victim to national security concerns in the US and one of the controversial transactions which led to the enactment of FINSA involved Chinese investment. On June 23, 2005, the state-owned China National Offshore Oil Corporation (CNOOC), which was the largest offshore oil and gas producer directly under the State-owned Assets Supervision and Administration Commission (SASAC) in China, announced its bid of US$18.5 billion to acquire the California-based energy firm Unocal Corporation (UNOCAL).[31] In the face of a congressional request fora national security review, the CNOOC voluntarily filed a notification to the CFIUS for such a review.[32] Although the voluntary application by CNOOC attempted to show good faith and an expectation of successfully gaining the national security review's approval,[33] the CFIUS never acted on this CNOOC filing. In the face of insurmountable congressional pushback, the CNOOC announced both the withdrawal of its national security review filing and the withdrawal of its bid to acquire UNOCAL.[34]

Soon after the proposed acquisition of UNOCAL by CNOOC, national security worries about Chinese investments began to be widely expressed in the US. Opponents of this Chinese transaction, such as the US-China Economic and Security

Review Commission, pointed out that the US was dependent on foreign supplies at this time, and it was inappropriate to sell businesses in the energy sector.

Within the Congress, there was staunch opposition to the CNOOC-UNOCAL transaction, resulting in House Resolution 344 which passed overwhelmingly, officially voiced Congress's concerns over the proposed acquisition and urged the president to block the transaction as it might pose a national security threat.[35] The national security objections were demonstrated in House Resolution 344 in the following four justified arguments.[36] First, the CNOOC deal was viewed as detrimental to US energy security and national security, as oil and natural gas resources are paramount strategic assets as regards the energy security of the US, especially at a time of high oil prices and tight supply.[37] Selling Unocal's oil assets to CNOOC would render UNOCAL's oil preferentially allocated to China or its oil reserves exclusively supplied to China, compromising US control over its own energy resources.[38] As CNOOC's acquisition of UNOCAL's strategic oil reserves spanning the globe from the Gulf of Mexico to the Caspian region to Southeast Asia, as well as Africa, Europe, and South America, represented a zero-sum reduction of US influence in those regional oil markets. Moreover, this deal would even have adverse consequences for the global energy market and damage US national security interests in the global context.[39]

Second, the term "Communist Chinese", cited by the Congress, showed special concerns determined by ideological conflicts about Chinese investment. The US perceived Chinese SOEs to receive preferential loans, such as non-commercial loans and subsidies, from their state-owned parent companies and state-owned banks in China, putting other bidders at a disadvantage in the competition and determined that Chinese SOEs did not behave as normal commercial companies.[40] As the Chinese government owned approximately 70 percent of CNOOC, that company was identified as an SOE rather than a pure and normal commercial presence.[41] This deal was regarded effectively as infiltrating the US economy and injecting a foreign power into it, unlike purely private foreign investment.

Third, the Congress viewed CNOOC's bid as revealing the Chinese government's increasingly voracious appetite for oil and its ambitious agenda to control the supply of oil and other important resources, as CNOOC would directly control nearly one-third of the world's excess oil supply.[42] The revenue generated from these resources would in turn strengthen the Chinese government.[43] It was perceived that, if CNOOC succeeded in acquiring UNOCAL, the falling into the control of the former or export to China of the sensitive and dual-use technologies originally held by the latter would threaten US national security.[44]

Fourth, similar transactions by US companies to acquire Chinese energy companies were not allowed in China's legal regime governing foreign investment. It was reasonable, on the basis of reciprocity, for the US to prohibit such an acquisition in the same industry.

Compared with the political and even hostile attitude expressed by Congress, the presidential attitude towards CNOOC's bid was much calmer.[45] On July 17, 2005, President Bush expressed his views on CNOOC's bid and announced that the

US government had procedures to analyze such a deal and its intentions, and that it was his duty to make this procedure work smoothly.

There were, moreover, other views in support of this bid. First, oil and natural gas could be replaced by other products, so that this transaction would not cause any national security implications resulting from lack of supply.[46] Second, as UNOCAL's share of global oil resources was quite low, the acquisition of CNOOC was unlikely to have much adverse impact on the global market.[47] Third, given the fact that Chinese enterprises had already mastered or might easily acquire the high technology owned by UNOCAL, CNOOC did not need to acquire the dual-use technologies that were at the heart of concerns.[48] Fourth, the CNOOC had already claimed that it would sell UNOCAL's assets in the Gulf of Mexico, attempting to eliminate US national security worries. Fifth, maintaining an open Chinese market and encouraging a liberalized investment policy were viewed as conducive to the interests of the US, and the prohibition of CNOOC's bid would signal investment protectionism, contravening the traditional open policy of the US.

4.1.2.3 The Role of CNOOC—UNOCAL in the FINSA

The CNOOC's acquisition of UNOCAL serves as a precise example of how congressional intervention supersedes a statutory national security review and successfully thwarts undesired foreign investment. This proposed transaction fed the Congress's perception of the CFIUS as a weak enforcement body and explained why the Congress had no choice but to intervene to protect US national security. The congressional intervention also indicated that the Congress could obstruct viable transactions in a capricious manner. On June 30, 2005, House Amendment 431, passed by 333 votes to 92 aimed at preventing the Department of the Treasury from using its funds to approve the CNOOC acquisition.[49] On the same day, the House of Representatives also passed the nonbinding House Resolution 334 with an overwhelming 398 to 15 vote, urging a national security review on CNOOC's transaction on the basis of the Exon-Florio Amendment, and pointing out threats to US national security posed by CNOOC control over UNOCAL.[50]

Both the Senate and the House of Representatives showed their congressional view that the CFIUS should prevent the acquisition. Representative Richard Pombo, who demonstrated his suspicion of the benefits of the transaction and was concerned that such a deal might bring disastrous consequences for US national security, wrote to the chairman of the Energy and Commerce Committee of the House of Representatives, and proposed to amend the draft energy law under consideration by Congress to add a clause to postpone the national security review of the CNOOC transaction prior to the completion of a detailed study of the deal by the DOE and other relevant departments.[51] Senator Byro Dorgan put forward another joint resolution, which advocated a law to prevent CNOOC's acquisition of UNOCAL, quoting all kinds of views against the deal and stating simply that CNOOC's purchase should be prohibited regardless of the provisions of other laws.[52]

The Congress attempted to make legal modifications to the process of national security review conducted by the CFIUS. A variety of bills which were haphazardly introduced by the Congress were directly aimed against the CNOOC deal, resulting in a political snowball, rendering prospects for the deal hopeless.[53] Both sides agreed in principle to the bill proposed by Dorgan through consultation, and accordingly, the Secretary of Energy, the Secretary of Defense and the Secretary of Homeland Security were required to study China's increasing energy demand and analyze its political and economic impact on US national security, which required the CFIUS to start its national security review after a 141-day study period.[54] Despite the fact that the arbitrary intervention by the Congress has fanned the fears of uncertainty among foreign investors ever since the CNOOC-UNOCAL debacle, the US has undergone various transformative changes as a result of FINSA, which regulated congressional involvement and established a more predictable process of national security review where the transaction did in fact implicate US national security interests.[55] The measures reflected in the FINSA to improve transparency and to clarify congressional involvement in national security review could be summarized as follows.

First, as the CNOOC failed to submit a notice about transactional risks that could trigger national security review, a preliminary national security review of all covered transactions and conducted by the CFIUS was mandated by the FINSA, in order to ensure that each transaction falling into the scope of national security review would receive sufficient attention from the CFIUS.[56] The parties to a proposed foreign merger, acquisition, or takeover can expect to provide preliminary information about the deal regardless of whether the CFIUS initiates the review or the parties themselves voluntarily seek government approval. This reflects a legislative attempt to avoid the CNOOC's plight of, firstly, not being reviewed by the CFIUS. The FINSA provides parties to a covered transaction with risk factors that have implicated US national security in the past. The CFIUS, for example, is required to issue guidelines on the types of reviewed foreign investment transactions that would present national security and critical infrastructure concerns.[57] The Implementing Regulations of FINSA, moreover, provide a number of examples to show what level of corporate control is sufficient to trigger CFIUS review.[58] The arbitrary congressional involvement that occurred in the CNOOC acquisition can be avoided with enhanced transparency of the CFIUS review.

Second, in an effort to limit congressional intervention in the national security review, the demands of legitimate and prudent congressional involvement have been satisfied by the introduction in the FINSA of requirements for the CFIUS to report to the Congress. Prior to FINSA, the Exon-Florio Amendment required only quadrennial reports to Congress, yet after an initial report in 1993, no such reports were submitted for the next dozen years.[59] Because of the lack of information about foreign investment and national security reviews, the Congress had to actively intervene in foreign investment activities during national security reviews, to realize its intentions of safeguarding national security. In the FINSA, therefore, the CFIUS is obliged to submit an annual report to Congress that summarizes trends and the foreign investment activities of the previous year and to provide notice and certification of its findings to the Congress during the additional phase of national security investigation, for pending transactions under review.[60] Congressional attempts to participate in national security reviews of foreign investments can be achieved in a transparent and legal manner, and capricious congressional intervention like that involving the CNOOC transaction can largely be avoided in practice.

4.1.3 *Foreign Investment Practices in the FIRRMA*

4.1.3.1 Increasing National Security Concerns About Chinese Investment

Driven by national security concerns, the CFIUS became a more influential watchdog on foreign investment after the establishment of the national security review by the Exon-Florio Amendment and the enactment of the FINSA.[61] In the face of China's meteoric economic growth, suspicions of perceived threats to US national security from foreign investment shifted to China. The US perceived Chinese investment to challenge its hegemony both economically and militarily within the narrative of globalization.[62] China topped the list in terms of CFIUS reviews of investment deals for potential national security risks, from President Obama onwards in the most recent decade, especially in the Trump and Biden administrations.[63] When Trump took office as president in 2017, For example, the Trump administration initiated China-specific measures, such as tariffs on goods from March 2018 under Section 301 of the Trade Act of 1974, driven by US national security worries which were referred to as the "Chinese theft of US intellectual property".[64] The CFIUS review was reformed by FIRRMA's targeting of Chinese investment for heightened scrutiny. Between 2005 and 2022, the CFIUS reviewed 2,852 foreign investment transactions, while there was an increase since 2017 (Figure 4.7).[65] Among them, the number of Chinese transactions under CFIUS review was 418 (Figure 4.8).[66]

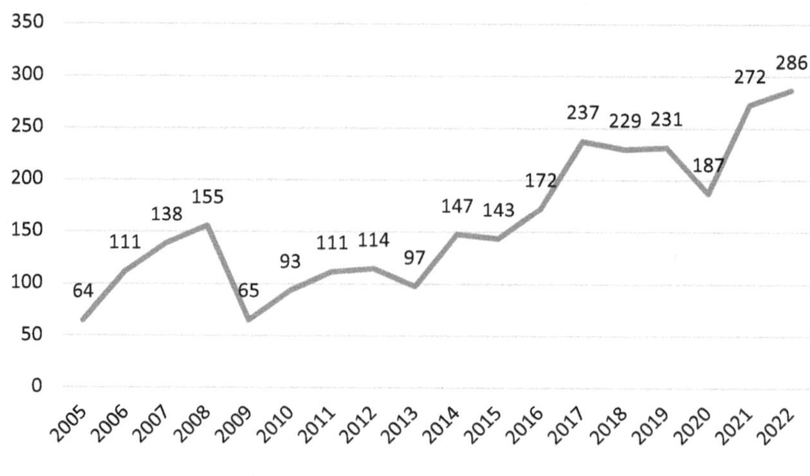

Figure 4.7 Covered Transactions from 2005 to 2022

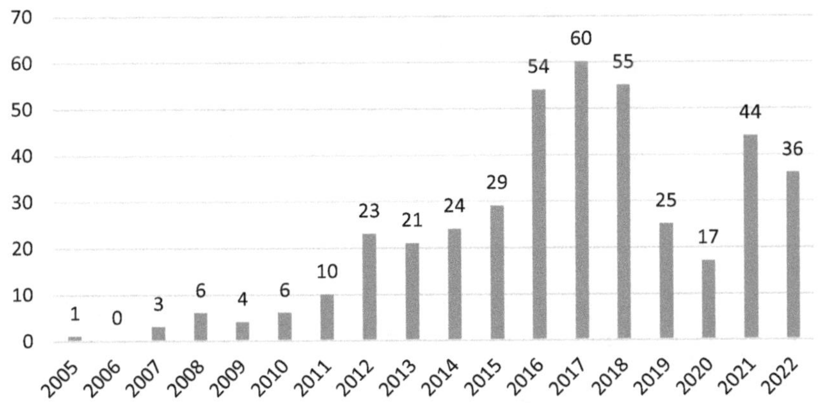

Figure 4.8 Covered Chinese Transactions from 2005 to 2022

Coincidentally, but not surprisingly, it can be seen that the total of seven transactions prohibited by presidential order in the history of national security reviews all involved Chinese buyers or Chinese-related factors.[67] Only the 1990 prohibition of CATIC's acquisition of MAMCO occurred before 2010, soon after the passage of the Exon-Florio Amendment. The rest were all prohibited after 2010 (Table 4.1). Compared with the relatively prudent attitude of President Obama in prohibiting Chinese investment, a negative impression towards Chinese investment emerges from the Trump administration, with an increasing number of prohibited Chinese investment projects. This indicates that President Trump perceived the regulatory mechanism of national security review as a normal measure to be used frequently to safeguard national security or national interests.

4.1.3.2 *Chinese Investment in US Telecommunication: Huawei vs. 3Com and Huawei vs. 3Leaf*

After the enactment of FINSA, two well-known transactions involving Huawei Technologies Co. Ltd. (Huawei) underwent US national security reviews. Although Huawei remains privately owned, it is perceived as a Chinese national champion, as the world's largest manufacturer and provider of key telecommunications networks.[75] On September 28, 2007, Bain Capital proposed a US$2.2 billion buyout of 3Com Corporation (3Com), a pioneering digital electronics maker known for networking products in the US.[76] Huawei planned to hold a minority stake in this contemplated deal at 16.5 percent and would not obtain any operational control or decision-making power over 3Com.[77] Learning from the failure of CNOOC's acquisition of UNOCAL, Bain Capital and Huawei voluntarily filed with the CFIUS a notice regarding this transaction for national security review. Despite the fact that Huawei made great efforts to negotiate alternative mitigations with the CFIUS over its national security concerns, the purchase of 3Com was eventually withdrawn in February 2008.[78] Three years later, in May 2010, Huawei proposed

Table 4.1 Transactions Blocked by US Presidential Action from 1988 to 2020

Acquirer	*Target*	*Sector*	*Alleged Threat to US National Security*	*Time*	*President*
China National Aero-Technology Import and Export Corporation (CATIC)[68]	Mamco Manufacturing Inc.	Airplane component manufacture	Acquirer likely to gain aircraft engine technology for military application	1990	George Bush
Ralls Corporation (US-based) and Sany Group (China-based)[69]	Terna Energy USA Holding	Wind farm	Target firm in proximity to a naval weapons systems training facility	2012	Barack Obama
Grand Chip Investment GmbH (Germany-based) and Fujian Grand Chip Investment Fund LP (China-based)[70]	Aixtron, Inc, US business	Semiconductor	Acquirer may misuse the sensitive missile defense system technology held by the target company	2016	Barack Obama
Canyon Bridge Capital (US-based company, with a Chinese investor as its sole limited partner)[71]	Lattice	Semiconductor	Acquirer was foreign government controlled. Target company involved in technologies with potential military applications.	2017	Donald Trump
Broaden (Singapore-based)[72]	Qualcomm	Semiconductor	US technology leadership in IT and communications may be challenged	2018	Donald Trump
Stayntouch, Inc.	Beijing Shiji Information Technology Co., Ltd.	Software supplier to the hospitality industry	Sensitive nature of the data it collects in its software for the hotel, food service, retail, and entertainment industries[73]	2020	Donald Trump
ByteDance Ltd[74]	Musical.ly (TikTok)	US social media app	Sensitive personal data	2020	Donald Trump

another bid, worth US$2 million, to 3Leaf Systems for intellectual property rights. Compared with 3Com, 3Leaf is a rather small server based in California.[79] This bid was approved by the Bureau of Industry and Security of the Department of Commerce, so Huawei did not file a notice to the CFIUS for an additional phase of national security review.[80] Later the DOD directed the CFIUS to request Huawei to file a notification regarding the consummated transaction and to initiate the review process, in order to determine whether this deal would trigger national security issues.[81] The CFIUS concluded after a national security investigation that Huawei must voluntarily divest itself of 3Leaf and recommended that President Obama reverse the transaction.[82] Huawei eventually decided that it would not wait for a final presidential decision, but instead agree to the divestiture and abandon the transaction.[83]

The failures of these Huawei investments in the US were a result of the US perception of the corporate identity of Huawei.[84] As Ren Zhengfei, its founder and leader, is a former People's Liberation Army (PLA) officer,[85] possible deep ties with the Chinese military posed a considerable roadblock to its aspirations to penetrate markets impinging on US national security interests and resulted in Huawei's failure to acquire 3Com and 3Leaf.[86] In addition, a US investigative report focused on national security implications that were presented by Chinese telecommunications companies.[87] The report complained that Huawei failed to cooperate fully with the investigation but was evasive and nonresponsive to questions at the heart of the security issues posed, and then forewarned that Chinese investment equipping US critical infrastructure would impose national security risks and undermine core national interests.[88] These failed transactions raised heightened attention to Chinese investment in the telecommunications industry, as an area of critical US infrastructure, and highlighted the need for a broader approach to defining national security in national security reviews.[89]

Inspired by the failed acquisitions by Huawei with its potential close ties to the Chinese military, the US began to strengthen its scrutiny in order to optimize avoidance of national security risks in foreign investments connected to foreign governments. In November 2012, the US-China Economic and Security Review Commission issued a report containing detailed perceptions about Chinese investment in the US. US industrial groups, lawmakers, and government officials recognized the potential for economic distortions and national security implications arising from China's economic growth backed by the state.[90] In particular, some observers argued that economic concerns focused on the possibility that state-backed Chinese companies choose to invest on the basis of strategic goals rather than market-based considerations and, with their generous state subsidies, are free from the normal constraints of market forces.[91]

One major recommendation for amending FINSA is to require a mandatory review of all prospective controlling transactions by Chinese state-owned and state-controlled companies investing in the US.[92] This suggestion had been carefully considered during the legislative process of the FIRRMA, with the purpose of allowing a shorter filing than a traditional CFIUS notice and a potentially expedited process for obtaining CFIUS clearance of a particular transaction. Circumstances requiring mandatory declarations, however, varied between the Senate and House versions of the bill. The Senate version required mandatory declarations for certain foreign government-backed transactions involving investments in critical infrastructure or critical technology, whereas the House version required them for certain government-backed transactions involving only critical technology.[93] In the end, foreign government controlled transactions relating not only to critical technology and critical infrastructure but also to sensitive personal data were covered within the scope of mandatory declarations.[94]

4.1.3.3 Chinese Investment in Real Estate: Ralls vs. Terna

On February 28, 2012, Ralls Corp. (Ralls), an affiliate of the Chinese heavy machinery manufacturing conglomerate Sany Group (Sany), proposed a purchase of wind farm assets from Terna Energy Corporation (Terna).[95] Ralls consummated the transaction to acquire the companies and properties without voluntarily filing a notification for a preliminary national security review. Later, on the basis of the national security threat posed by these four wind farm properties close to a restricted airbase and bombing zone deployed by the US Navy for the test flight of an advanced electronic warfare aircraft, the CFIUS requested that Ralls file a voluntary notification.[96] The CFIUS then reached a conclusion that such a transaction would threaten US national security and required Ralls to cease all construction and operations at certain project sites, as well as all access to the project sites immediately.[97] On September 13, the CFIUS concluded its investigation and forwarded a report to President Obama, who, on September 28, 2012, decided to prohibit the transaction and order an immediate divestiture.[98]

Prior investment by investors from Denmark and Germany in other wind turbines near such a claimed restricted airspace, however, had not been blocked in this way.[99] Ralls decided to file a lawsuit against the CFIUS, as well as the president, in the DC District Court, and to seek the court's declaration that the orders made by both the CFIUS and the president were invalid. In fact, the court ruled in favor of the defendant's motion to dismiss the plaintiff's complaint for lack of jurisdiction.[100] Ralls then lodged an appeal to the DC Circuit Court on May 5, 2014,[101] challenging the dismissal of its due process claims against the presidential order and its claims against the CFIUS order.[102] The Court of Appeals ruled on July 15, 2014, and reversed the lower court's verdict, concluding that the President's Order violated the due process clause of the Fifth Amendment by depriving Ralls of property without providing adequate opportunity to be heard or an adequate explanation of the reasons for the decision.[103] On November 4, 2015, attorneys for Ralls announced that they had settled the lawsuit with the US government. Under the settlement terms, Ralls might sell the wind farm assets to a third party of its choosing, an arrangement to which the CFIUS had previously objected. Furthermore, the CFIUS acknowledged that the transaction did not raise national security risks and that both Ralls and Sany were free to submit future transactions and investments to the CFIUS for review.[104]

Since the 911 attacks, the US has paid attention to ensuring the security of various facilities, such as ports, chemical factories, and airports, either commercial or military. Critical infrastructure and real estate facilities located in sensitive places or in close proximity to military facilities raises national security worries. This decision of the CFIUS and president in relation to the transaction of Terna by Ralls in 2012 indicates not only continual US hostility towards Chinese investment but also its heightened concerns about security of critical infrastructure and certain real estate. The targeted company's physical proximity to military installations or sensitive facilities raised red flags for national security, as this attribute increases the potential for economic or military espionage.

In order to avoid the embarrassment of a lawsuit filed by Ralls and ensure the authority of decisions made by the CFIUS and the president, the reformed regulatory mechanism of national security review attempts to address the concerns related to sensitive facilities. As a consequence, the scope of foreign investments subject to national security review in the legal regime of the FIRRMA includes greenfield real estate transactions; that is, the purchase or lease by, or concession to, a foreign person of private or public real estate located in the US, when such a transaction is located within or functioning as part of specified ports, either airports or maritime ports, or in close proximity to military installations and other facilities of the US government.[105] The FIRRMA provides a detailed definition of the term "close proximity" as the area that extends outward one mile from the boundary of a military installation, facility, or property of the US government.[106] Three characteristics are explained in the FIRRMA with respect to military installations or other facilities or property of the US government. The first is that the real estate is in close proximity to military installations and other facilities of the US government that are sensitive for reasons relating to national security.[107] The second is that the real estate might reasonably provide the foreign person with the ability to collect intelligence on activities being conducted at such an installation, facility, or property.[108] The third is that it could otherwise expose national security activities at such an installation, facility, or property to the risk of foreign surveillance.[109]

4.2 Practices of National Security Review in China

4.2.1 Foreign Investment Under the Conservative Perspective

Traditionally, China maintained a conservative attitude towards foreign investment. Prior to the policy of reform and opening up in 1978, it was hard to find commercial entities established by foreign investment in China. Since the reform and opening up policy was initiated in 1978, foreign investment began to be allowed in China, and the earliest law concerning foreign investment, namely, the EJV Law, was adopted accordingly. During the first decade, foreign investors had to choose the form of joint venture with Chinese partners to establish an FIE. In the late 1990s, industrial sectors were partly open to foreign investments, which were specifically categorized into four clusters: encouraged, permitted, restricted, and prohibited. Even though the legal regime of FIE Laws had already basically been established, foreign investment was continuously under the strict scrutiny of the Chinese government, through several layers of approval review at the market access, for the establishment of FIEs and foreign investment projects.

After the policy of reform and opening up was adopted in China, foreign investment inflows increased steadily and rapidly between 1978 and 1992.[110] From 1979 to 1988 the value of China's FDI inflows was US$12.5 billion, and in 1999, the value increased to about US$40 billion.[111] In order to sustain growth momentum in the economy, China continually attempted to secure the critical input factor, that is, the growth of foreign investment. In the 1990s, therefore, a series of regulations were adopted to further attract foreign investment, providing preferential measures to foreign investors to encourage industrial sectors in particular. In 2002, the value of FDI in China jumped to US$52.7 billion, and since then, annual foreign investment inflows have been increasing continually.[112] In 2010, the value of inward foreign investment reached US$105.7 billion.[113] We can see, then, that in the decade since China's accession to the WTO, the annual value of FDI inflows into China has doubled.[114]

The policy of reform and opening up created enormous benefits for foreign investment in China. It was reported that, in the year 1994, joint ventures accounted for a third of China's imports and almost 20 percent of its exports, and wholly foreign owned enterprises (WFOEs) accounted for 12 percent of imports and 9 percent of exports.[115] At the initial stage in the legal regime of FIE Laws, however, foreign investment M&As were largely prohibited, as the FIE Laws at that time allowed a commercial presence only through FIEs. Along with the significant contributions of foreign investment M&As in China, there were many worries about foreign investment M&As as they were given too many advantages in the emerging market, without adequate regulation by the central government, might gain access to capacity and market share in China.[116]

4.2.2 US Investments and M&A Security Reviews in China: Carlyle vs. Xugong

Propelled by the global M&A wave initiated in the early 1990s and peaking in the year 2000, a dramatic surge in foreign investment M&As took place in China. In 2003, the reported value of takeovers of firms within China by foreign investment was slightly over US$1.6 billion, approximately 3 percent of total FDI inflows as reported inward FDI flow.[117] The growth of foreign investment in the form of M&As continued in the following decade. In the year 2012, the value of cross-border M&As accounted for around 8.8 percent of total inward FDI flow in China.[118]

M&As became a favorable option enabling foreign investors to escape strict approval reviews at the market access in the FIE Laws and the guidance system.[119] Some foreign investment M&A transactions were strategically aimed at purchasing top Chinese companies or obtaining Chinese essential assets, giving rise to the criticism that they endangered China's vulnerable domestic national security enterprises and put China's national security in jeopardy.[120] From 2003 to 2007, the proportion of market control from foreign investment over China's industry exceeded 30 percent, and the equity control of foreign investment over China's industry from 2007 to 2010 was close to 30 percent.[121]

When China found later that foreign investment by means of M&As was deeply entrenched in almost every aspect of its economy, its sensitivities about national security and economic security were pricked.[122] At the same time, certain overseas acquisitions conducted by Chinese investors failed because of national security reviews, especially in the US. The regulatory mechanism of national security review of foreign investment M&As in the US inspired China to establish a similar template for better addressing its national security worries.

In 2005, the Carlyle Group (Caryle), a US-based private equity firm, announced its offer to buy 85 percent of the stock in Xugong, an SOE wholly owned by Xuzhou People's Government and China's largest construction machinery manufacturer, at the price of US$375 million.[123] After being rashly announced to the public, the deal was submitted to MOFCOM for approval and underwent a lengthy three-year review process.[124] Even though Carlyle made concessions, revised its offer twice and scaled back its initial investment, which resulted in a substantial reduction in Carlyle's proposed stake in Xugong, from 85 percent to 45 percent, in response to competition from a rival Chinese bidder, Sany. It failed to address national security concerns which were widely expressed in China.[125] Some Chinese nationalists complained that the sale of strategic assets at knock-down prices would threaten China's national economic security.[126] In the face of growing public discontent, MOFCOM suspended the approval review for this acquisition at the market access, placing it in bureaucratic limbo for over three years.[127] The deal could not be implemented because the period of three years signed in the acquiring agreements between Carlyle and Xugong had expired. In July 2008, the deal fell through. MOFCOM had effectively used its review discretion on M&As to quash the politically sensitive takeover bid of Xugong by Carlyle. No official explanations have ever been released regarding this deal, leaving much space for conjecture as to what MOFCOM's real concern was for spending almost three years reviewing one deal and ending with no finding at all.[128]

There was heated, apparently rather polarized, debate about the transaction's failure.[129] On the one hand, some scholars praised MOFCOM's resolute effort to protect national economic security by preventing a potentially dangerous sell-out of strategic state assets.[130] From their point of view, Carlyle's insidious attempt to acquire Xugong was nothing but a potential annihilation of a Chinese national champion, a convenient sacrifice of Chinese state assets, and a hostile and appalling attempt to exploit a successful Chinese company under the guise of regular commercial activities.[131] On the other hand, other arguments denied that Xugong was merely a heavy machinery manufacturer without any sensitive or strategic significance, and held that it was hard to see national security implications.[132] They contended that MOFCOM simply acted in retaliation and in response to a nationalistic backlash because of the debacle of CNOOC's acquisition of UNOCAL only a few months earlier.[133]

This was before the M&A Provisions of 2003 which officially established the regulatory mechanism of national security review in balancing the tension between foreign investment liberalization, political pressure, and national security protection. It is understandable that MOFCOM's hands were tied because of the inadequate legal grounds on which to forbid Carlyle's deal, but it seems difficult, if not impossible, to figure out the true intentions behind MOFCOM's action. In the same year that Carlyle was thwarted, 2006, however, MOFCOM revised the M&A Regulations. This legal behavior indicates that new provisions concerning security review for foreign investment M&As were enacted in response to the Carlyle acquisition and perceived hypocrisy in US treatment of foreign investments.[134] To some extent, the real purpose of preventing the Carlyle transaction—national security—would be evidenced by this signal.

4.2.3 US Investment and M&A Security Reviews in China: Coco-Cola vs. Huiyuan

In September 2008, the Coca-Cola Company (Coca-Cola), a world-renowned multinational enterprise based in the US, proposed to wholly acquire Huiyuan Fruit Juice Group Limited (Huiyuan), a leading Chinese brand in juice beverage production, for US$2.3 billion.[135] Coca-Cola voluntarily submitted the paperwork to MOFCOM for an anti-monopoly review, in accordance with the AML promulgated in 2007.[136] Similar to the Carlyle-Xugong deal, this proposed takeover quickly attracted public attention and raised heated discussion. Opposition views were widely expressed and represented the majority, in the face of the possibility of the gradual disappearance of a national champion.[137] Notably, in contrast to MOFCOM's three-year reaction in the form of the review process over Carlyle's proposed acquisition of Xugong, MOFCOM only took six months to reach a decision, and the prohibition of the deal was made in March 2009.[138] In contrast to its silence on the Carlyle deal, moreover, MOFCOM provided an official announcement of its decision and explained that the prohibition decision was made in accordance with Article 28 of AML, proclaiming that the concentration of operators caused by the proposed deal would restrict or might restrict market competition.[139] It was viewed as a milestone in China's regulatory regime of foreign investment, as the first legitimate and laudable action made by MOFCOM.[140]

It seems at first glance that Coco-Cola's bid for Huiyuan barely impinged on national security, as MOFCOM specifically stated that the prohibition was based on competition issues. Suspicions and criticisms emerged, however, soon after MOFCOM's explanation that its account also involved national security concerns, such as the political purpose of preserving a nationally well-known brand.[141] The consideration of competition concerns alone could not suffice to justify the prohibition decision.[142] According to the M&A security review described in the M&A Provisions of 2006, safeguarding Chinese champions from foreign investment is one of the factors triggering M&A security reviews. In this case, even though no M&A security review had been initiated on this deal, the concerns about national security were undeniable.[143] Interestingly, the episode shows that MOFCOM was reluctant to express its national security concerns explicitly to justify this final decision, on the basis of Article 31 of AML. It is reasonable to explore the possibility that the real reason behind this decision was national security, although it had undergone a legitimate competition review. One might presume that, at least one of the most plausible considerations about this question is that MOFCOM deliberately avoided pursuing a national security review under Article 31 of AML, in order to avoid greater ambiguity and yet more public skepticism.[144] Another possible reason is that the description of M&A security review in Article 31 of AML is quite vague and broad; merely a conceptualization, far from a feasible and practical enforcement mechanism. In this case, without detailed guidelines, it would have been difficult for MOFCOM to enforce a national security review in practice.

The difficulty of implementing national security review in relation to foreign investment M&As was revealed by this transaction, as China provided only general principles on M&A security review at this stage. On the one hand, the lack of detailed rules on national security review made implementation unrealistic. On the other hand, there was an institutional deficiency between anti-monopoly review and national security review in the governance of foreign investment M&As.[145] Even though some scholars contended that an independent national security review was not needed because a considerably intertwined and highly regulated foreign investment regime with repetitive references to national security concerns had existed for decades, the majority argued that previous regulatory approval reviews on foreign investment at the market access did not cover inbound M&As. The necessity and significance—when national security concerns appeared in certain foreign investment M&As—of a national security review regime with detailed and formalized rules, moreover, is solidly evidenced by the embarrassment and dilemma Chinese authorities faced in this transaction, in which, because there was no statutory national security review mechanism, authorities had to turn to the inappropriate approach, such as anti-monopoly review.[146]

In order to ensure the feasibility and effectiveness of M&A security review as an independent regulatory system, a succession of doubts has to be answered. What, for example, is the definition of national security? Why does certain foreign investment fall within the purview of national security review? Who has the authority to conduct a national security review? What is the detailed procedure for conducting a national security review? These questions have been addressed in the State Council Circular 6 on M&A security review which was introduced in 2011, in which the review scope, criteria, procedure, as well as review body were fleshed out.

4.2.4 Foreign Investment in National Security Review in the FIL: Yonghui vs. Zhongbai

Yonghui Superstores Co. Ltd. (Yonghui), a supermarket operator, was the second largest shareholder—with a 29.9 percent stake—in Zhongbai Holdings Group Co. Ltd., (Zhongbai), a central China regional supermarket chain.[147] According to a statement dated April 12, 2019, Yonghui offered CNY¥ 8.10 per share to raise its stake in Zhongbai to 40 percent from nearly 30 percent, in a deal valued at CNY¥ 559 million.[148]

This planned investment was expected to make Yonghui the controlling shareholder in Zhongbai and boost Yonghui's presence in Hubei province, the home market of Zhongbai.[149] Two days after the State Administration for Market Regulation (SAMR) had given its merger control clearance for Yonghui's bid,[150] the NDRC requested Yonghui to submit a filing for a foreign investment security review and supplementary documents.[151] In December 2019, Yonghui announced the dropping of its proposed acquisition of Zhongbai and abandoned the deal altogether, without disclosing whether its decision was made as a result of a national security review.[152]

It is rare for national security concerns to be cited in the course of reviews of deals in the retail sector. Even though the exact nature of the national security review in this case is unknown, as the NDRC made no public official confirmation or explanation as to its concerns about the deal or the standards it applied to assess it, the fact that Yonghui's largest shareholder was Dairy Farm International, a subsidiary of the British conglomerate Jardine Matheson, may have triggered the invocation of the national security review.[153] Additionally, the threshold for the control element to initiate a national security review was absent, as Yonghui sought to acquire only 40 percent of Zhongbai's shares, and there was no evidence to indicate that it would gain de facto control of Zhongbai. Even though the bid might result in Yonghui's de facto control of Zhongbai as its biggest shareholder, the retail sector does not fall within the scope of national security unless a foreign investor is seeking a controlling interest in the target company.[154] To some extent, there were some suspicions that the national security review that took place in relation to this transaction might involve national defense concerns. Even though the retail sector appears irrelevant to the security of national defense, it was undeniable that Zhongbai was the major provider of warehousing and distribution as part of the catering services for the 2019 Military World Games in October 2019.[155] Zhongbai, moreover, had a large number of stores located in certain military colleges in Wuhan. Notably, Wuhan State-Owned Assets Management, which was wholly owned by Wuhan State-Owned Assets Supervision and Administration Commission had a 34.9 percent stake in Zhongbai, making it its biggest shareholder. The increase in Yonghui's stake in Zhongbai from 29.9 percent to 40 percent would result in the loss of the controlling position of Wuhan State-Owned Assets Management in Zhongbai, and ultimately affect the economic interests of Wuhan Municipal Government, which might indirectly affect governmental control over the retail sector.

The acquisition of Zhongbai by Yonghui is the first and only known case to undergo the process of national security review in China.[156] This was before the Measures had been issued and the national security review had to be conducted in accordance with State Council Circular 6, MOFCOM Announcement 53, and State Council Circular 24. Under those previous rules, Yonghui's acquisition would fall outside of the prescribed sectoral scope, as it involved the operation of supermarkets in the retail sector. It was therefore difficult, if not impossible, for the NDRC to give any specific or legitimate grounds for its request for national security review or for its decisive role in thwarting such a deal.

For the purpose of addressing the problems revealed in the national security review conducted on this deal, it is widely acknowledged in China that the previous rules on national security review should be unified and reformed under the updated legal regime of the FIL. On the basis of previous rules on national security review and the legal spirit of the FIL, the Measures were finally issued in late 2020, in the context of the FIL. Pursuant to the Measures, in addition to specifying several sectors which are essential to national security, foreign investment in other critical sectors with actual control falls within the scope of national security review.[157] This legal arrangement attempts to avoid the embarrassment of the Yonghui acquisition in the retail sector, which was not listed among sectors subject to national security review in previous rules. It is also designed to avoid national security risks caused by foreign investment in other unpredictable or emerging sectors which have not been listed in the legal texts but might become essential to national security in the future. As any potential foreign investment could be described as falling within the scope of other critical sectors, this provision seems to cover an all-inclusive range of foreign investment.

4.3 An Oriented Process of National Security Reviews in China and the US

4.3.1 How do US Investments in China Affect US Ideas About CFIUS Reviews and Chinese Investments in the US?

There is a long history of discrimination against US investment in China. Under the legal regime of FIE Laws, the several approval reviews set up at the market access for foreign investment, such as those for FIEs or for foreign investment projects, have made it difficult for US investors to establish enterprises or enter into numerous industries. Chinese industrial sectors have been gradually opened in the past decades, when a large number of sectors were prohibited or restricted. The traditional policy on foreign investment in China created great obstacles to foreign investment activities. Many MNEs based in the US failed in their efforts to enter the Chinese market in the initial stage. Some US investors had to establish joint ventures with Chinese partners, in order to succeed in their investment plans. Under the legal regime of FIE Laws, any FIE established at the market access was required to be approved by MOFCOM and registered by the State Administration for Industry and Commerce. The review criteria for FIE establishment was never mentioned in legal texts, so it was quite hard for US investors to know whether their investment met this simple and general requirement. In the 1990s, China's Guidance System was established as an important legal supplement within the context of FIE Laws, to further encourage and govern foreign investment. China produced a long list of restricted and prohibited sectors for foreign investment, and all foreign investment projects as well as activities by the established FIEs had to be reviewed if they were related to these sectors. Foreign investment had to go through a strict and non-transparent process of approval review at the market access before entry into these restricted or prohibited industrial sectors. Undoubtedly, these regulatory layers of approval reviews at the market access contributed to great inconvenience to foreign investors in the absence of any transparency or efficiency. US investors incurred great costs, including time and effort, to survive these approval reviews without any predicted signals. The links between these regulatory reviews at the market access and national security concerns are undeniable. National security concerns reflected in the legal regime of FIE Laws were mixed with pure national security-related issues, such as military security, security of national defense, economic security, and other security matters involving preserving the socialist regime under the CPC's leadership. The internal ideas on national security and foreign investment in China, which are also affected by socialism, played a decisive role in formulating Chinese regulatory reviews of foreign investment at the market access. Since China's accession to the WTO, moreover, China's domestic market has been further opened and reformed under a market-oriented approach, and the M&A method of foreign investment, under which Chinese assets or stakes are relatively easily acquired, has been permitted in China. The regulatory mechanisms of M&A review and M&A security review, however, revealed the Chinese government's remaining concerns on national security and economic activities, but arbitrary intervention in foreign investment activities was perceived to be carried out with the purpose of protecting economic security. In order to avoid criticisms of governmental intervention in foreign investment, certain foreign investment M&As were blocked during anti-monopoly review in the name of competition concerns, rather than national security concerns. The frequently enforced approach of anti-monopoly review mixed with national security worries rendered the regulatory mechanism of anti-monopoly review unjustifiable.

Because of these regulatory layers at the market access, foreign investors, especially those from the US, have, in past decades, complained extensively about the legal regime of FIE Laws for FIEs, foreign investment projects, and foreign investment M&As. The US domestic market is wide open to foreign investment under the traditional open policy because of the historical benefits accruing to the US from foreign investment therein. Chinese investment in the US was not treated in the way US investment was treated in China, but given equal treatment to domestic investment. Unlike the pure market players, such as private enterprises in the US, however, some Chinese overseas enterprises were state-owned or had close ties with government. Their investment plans in the US may be perceived to be influenced by strategic goals of the Chinese government.

In the face of China's extraordinary economic development, moreover, the US has gradually come to view China as a strategic competitor, or even a threat to US superpower status.[158] A major ingredient of China's remarkable and unprecedented economic growth is its dramatic and increasing investment.[159] Indeed, an increasing number of Chinese investments can be found in the US, raising serious national security concerns about Chinese investment in the US. Along with US worries about China's meteoric rise and challenges to its dominance in international markets, Chinese investment in American companies, particularly in relation to high technologies, are deemed as potential threats to US national security, which might not only corrupt manufacturing and distribution processes that serve the US government, but also challenge US economic and technological leadership.[160] It is perceived in the US that domestic US products or services could be compromised to enable foreign powers to eavesdrop, copy, or steal sensitive data or technology.[161] These concerns have been evidenced, for example, by the failures of Huawei's repeated acquisitions of US companies in the telecommunications sector following US national security reviews. To be specific, in the attempted acquisition of 3Com by Huawei, a specific concern about Huawei in the national security review was that it would gain access to the equipment maker's technology, which is used by the DOD.[162] Accordingly, in response to perceived threats from Chinese investment, the US has crafted an elaborate legislative framework to review foreign mergers and acquisitions for national security implications, including the risk of economic espionage, which is an increasing concern within the US national security apparatus.[163] While China has focused heavily on economic growth through trade partnerships, its success has translated into a dramatic increase in its power potential relative to the US.[164] A broader scope of foreign investment subject to national security review, moreover, has been covered in the FIRRMA. In addition to traditional security, such as military and national defense security, other dimensions of security, such as security of critical infrastructure, technological security, information security, and cybersecurity are taken into consideration in the national security review. Under the FIRRMA, foreign investment transactions in relation to critical infrastructure, critical technology and sensitive personal data, undergo stricter national security review scrutiny, even though they are non-controlling deals. The type of foreign investment under national security review, moreover, is no longer limited to M&As. Greenfield investments, such as real estate transactions, would also trigger national security reviews. These approaches to involving a massive range of foreign investment in US national security reviews have, in almost every respect, become gradually similar to China's all-inclusive means, in the legal system of FIE Laws, of supervising foreign investment on national security grounds at the market access.

4.3.2 How do Chinese Investments in the US Affect Chinese Ideas on National Security Reviews and US Investments in China?

As mentioned previously, because of the traditional open US policy towards foreign investment, Chinese investments can be found in a wide range of US industries. Only a small number of acquisitions by Chinese investments have been blocked by national security reviews. All the presidential orders on foreign investments have been made on investments from China or in relation to China. One highly likely reason for this is that the Chinese domestic market failed to give equal treatment based on the principle of reciprocity to US investment in corresponding sectors. In turn, Chinese investment in the US is very likely to be treated in a stricter manner when national security reviews are carried out. Even though the details of considerations arising in the process of assessing national security implications on Chinese investment are unknown, this presumption is supported, by failed Chinese investment in transactions similar to others from other foreign origins which were approved without national security review. In the acquisition of Ralls by Terna, for example, the properties of certain facilities owned by Chinese investment were claimed to be located in a restricted area, and had to be divested by presidential order, while similar facilities located in the same zone but owned by other foreigners were allowed. This case indicates a more conservative attitude on the part of the US towards Chinese investment than towards investment from other countries.

In order to address US discriminatory and hostile attitudes towards Chinese investment, China attempted to further reform and open its domestic market to US investment, in line with international investment rules advocated by the US. China has been undertaking economic reform for several decades and created more market-oriented rules for foreign investors, such as FIE laws and supplementary industrial policies which introduced some liberalized principles and adopted international practices, to follow international rules and adapt to economic conditions. Even though there were some criticisms that they were often not effectively implemented and failed to provide the protection and predictability associated with the rule of law, China's ambition to improve the environment for foreign investment is undeniable. The poor performance of the FIE laws mainly results from the practical obstacles and inconsistencies inherently rooted in Chinese domestic ideology and weak legal infrastructure, contributing to a lack of systematic and unified law governing foreign investment. To respond to these criticisms, China has, on several occasions, adopted rules and taken measures to create a level playing field for foreign investment, by amending the FIE Laws and establishing pilot FTZs.[165] In 2020, a unified FIL came into force, which grants equal national treatment to foreign investment, in line with the principle of national treatment advocated by the US. To be specific, a legal document on national security review in China under the FIL legal regime was issued in late 2020, in the form of the Measures. These two remarkable legal efforts fully indicate China's desire to respond positively to US criticisms and complaints about the legal system governing foreign investment in China, and its ambition to comply with the rule of law, the rule of international law, and international customary practices.

It can be concluded that the failures of Chinese investments in US national security reviews accelerated the pace at which China improved its domestic law governing foreign investment and established a legitimate and enforceable regulatory mechanism to safeguard national security, rather than an arbitrary and capricious mechanism with unjustified and unconvincing decisions on foreign investment. In this way, the credibility and reliability of national security concerns in the FIL has been largely achieved.

4.3.3 The Transition of China's All-inclusive Idea and US Idea to a Comprehensive Idea on National Security Reviews

As discussed previously, China held a conservative attitude towards foreign investment. Under the legal regime of FIE Laws, there were several regulatory tools to enable government to assess national security impacts during the approval review at the market access for the establishment of FIEs, foreign investment projects, or foreign investment M&As. National security concerns were not distinguished from political and economic concerns. Not only the traditional security of the military and national defense, therefore, but also the stability of the socialist regime, the capacity for centralized planning and the independence and sustainable development of the national economy, were all treated together as national security concerns hidden behind a variety of regulatory reviews for different types of foreign investment at the market access. In particular, national economic security was even expressly specified in the M&A security review for foreign investment M&As, which indicates that China placed great emphasis on safeguarding the stability and development of the national economy. This kind of all-inclusive approach, either purely or partly related to national security, was taken into account in reviews of foreign investment. This approach to defining national security and foreign investment, however, left a negative impression of China's legal regime governing foreign investment and created a discriminatory environment for foreign investment. China's excessive concern and prudence on foreign investment, moreover, also in turn resulted in failures of Chinese overseas investment in the course of the host country's national security review. The significance and benefits of foreign investment to economic growth in China have been widely acknowledged in China. The experience of Chinese investment in other countries, especially in the US, made China aware of the necessity of defining national security concerns in a transparent and legitimate way. China therefore established the regulatory mechanism of the national security review for foreign investment and also enacted the National Security Law. National security concerns have been integrated and developed into the overall national security concept. Not only traditional security, but also security in emerging sectors, such as information security, has been comprehensively integrated into this concept. Foreign investment in China shall only fall within the scope of national security review in accordance with the manner described in the relevant legal texts, rather than by subjective decision or as a result of a regulator's views on national security and foreign investment.

In stark contrast to China, which was originally unwelcoming of foreign investment, the US had long been positioned as an exporting state. This traditional opening policy played an essential role in US economic prosperity early on. In the early twentieth century, at the outset of World War I, US concerns about national security regarding foreign investment were raised in relation to the level of foreign investment in industry and the economy.[166] When the US moved toward entering World War I, the growing antagonism between the US and Germany led to national security worries posed by German-controlled investments.[167] Consequently, the intention to preserve military security contributed to the passage of the Trading with the Enemy Act (TWEA) as well as other sectoral restrictions. It was military security in wartime that resulted in the sectoral legislation on restricting foreign investment.

The national security review established in the Exon-Florio Amendment served as a bottom line and last resort in safeguarding national security from foreign investment, and would only be triggered when other laws and regulations, other than the International Emergency Economic Powers Act (IEEPA), failed to work effectively. Pursuant to the Exon-Florio Amendment, one of the conditions for a presidential decision is that neither the amendment, the IEEPA, or any other law could provide adequate power to the president to preserve national security.[168] The last provision of the Exon-Florio Amendment clearly stipulates that the amendment's content should not be interpreted as any change or adjustment to the existing powers, procedures, provisions, investigations, enforcement measures, or review provided in other laws.[169] In the absence of a clear definition of national security, it is the CFIUS and the president that are granted discretionary power to define national security without judicial review. The Exon-Florio Amendment did not explicitly use the term "national economic security", indicating that the US did not intend to undercut its traditional commitment to an open investment policy. To some extent, however, the national security review introduced by the Exon-Florio Amendment can be easily used in practice as a tool of economic protectionism.

Later, national economic security was emphasized indirectly in the FINSA. Instead of clearly stating national economic security as an independent standard to trigger national security review, the FINSA adopted the approach of bringing economic security factors within the purview of national security review, as a result of a debate on whether to bring economic factors into the discussion over the national security review.[170] The approach of listing national economic security as a review standard would have led the CFIUS to focus too much on economic issues, and the CFIUS would inevitably have become overwhelmed with reviews, affecting its ability to protect national security.[171] In addition, the inclusion of economic reviews as a standard would have weakened its original functions as well as its legislative spirit of protecting national security, in contrast to the openness of US policy on foreign investment. The suggestion of listing economic security as an independent review criterion, moreover, would have led to a decrease in investment inflows in the US, as well as increasing market access barriers or retaliatory measures imposed by other countries on US overseas investment.[172] This would in turn have damaged the US national security interest of maintaining the status of an economic superpower in an increasingly competitive global economy.

The FIRRMA views national security through a much broader lens.[173] Non-controlling foreign investment in relation to critical infrastructure, critical technology, sensitive personal data, and real estate in sensitive locations, would fall within the scope of national security review, rendering such scope quite different from the traditional one for controlling foreign investment involving national security threats. Along with this broader definition of national security and foreign investment in the FIRRMA, it was acknowledged that critical infrastructure, critical technology, and personal data of US citizens were perceived to be relevant to US national security and in turn fundamental to longer-term objectives related to national security.[174]

As a result, both for offensive and defensive reasons, national security factors in national security review were expanded. Not only economic factors of national security, but also concerns in the fields of information, infrastructure, and technology involving national security apparatuses would be carefully assessed in the national security review, under the reformed legal regime of the FIRRMA. Even though national security has not been clearly defined in US foreign investment legislation, its meaning has been developed, expanding from traditional security of military and national defense to as large as possible a scope involving nontraditional security, such as technological security, cybersecurity, information security. This seemingly all-inclusive approach to national security review of foreign investments seems similar to the legal approach to national security reflected in China's national security review under the ideological context of the overall national security concept. Similar to the 11 types of national security specified as comprising the overall national security concept, US national security in national security review is also specified in the FIRRMA in a detailed manner, which provides explanations of key terms related to national security, such as critical infrastructure, critical technology, sensitive personal data, close proximity, or even gives examples for better understanding and guidance in practice.

4.3.4 From Political Intervention to a Legalized Approach

In China, practical tensions and ideological confusion about foreign investment legislation often surrounded efforts to attract foreign investment because of concerns about national security and security of the socialist economy. National security concerns were not explicitly stated in FIE Laws, but always served as the common consensus for governmental officials reviewing or examining and deciding whether to approve such a foreign investment. Foreign investors could not get any information about national security concerns during the approval process for the establishment of their FIEs and foreign investment projects at the market access. At the early stage, for example, when the Wholly-foreign-owned Enterprises Law (WFOE Law) was published in 1986, WFOE were permitted and became the most favored form for foreign investors. During the approval process at the market access, however, the Chinese government preferred to issue approval licenses to joint ventures with Chinese parties. As a result, the credibility and reasonableness of security concerns for foreign investment in the FIE Laws were poor. It was hard to win foreign investors' full trust of Chinese legislation for attracting foreign investment and the policy of reform and opening up. These negative consequences were largely overridden by stipulating national security review in relation to foreign investment in the FIL, which attempted to improve transparency and predictability for foreign investment through the issuance of the Measures. Some legal arrangements established by US national security review have been employed in China's national security review, while certain underlying fundamentals have been rejected to accommodate existing ideologies and institutions.[175] The first enforcement case of China's national security review, moreover, the Zhongbai case indicated that China's national security review under the FIL would be used frequently to govern foreign investment, like the US national security reviews conducted by the CFIUS. China attempts to address national security concerns on foreign investment in a legitimate and reasonable way. Undoubtedly, it is hard and takes a long time to enforce national security review perfectly, since changing ideas about national security and foreign investment rooted in domestic ideology under the context of China's socialist market economy is not as easy as changing the words of legal texts. At least it is predictable that the enforcement of national security reviews in China will continue to follow the rule of law, abandoning the previous approach of governmental intervention without legitimate reasons and procedures, but will not abandon its inherent internal ideas.

In the US, in the initial stage of national security review, a small number of foreign investment transactions were reviewed since the CFIUS was established in 1975. Prior to the Exon-Florio Amendment, fewer than 30 transactions were reviewed by the CFIUS and most were related to foreign governments, while the CFIUS had never determined any foreign investment to harm national security.[176] Neither substantive measures against foreign mergers and acquisitions, nor procedural requirements of national security review for foreign investment which required transaction parties to submit a review notice, moreover, were formulated to scrutinize foreign investment and protect national security in the US before the passage of the Exon-Florio Amendment. National security review was basically a political procedure routinely conducted by a bureaucratic organization, rather than a legal process.

The political nature of the CFIUS procedures and national security reviews would be evidenced by the review process and result of the Fujitsu case. Since then, the Exon-Florio Amendment has provided a legal mechanism for the president to make final decisions on national security reviews. It is undeniable that the legalization of national security concerns in foreign mergers and acquisitions through the Exon-Florio Amendment has considerable positive significance. The CFIUS was vested with institutional functions and substantive powers, as it could even recommend the president to prohibit or suspend certain foreign investments. The lawmaking for national security review, which clearly set up clear procedures and requirements for foreign investors, the CFIUS, the president, and the Congress, made the review transparent, predictable, and feasible, largely avoiding potential arbitrary political intervention. The Exon-Florio Amendment shows that the US desires to eliminate or reduce political considerations in national security review and provide maximum protection to foreign investment when preserving national security, in a legalized and normalized approach.

Amid a lack of statutory congressional oversight on national security review and foreign investment, the Congress would intervene in practice anyway, leading to the failures of CNOOC's bid for UNOCAL. FINSA was introduced to regulate the role of Congress in national security review, by imposing heightened congressional reporting requirements on such reviews conducted by the CFIUS.[177] In addition to annual reporting obligations on the part of the CFIUS, the FINSA contained one article specifically requiring the CFIUS to respond promptly with briefings at the request of the Congress.[178] To be specific, the CFIUS needs to submit a written report to the Congress at the completion of the preliminary, national security stage, where generally, the CFIUS will lead to two findings. The first either confirms or denies that the transaction in question poses a national security risk. Notably, there are two situations in which there is no national security risk. One is that the transaction itself poses no national security risk it will be permitted immediately and the national security review completed forthwith. The other situation in which there is no national security risk is that a national security risk is deemed to exist but such risk has been addressed through mitigation measures. In such a situation the

Secretary of the Treasury and the head of the lead agency should jointly conclude that there is no national security risk and submit a written notice to the Congress; otherwise, signature power in relation to such a written report to the Congress could also be given to personnel entrusted by the Secretary of the Treasury and the head of the lead agency, or by the president, and approved by the Senate.[179] It is notable that the requirements for identifying agents for reporting to the Congress are quite strict. The CFIUS must exercise full responsibility and accountability when reaching a finding and signing a written notice. This in turn places great pressure on the CFIUS to avoid arbitrary judgments. This reporting requirement concerning the preliminary national security review indicates the high level of congressional involvement in national security review. The second judgment is whether or not to proceed to investigation if national security risks have not yet been mitigated.[180] The FINSA also stipulates that a report must be submitted to the Congress at the beginning of the investigation stage. Upon completion of the investigation, there are also generally two findings. The first is a finding of no national security risk, which has to be made in the context of the implementation of mitigation measures. In this regard, the Secretary of the Treasury and the head of the lead agency shall also jointly submit a written report to the Congress.[181] In terms of entrusting agents to sign such a written report and reporting it to the Congress in the phase of national security investigation, the requirement is, as previously mentioned, much stricter than that in the preliminary national security review. The Secretary of the Treasury could empower only the deputy secretary of the Treasury, and the person in charge of the lead agency could transfer his power only to the deputy head of such a lead agency or other personnel of the same level.[182] The second possible finding is that the transaction does indeed pose a national security risk, whereupon the transaction would be transferred to the president for a final decision. The written report to the Congress is not specifically mentioned in the FINSA. On the one hand, this legal arrangement shows congressional compromise to grant the greatest discretion and independence to presidential authority on invoking a national security review of a foreign investment.[183] On the other hand, the Exon-Florio Amendment had already stipulated a requirement for reporting to the Congress about the presidential decision, which did not require repeat stipulation by the FINSA.

The reporting requirement added in the FINSA indicated that the Congress intended to strengthen its oversight of national security review. Regardless of whether judgment is reached in the preliminary national security review or the national security investigation, if it holds that there is no national security risk, a written report must be submitted to the Congress so that the Congress can supervise and give suggestions in a timely manner. The requirements, moreover, for empowering the agency to sign the report about such a determination are strict, in order to ensure the strength of the tracking and supervision of the process of national security review under congressional oversight and indicate prudent attitudes towards the issue of national security and foreign investment. Additionally, the rules on reporting on national security review to the Congress demonstrate that the Congress is mainly concerned about foreign investment transactions approved by the CFIUS, but not greatly concerned about the CFIUS's determinations that certain transactions pose national security risks, as they might be mitigated with appropriate measures by the CFIUS or be prohibited or suspended by the president. The reporting requirement applicable in two phases of national security review, therefore, shows the obvious tendency of the Congress to restrict foreign investment and to supervise the whole process of national security review.

There is no further requirement for reporting to the Congress in the FIRRMA. To some extent, this shows that the detailed reporting requirement to the Congress stipulated in the FINSA has already ensured the congressional oversight over national security review of foreign investments. The reporting requirement provides a legal and prudent means for the Congress to satisfy its desire to supervise foreign investment and safeguard national security, on the one hand, and ensure the greatest authority of the CFIUS and the president in the process of national security review on the other. In this way, arbitrary intervention of the Congress in national security review, as in the transaction involving UNOCAL and CNOOC, will become less possible. Through an oriented process of law-making on national security reviews for foreign investment, it can be concluded that national security reviews both in China and the US are moving towards a much more legalized and normalized path, a process which is expected to continue in the coming years.

Notes

1 Andrews, Gregory E. "An Evaluation of the Need for Further Statutory Controls on Foreign Direct Investment in the United States." *Vanderbilt Journal of Transnational Law* 8 (1974): 152; Mundheim, Robert H. and Heleniak, David W. "American Attitudes Toward Foreign Direct Investment in the United States." *Journal of Comparative Corporate Law and Securities Regulation* 2, no. 4 (1979): 221, 235.

2 Weimer, Christopher M. "Foreign Direct Investment and National Security Post-FINSA 2007." *Texas Law Review* 87, no. 3 (2009): 664–666; Saha, Souvik. "CFIUS Now Made in China: Dueling National Security Review Frameworks as a Countermeasure to Economic Espionage in the Age of Globalization." *Northwestern Journal of International Law & Business* 33, no. 1 (2012): 234.

3 Saha, Souvik. "CFIUS Now Made in China: Dueling National Security Review Frameworks as a Countermeasure to Economic Espionage in the Age of Globalization." *Northwestern Journal of International Law & Business* 33, no. 1 (2012): 234.

4 Graham, Edward M. and Marchick, David Matthew. *US National Security and Foreign Investment*. Washington, DC: Institute for International Economics, 2006, 99.

5 Mira, Wilkins. *The Maturing of Multinational Enterprise: American Business Abroad from 1914 to 1970*. Cambridge: Harvard University Press, 1974; Mira, Wilkins. *The History of Foreign Investment in the United States 1914–1945*. Cambridge: Harvard University Press, 1989.

6 Hymer, Stephen H. "The International Operations of National Firms: A Study of Direct Foreign Investment." Doctoral thesis of Massachusetts Institute of Technology, 1960.

7 Graham, Edward M. and Marchick, David Matthew. *US National Security and Foreign Investment*. Washington, DC: Institute for International Economics, 2006, 9; Institute for International Economics. US National Security and FDI. https://piie.com/publications/chapters_preview/3918/01iie3918.pdf, 8.

8 Mundheim, Robert H. and Heleniak, David W. "American Attitudes toward Foreign Direct Investment in the United States." *Journal of Comparative Corporate Law and Securities Regulation* 2, no. 4 (1979): 222.

9 Ronald Reagan Presidential Library & Museum. "Statement on International Investment Policy." www.reaganlibrary.gov/archives/speech/statement-international-investment-policy.
10 Graham, Edward M. and Marchick, David Matthew. *US National Security and Foreign Investment*. Washington, DC: Institute for International Economics, 2006, 21; Data from Bureau of Economic Analysis (BEA). www.bea.gov/data.
11 Graham, Edward M. and Marchick, David Matthew. *US National Security and Foreign Investment*. Washington, DC: Institute for International Economics, 2006, 21; Data from Bureau of Economic Analysis (BEA). www.bea.gov/data.
12 Committee on Government Operations. "The Adequacy of the Federal Response to Foreign Investment in the United States." Rept. No. 96–1216, 1980: 166–184.
13 Long, William J. "The US-Japan Semiconductor Dispute: Implications for US Trade Policy." *Maryland Journal of International Law* 13, no. 1 (1988): 9; Alvarez, Jose E. "Political Protectionism and United States International Investment Obligations in Conflict: The Hazards of Exon-Florio." *Virginia Journal of International Law* 30, no. 1 (1989): 57.
14 Walters, Donna K. H. "Deal to Sell Fairchild Semiconductor to Fujitsu Canceled." 1987. www.latimes.com/archives/la-xpm-1987-03-17-fi-12290-story.html.
15 Walters, Donna K. H. "Deal to Sell Fairchild Semiconductor to Fujitsu Canceled." 1987. www.latimes.com/archives/la-xpm-1987-03-17-fi-12290-story.html.
16 Walters, Donna K. H. "Deal to Sell Fairchild Semiconductor to Fujitsu Canceled." 1987. www.latimes.com/archives/la-xpm-1987-03-17-fi-12290-story.html.
17 Alvarez, Jose E. "Political Protectionism and United States International Investment Obligations in Conflict: The Hazards of Exon-Florio." *Virginia Journal of International Law* 30, no. 1 (1989): 58–59.
18 Exon, Metzenbaum. "Attack Firchild-Fujitsu Deal, Defense and Antitrust Concerns Raised." *International Investment & Trade Representative* 4 (1987).
19 Exon, Metzenbaum. "Attack Firchild-Fujitsu Deal, Defense and Antitrust Concerns Raised." *International Investment & Trade Representative* 4 (1987).
20 Exon, Metzenbaum. "Attack Firchild-Fujitsu Deal, Defense and Antitrust Concerns Raised." *International Investment & Trade Representative* 4 (1987).
21 Rampel, William C. and Walters, Donna K. H. "The Fairchild Deal: Trade War: When Chips Were Down." www.latimes.com/archives/la-xpm-1987-11-30-mn-16900-story.html.
22 United States Acquisitions Hearing (see n 445); *Monthly Catalog of US Government Publications*. Washington, DC: US Government Printing Office, 1987, 157.
23 Exon, Metzenbaum. "Attack Firchild-Fujitsu Deal, Defense and Antitrust Concerns Raised." *International Investment & Trade Representative* 4 (1987); Waldeck, Cecelia M. "Proposals for Limiting Foreign Investment Risk under the Exon-Florio Amendment." *Hastings Law Journal* 42, no. 4 (1991): 1182–1186.
24 Exon, Metzenbaum. "Attack Firchild-Fujitsu Deal, Defense and Antitrust Concerns Raised." *International Investment & Trade Representative* 4 (1987); Waldeck, Cecelia M. "Proposals for Limiting Foreign Investment Risk under the Exon-Florio Amendment." *Hastings Law Journal* 42, no. 4 (1991): 1182–1186.
25 100th Congress, S.907, Technology Competitiveness Act (1987); Alvarez, Jose E. "Political Protectionism and United States International Investment Obligations in Conflict: The Hazards of Exon-Florio." *Virginia Journal of International Law* 30, no. 1 (1989): 63.
26 Data from Bureau of Economic Analysis. www.bea.gov/data.
27 Graham, Edward M. and Marchick, David Matthew. *US National Security and Foreign Investment*. Washington, DC: Institute for International Economics, 2006, 53.
28 "CFIUS Annual Report to Congress." https://home.treasury.gov/policy-issues/international/the-committee-on-foreign-investment-in-the-united-states-cfius/cfius-reports-and-tables.
29 Graham, Edward M. and Marchick, David Matthew. *US National Security and Foreign Investment*. Washington, DC: Institute for International Economics, 2006, 53.

30 Graham, Edward M. and Marchick, David Matthew. *US National Security and Foreign Investment*. Washington, DC: Institute for International Economics, 2006, 53.
31 Jackson, James K. "Exon-Florio Foreign Investment Provision: Comparison of H.R. 556 and S. 1610." www.fas.org/sgp/crs/natsec/RL34082.pdf; Young, Kristy E. "The Committee on Foreign Investment in the United States and the Foreign Investment and National Securities Act of 2007: A Delicate Balancing Act That Needs Revision." *U.C. Davis Journal of International Law & Policy* 15, no. 1 (2009): 52; Barboza, David and Sorkin, Andrew Ross. "Chinese Company Drops Bid to Buy U.S. Oil Concern." www.nytimes.com/2005/08/03/business/worldbusiness/chinese-company-drops-bid-to-buy-us-oil-concern.html.
32 Sud, Gaurav. "From Fretting Takeovers to Vetting CFIUS: Finding a Balance in U.S. Policy Regarding Foreign Acquisitions of Domestic Assets." *Vanderbilt Journal of Transnational Law* 39, no. 4 (2006): 1313.
33 Young, Kristy E. "The Committee on Foreign Investment in the United States and the Foreign Investment and National Securities Act of 2007: A Delicate Balancing Act That Needs Revision." *U.C. Davis Journal of International Law & Policy* 15, no. 1 (2009): 52.
34 Saha, Souvik. "CFIUS Now Made in China: Dueling National Security Review Frameworks as a Countermeasure to Economic Espionage in the Age of Globalization." *Northwestern Journal of International Law & Business* 33, no. 1 (2012): 221.
35 Rep. Pombo Richard W., H.R Res. 344, 109th Congress. "Expressing the Sense of the House of Representatives that a Chinese State-owned Energy Company Exercising Control of Critical United States Energy Infrastructure and Energy Production Capacity Could Take Action That Would Threaten to Impair the National Security of the United States." 2005. www.congress.gov/bill/109th-congress/house-resolution/344 (H.R Res. 344).
36 H.R Res. 344.
37 H.R Res. 344.
38 Graham, Edward M. and Marchick, David Matthew. *US National Security and Foreign Investment*. Washington, DC: Institute for International Economics, 2006, 130.
39 H.R Res. 344.
40 H.R Res. 344, H5570; Petrusic, Michael. "Oil and National Security: CNOOC's Failed Bid to Purchase Unocal." *North Carolina Law Review* 84, no. 4 (2006): 1379; Saha, Souvik. "CFIUS Now Made in China: Dueling National Security Review Frameworks as a Countermeasure to Economic Espionage in the Age of Globalization." *Northwestern Journal of International Law & Business* 33, no. 1 (2012): 222.
41 H.R Res. 344, H5570.
42 H.R Res. 344.
43 H.R Res. 344.
44 Petrusic, Michael. "Oil and National Security: CNOOC's Failed Bid to Purchase Unocal." *North Carolina Law Review* 84, no. 4 (2006): 1379; Saha, Souvik. "CFIUS Now Made in China: Dueling National Security Review Frameworks as a Countermeasure to Economic Espionage in the Age of Globalization." *Northwestern Journal of International Law & Business* 33, no. 1 (2012): 222; Mamounas, Joseph. "Controlling Foreign Ownership of US Strategic Assets: The Challenge of Maintaining National Security in a Globalized and Oil Dependent World." *Law and Business Review of the Americas* 13, no. 2 (2007): 405.
45 Nanto, Dick K. *China and the CNOOC Bid for Unocal: Issues for Congress: Issues for Congress*. Washington, DC: United States Congressional Research Service, 2006, 14.
46 Graham, Edward M. and Marchick, David Matthew. *US National Security and Foreign Investment*. Washington, DC: Institute for International Economics, 2006, 130–131.
47 Graham, Edward M. and Marchick, David Matthew. *US National Security and Foreign Investment*. Washington, DC: Institute for International Economics, 2006, 130–131.

48 Graham, Edward M. and Marchick, David Matthew. *US National Security and Foreign Investment*. Washington, DC: Institute for International Economics, 2006, 130–131.
49 Graham, Edward M. and Marchick, David Matthew. *US National Security and Foreign Investment*. Washington, DC: Institute for International Economics, 2006, 131; H.R. Con. amend. 431, 109th Congress (2005); Casselman, Joshua W. "China's Latest 'Threat' to the United States: The Failed CNOOC-UNOCAL Merger and Its Implications for Exon-Florio and CFIUS." *Indiana International & Comparative Law Review* 17, no. 1 (2007): 163.
50 Graham, Edward M. and Marchick, David Matthew. *US National Security and Foreign Investment*. Washington, DC: Institute for International Economics, 2006, 131; H.R. Con. amend. 431, 109th Congress (2005); Casselman, Joshua W. "China's Latest 'Threat' to the United States: The Failed CNOOC-UNOCAL Merger and Its Implications for Exon-Florio and CFIUS." *Indiana International & Comparative Law Review* 17, no. 1 (2007): 163; H.Amdt.431, 109th Congress, 1st Session, 151 Cong. Rec. H5515.
51 Baker, David R. "Chinese Bid Seen As Too Risky/Filing Shows Unocal Thought Lower Chevron Offer Was Safer." 2005. www.sfgate.com/business/article/Chinese-bid-seen-as-too-risky-Filing-shows-2620430.php; Holt, Thomas P. "CNOOC-UNOCAL and the WTO: Discriminatory Rules in the China Protocol Are a Latent Threat to the Rule of Law in the Dispute Settlement Understanding." *Pacific Rim Law & Policy Journal* 15, no. 2 (2006): 458; Casselman, Joshua W. "China's Latest 'Threat' to the United States: The Failed CNOOC-UNOCAL Merger and Its Implications for Exon-Florio and CFIUS." *Indiana International & Comparative Law Review* 17, no. 1 (2007): 163; Energy Policy Act, H.R. 6, 109th Congress, § 1837 (2005); Zhang, Angela Huyue. "Foreign Direct Investment from China: Sense and Sensibility." *Northwestern Journal of International Law & Business* 34, no. 3 (2014): 429.
52 Casselman, Joshua W. "China's Latest 'Threat' to the United States: The Failed CNOOC-UNOCAL Merger and Its Implications for Exon-Florio and CFIUS." *Indiana International & Comparative Law Review* 17, no. 1 (2007): 163; S. 1412, 109th Congress (2005).
53 Nanto, Dick K. *China and the CNOOC Bid for Unocal: Issues for Congress: Issues for Congress*. Washington, DC: United States Congressional Research Service, 2006, 15–16; Mamounas, Joseph. "Controlling Foreign Ownership of US Strategic Assets: The Challenge of Maintaining National Security in a Globalized and Oil Dependent World." *Law and Business Review of the Americas* 13, no. 2 (2007): 412.
54 Nanto, Dick K. *China and the CNOOC Bid for Unocal: Issues for Congress: Issues for Congress*. Washington, DC: United States Congressional Research Service, 2006, 51; Mouawad, Jad. "Congress Calls for a Review of the Chinese Bid for Unocal." 2005. www.nytimes.com/2005/07/27/business/congress-calls-for-a-review-of-the-chinese-bid-for-unocal.html; Casselman, Joshua W. "China's Latest 'Threat' to the United States: The Failed CNOOC-UNOCAL Merger and Its Implications for Exon-Florio and CFIUS." *Indiana International & Comparative Law Review* 17, no. 1 (2007): 163.
55 Saha, Souvik. "CFIUS Now Made in China: Dueling National Security Review Frameworks as a Countermeasure to Economic Espionage in the Age of Globalization." *Northwestern Journal of International Law & Business* 33, no. 1 (2012): 224–225.
56 Foreign Investment and National Security Act of 2007 (FINSA), Pub. L. No. 110–49, 121 Stat. 246 (2007), Sec.2. (b)(1).
57 Foreign Investment and National Security Act of 2007 (FINSA), Pub. L. No. 110–49, 121 Stat. 246 (2007), Sec.2. (b)(1).
58 Regulations Pertaining to Mergers, Acquisitions, and Takeovers by Foreign Persons, 31 C.F.R Part § 800.204.
59 Sullivan, Matthew C. "CFIUS and Congress Reconsidered: Fire Alarms, Police Patrols, and a New Oversight Regime." *Willamette Journal of International Law and Dispute Resolution* 17, no. 2 (2009): 234.

60 Foreign Investment and National Security Act of 2007 (FINSA), Pub. L. No. 110–49, 121 Stat. 246 (2007), Sec. 7 (b).
61 Ma, Winston and Downs, Paul. *The Hunt for Unicorns: How Sovereign Fund are Reshaping Investment*. New Jersey: Wiley Press, 2021, 246.
62 Saha, Souvik. "CFIUS Now Made in China: Dueling National Security Review Frameworks as a Countermeasure to Economic Espionage in the Age of Globalization." *Northwestern Journal of International Law & Business* 33, no. 1 (2012): 202–205; Grosse, Robert, Gamso, Jonas and Nelson, Roy C. "China's Rise, World Order, and the Implications for International Business." *Management International Review* 61 (2021): 1–26. https://doi.org/10.1007/s11575-020-00433-8.
63 Walshe, Taylor and Tan, Shining. "TikTok on the Clock: A Summary of CFIUS's Investigation into ByteDance." www.csis.org/blogs/trustee-china-hand/tiktok-clock-summary-cfiuss-investigation-bytedance.
64 Diamond, Jeremy. "Trump Hits China with Tariffs, Heightening Concerns of Global Trade War." 2018. https://edition.cnn.com/2018/03/22/politics/donald-trump-china-tariffs-trade-war/index.html.
65 "CFIUS Reports and Tables." https://home.treasury.gov/policy-issues/international/the-committee-on-foreign-investment-in-the-united-states-cfius/cfius-reports-and-tables.
66 "CFIUS Reports and Tables." https://home.treasury.gov/policy-issues/international/the-committee-on-foreign-investment-in-the-united-states-cfius/cfius-reports-and-tables.
67 Ma, Winston and Downs, Paul. *The Hunt for Unicorns: How Sovereign Fund are Reshaping Investment*. New Jersey: Wiley Press, 2021, 246.
68 The White House. "Order on the China National Aero-Technology Import and Export Corporation Divestiture of MAMCO Manufacturing, Incorporated." 1990. www.presidency.ucsb.edu/documents/order-the-china-national-aero-technology-import-and-export-corporation-divestiture-mamco.
69 The White House. "Order Signed by the President Regarding the Acquisition of Four U.S. Wind Farm Project Companies by Ralls Corporation." 2012. https://obamawhitehouse.archives.gov/the-press-office/2012/09/28/order-signed-president-regarding-acquisition-four-us-wind-farm-project-c.
70 The White House. "Presidential Order Regarding the Proposed Acquisition of a Controlling Interest in Aixtron SE by Grand Chip Investment GMBH." 2016. https://obamawhitehouse.archives.gov/the-press-office/2016/12/02/presidential-order-regarding-proposed-acquisition-controlling-interest.
71 The White House. "Order Regarding the Proposed Acquisition of Lattice Semiconductor Corporation by China Venture Capital Fund Corporation Limited." 2017. https://trumpwhitehouse.archives.gov/presidential-actions/order-regarding-proposed-acquisition-lattice-semiconductor-corporation-china-venture-capital-fund-corporation-limited/.
72 The White House. "Presidential Order Regarding the Proposed Takeover of Qualcomm Incorporated by Broadcom Limited." 2018. www.govinfo.gov/app/details/DCPD-201800154.
73 Bench, Jonathan. "CFIUS in the News Again for Overturning China Deals Involving Sensitive Data." https://harrisbricken.com/chinalawblog/cfius-in-the-news-again-for-overturning-china-deals-involving-sensitive-data/.
74 The White House. "Order Regarding the Acquisition of Musical.ly by ByteDance Ltd." 2020. www.govinfo.gov/app/details/DCPD-202000608/.
75 Weber, Jonathan. "Explainer: What Is China's Huawei Technologies and Why Is IT Controversial." www.reuters.com/article/us-usa-china-huawei-explainer-idUSKBN1O5172.
76 Waters, Richard and Politi, James. "Huawei-3Com Deal Finally Collapses." www.ft.com/content/c2091814-f6b5-11dc-bda1-000077b07658.
77 Waters, Richard and Politi, James. "Huawei-3Com Deal Finally Collapses." www.ft.com/content/c2091814-f6b5-11dc-bda1-000077b07658.

78 Bian, Cheng. *National Security Review of Foreign Investment: A Comparative Legal Analysis of China, the United States and the European Union*. London: Routledge, 2020, 125.

79 Kan, Michael. “China’s Huawei to Reverse Controversial Deal for 3Leaf.” www.pcworld.com/article/220183/article.html#tk.mod_stln.

80 Brown, Mayer. “CFIUS Disapproval of Huawei-3Leaf Systems Deal Puts New Focus on US Controls over Cloud Computing Technology.” 2011. www.lexology.com/library/detail.aspx?g=29b6dfbb-d45e-44ff-9d73-934415753a9c; Carew, Sinead and Wohl, Jessica. “Huawei Backs away from 3Leaf Acquisition.” 2011. www.ciol.com/huawei-backs-away-3leaf-acquisition/.

81 Flicker, Scott M. and Parsons, Dana M. “Huawei-CFIUS Redux: Now It Gets Interesting.” 2011. www.paulhastings.com/insights/client-alerts/huawei-cfius-redux-now-it-gets-interesting; Kan, Michael. “Report: U.S. Panel to Recommend Reversing Huawei Deal.” www.pcworld.com/businesscenter/article/219414/report_us_panel_to_recommend_reversing_huawei_deal.html#tk.mod_rel.

82 Nicholson, Chris V. “The Big Chill: Huawei Imbroglio Puts Countries at Odds.” 2011. https://dealbook.nytimes.com/2011/02/18/the-big-chill-huawei-imbroglio-puts-countries-at-odds/.

83 Jiang, Jingli and Li, Gen. “CFIUS: For National Security Investigation or for Political Scrutiny?” *Texas Journal of Oil, Gas and Energy Law* 9, no. 1 (2013): 90–91; Hunnicutt, Charles A. “$2 Million Deal=Big CFIUS Mistake.” 2011. www.troutman.com/insights/2-million-deal-big-cfius-mistake.html.

84 Carew, Sinead and Wohl, Jessica. “Huawei Backs Away from 3Leaf Acquisition.” 2011. www.reuters.com/article/us-huawei-3leaf-idUSTRE71I38920110219.

85 Hille, Kathrin. “China and the US: Access Denied.” www.ft.com/intl/cms/s/0/9080ccaa-614d-11e0-ab25-00144feab49a.html#axzz1lcpMcarP.

86 Saha, Souvik. “CFIUS Now Made in China: Dueling National Security Review Frameworks as a Countermeasure to Economic Espionage in the Age of Globalization.” *Northwestern Journal of International Law & Business* 33, no. 1 (2012): 230.

87 US House of Representatives, 112th Congress. “Investigative Report on the U.S. National Security Issues Posed by Chinese Telecommunications Companies Huawei and ZTE.” https://republicans-intelligence.house.gov/sites/intelligence.house.gov/files/documents/huawei-zte%20investigative%20report%20(final).pdf.

88 Bian, Cheng. *National Security Review of Foreign Investment: A Comparative Legal Analysis of China, the United States and the European Union*. London: Routledge, 2020, 126.

89 Saha, Souvik. “CFIUS Now Made in China: Dueling National Security Review Frameworks as a Countermeasure to Economic Espionage in the Age of Globalization.” *Northwestern Journal of International Law & Business* 33, no. 1 (2012): 230.

90 US-China Economic and Security Review Commission. “2012 Report to Congress, Executive Summary and Recommendations.” 2012. www.uscc.gov/sites/default/files/annual_reports/2012-Report-to-Congress-Key%20Recs.pdf.

91 US-China Economic and Security Review Commission. “2012 Report to Congress, Executive Summary and Recommendations.” 2012. www.uscc.gov/sites/default/files/annual_reports/2012-Report-to-Congress-Key%20Recs.pdf.

92 US-China Economic and Security Review Commission. “2012 Report to Congress, Executive Summary and Recommendations.” 2012. www.uscc.gov/sites/default/files/annual_reports/2012-Report-to-Congress-Key%20Recs.pdf.

93 Jalinous, Farhad, Mildorf, Karalyn, Schomig, Keith and Sowerby, Stacia. “National Security Review 2018: United States.” 2018. www.jdsupra.com/legalnews/national-security-reviews-2018-united-20400/.

94 31 C.F.R. Part 800.

95 Jiang, Jingli and Li, Gen. "CFIUS: For National Security Investigation or for Political Scrutiny?" *Texas Journal of Oil, Gas and Energy Law* 9, no. 1 (2013): 91; Fitzpatrick, Christopher M. "Where Ralls Went Wrong: CFIUS, the Courts, and the Balance of Liberty and Security." *Cornell Law Review* 101, no. 4 (2016): 1092.

96 Deeley, Hunter. "The Expanding Reach of the Executive in Foreign Direct Investment: How Ralls V. CFIUS Will Alter the FDI Landscape in the United States." *American University Business Law Review* 4, no. 1 (2015): 136; L'opez-Casero, Alexandra. "A Year in Review: More Transactions Run into CFIUS Trouble." 2014. www.nixonpeabody.com/-/media/Files/Alerts/167021_M_and_A_16JAN2014.ashx.

97 Fitzpatrick, Christopher M. "Where Ralls Went Wrong: CFIUS, the Courts, and the Balance of Liberty and Security." *Cornell Law Review* 101, no. 4 (2016): 1093; Ralls Corp. vs. Committee of Foreign Investment in the United States, 305; Ralls Corp. vs. Committee on Foreign Investment in the United States, Civil Action No. 12–1513 (ABJ), United States District Court for the District of Columbia, 926 F.Supp.2d 71 (2013), Amended Memorandum Opinion, 26 February 2013 (Civil Action No. 12–1513), 7.

98 Ralls Corp. vs. Committee of Foreign Investment in the United States, 305; The White House. "Order Signed by the President Regarding the Acquisition of Four U.S. Wind Farm Project Companies by Ralls Corporation." 2012. https://obamawhitehouse.archives.gov/the-press-office/2012/09/28/order-signed-president-regarding-acquisition-four-us-wind-farm-project-c.

99 Ralls Corp. v. CFIUS (see n 680), pp. 304–305; Nin-Hai Tseng. "Sany's Bold U.S. Move." https://fortune.com/2013/06/17/sanys-bold-u-s-move/ (visited 16 April 2021); Wan, William and Finn, Peterm. "Global Race on to Match U.S. Drone Capabilities." 2011. www.washingtonpost.com/world/national-security/global-race-on-to-match-us-drone-capabilities/2011/06/30/gHQACWdmxH_story.html.

100 Civil Action No. 12–1513, 6; Fitzpatrick, Christopher M. "Where Ralls Went Wrong: CFIUS, the Courts, and the Balance of Liberty and Security." *Cornell Law Review* 101, no. 4 (2016): 1094.

101 Bian, Cheng. *National Security Review of Foreign Investment: A Comparative Legal Analysis of China, the United States and the European Union*. London: Routledge, 2020, 127.

102 Ralls vs. Committee of Foreign Investment in the United States (No. 1: 12-cv-01513), United States Court of Appeals for the District of Columbia Circuit. www.cadc.uscourts.gov/internet/opinions.nsf/B27E81AF31E360DA85257D16004E43E7/$file/13-5315-1502552.pdf.

103 Ralls vs. Committee of Foreign Investment in the United States (No. 1: 12-cv-01513), United States Court of Appeals for the District of Columbia Circuit. www.cadc.uscourts.gov/internet/opinions.nsf/B27E81AF31E360DA85257D16004E43E7/$file/13-5315-1502552.pdf (visited 17 April 2021), 47.

104 Heifetz, Stephen. "Ralls and U.S. Government Settle Only CFIUS Suit in History." www.steptoeinternationalcomplianceblog.com/2015/10/ralls-and-u-s-government-settle-only-cfius-suit-in-history/; Bian, Cheng. *National Security Review of Foreign Investment: A Comparative Legal Analysis of China, the United States and the European Union*. London: Routledge, 2020, 127.

105 50 U.S.C. § 4565 (a)(4)(B)(ii)(I); 50 U.S.C. § 4565 (a)(4)(B)(ii)(II)(aa); 31 C.F.R. Part § 802.211(a).

106 31 C.F.R. Part § 802.203.

107 50 U.S.C.§4565 (a)(4)(B)(ii)(II)(bb)(AA); 31 C.F.R. Part § 802.211(b)(1).

108 50 U.S.C. § 4565 (a)(4)(B)(ii)(II)(bb)(BB).

109 50 U.S.C. § 4565 (a)(4)(B)(ii)(II)(bb)(CC).

110 Davis, Ken. "China Investment Policy: An Update." OECD Working Papers on International Investment, OECD Publishing. http://dx.doi.org/10.1787/5k4691lhmvbt-en.

111 National Bureau of Statistics of China. www.stats.gov.cn/english/Statisticaldata/AnnualData/; Data from World Bank website. https://data.worldbank.org/indicator/BX.KLT.DINV.WD.GD.ZS?locations=CN; Data from MOFCOM website. http://english.mofcom.gov.cn/article/statistic/foreigninvestment/.

112 Cheong, Young Rok. "Global Capital Flows and the Position of China: Structural and Institutional Factors and Their Implications." *FONDAD-KIEP-SNU Conference*. 2003. www.econ.hku.hk/~xiaogeng/research/Paper/Cheong-Xiao%20FONDAD%20paper%20and%20tables.pdf; Chang, Gordon G. "China's Seven-Percent Solution, Part I." *China Brief* 3, no. 2 (2003). https://jamestown.org/program/chinas-seven-percent-solution-part-i/

113 Data from World Bank website. https://data.worldbank.org/indicator/BX.KLT.DINV.WD.GD.ZS?locations=CN.

114 Li, Yuwen and Bian, Cheng. "A New Dimension of Foreign Investment Law in China: Evolution and Impacts of the National Security Review System." *Asia Pacific Law Review* 24, no. 2 (2016): 152.

115 Gao, Shan. "The Evolution of China's Foreign Investment Policy and Law (1978–2016)." Doctoral thesis of the Pennsylvania State University, 2017, 134; World Bank. *China 2020: China Engaged*. Washington, DC: IMF, 1997. https://documents1.worldbank.org/curated/en/656981468743976946/pdf/multi0page.pdf.

116 Jensen, Eric. "Balancing Security and Growth: Defining National Security Review of Foreign Investment in China." *Pacific Rim Law & Policy Journal Association* 19, no. 1 (2010): 166.

117 Wang, Yan. *Chinese Legal Reform: The Case of Foreign Investment Law*. London: Routledge, 2002, 100; Graham, Edward M. and Marchick, David Matthew. *US National Security and Foreign Investment*. Washington, DC: Institute for International Economics, 2006, 100.

118 Zhang, Jinxing. "Report on China's M&A Market 2014." 2014. http://special.ceweekly.cn/2014/0923/93486.shtml.

119 Li, Menggang. *Annual Report on China's FDI Industrial Control (2011–2012)*. Beijing: Social Science Academic Press, 2012, 26–32.

120 Liu, Ziyu. "Security Review in the Evolution of Foreign Investment Law with Chinese Characteristics: Part I." *Business Law Review* 41, no. 5 (2020): 173.

121 Liu, Ziyu. "Security Review in the Evolution of Foreign Investment Law with Chinese Characteristics: Part I." *Business Law Review* 41, no. 5 (2020): 173.

122 China News. "Review of Coco-Cola's Acquisition of Huiyuan: Opposed by More Than 80% of the Audience." 2009. www.chinanews.com/cj/cyzh/news/2009/03-18/1607385.shtml.

123 People's Daily Online. "War of Words in Company Takeover Battle." 2006. http://english.peopledaily.com.cn/200606/16/eng20060616_274537.html.

124 Li, Yuwen and Bian, Cheng. "A New Dimension of Foreign Investment Law in China: Evolution and Impacts of the National Security Review System." *Asia Pacific Law Review* 24, no. 2 (2016).

125 Jensen, Eric. "Balancing Security and Growth: Defining National Security Review of Foreign Investment in China." *Pacific Rim Law & Policy Journal Association* 19, no. 1 (2010): 166.

126 Flannery, Russell. "A China That Can Say No." 2006. www.forbes.com/global/2006/0918/096.html.

127 Flannery, Russell. "A China That Can Say No." 2006. www.forbes.com/global/2006/0918/096.html.

128 Li, Yuwen and Bian, Cheng. "A New Dimension of Foreign Investment Law in China: Evolution and Impacts of the National Security Review System." *Asia Pacific Law Review* 24, no. 2 (2016): 157.

129 Li, Yuwen and Bian, Cheng. "A New Dimension of Foreign Investment Law in China: Evolution and Impacts of the National Security Review System." *Asia Pacific Law Review* 24, no. 2 (2016): 157.
130 Du, Yang. "A Domestic Gradation Analysis of Economy Securitization of China: A Carlyle Acquiring Xugong Case Study." *Foreign Affairs Review* 27, no. 3 (2010): 133.
131 Chen, Yugang and Sun, Xiaohui. "A Failed Acquisition: Protectionism of Regulators or Disarming National Security Threats? A Carlyle Acquiring Xugong Case Study." *Contemporary Economy and Management* 31, no. 11 (2009).
132 Li, Yuwen and Bian, Cheng. "A New Dimension of Foreign Investment Law in China: Evolution and Impacts of the National Security Review System." *Asia Pacific Law Review* 24, no. 2 (2016): 157.
133 Goldstein, Kevin B. "Reviewing Cross-Border Mergers and Acquisitions for Competition and National Security: A Comparative Look at How the U.S.A., Europe and China Separate Security Concerns from Competition Concerns in Reviewing Acquisitions by Foreign Entities." *Tsinghua China Law Review* 3, no. 2 (2011): 247; Tucker, Sundeep, Hill, Andrew and Thornhill, John. "Carlyle-Xugong Saga Has Become a Never-Ending Story." www.ft.com/content/3084bd7c-4920-11dd-9a5f-000077b07658.
134 Duron, Destiny. "The Costs of Perceived Hypocrisy: The Impact of U.S. Treatment of Foreign Acquisitions of Domestic Enterprises." *Duke Law Journal* 57 (2008): 1795.
135 Soomro, Nishan-E-Hyder, Khan, Asif and Arafa, Ahmed. "Anti-Monopoly Law of China: A Case Study of Coco Cola's Proposed Merger with Huiyuan." *International Journal of Business and Economic Research* 10, no. 1 (2021): 34–39; Li, Yuwen and Bian, Cheng. "A New Dimension of Foreign Investment Law in China: Evolution and Impacts of the National Security Review System." *Asia Pacific Law Review* 24, no. 2 (2016): 159.
136 Li, Yuwen and Bian, Cheng. "A New Dimension of Foreign Investment Law in China: Evolution and Impacts of the National Security Review System." *Asia Pacific Law Review* 24, no. 2 (2016): 159.
137 Li, Yuwen and Bian, Cheng. "A New Dimension of Foreign Investment Law in China: Evolution and Impacts of the National Security Review System." *Asia Pacific Law Review* 24, no. 2 (2016): 159.
138 Li, Yuwen and Bian, Cheng. "A New Dimension of Foreign Investment Law in China: Evolution and Impacts of the National Security Review System." *Asia Pacific Law Review* 24, no. 2 (2016): 159.
139 MOFCOM Announcement (2009) No. 22: Announcement Barring Acquisition of Huiyuan by Coca-Cola (Issued by the Anti-Monopoly Bureau of MOFCOM on 18 March 2009, effective immediately).
140 Li, Yuwen and Bian, Cheng. "A New Dimension of Foreign Investment Law in China: Evolution and Impacts of the National Security Review System." *Asia Pacific Law Review* 24, no. 2 (2016): 159.
141 Q&A Conference on the Anti-Monopoly Review of the Coca-Cola-Huiyuan Merger Case by the Spokesman of MOFCOM Jian Yao (Issued by MOFCOM on 25 March 2009).
142 Pan, Zhicheng. "An Analysis of Relevant Reasons Why MOFCOM Banned the Acquisition of Huiyuan by Coca-Cola." *Law Science* 32, no. 7 (2009); Goldstein, Kevin B. "Reviewing Cross-Border Mergers and Acquisitions for Competition and National Security: A Comparative Look at How the U.S.A., Europe and China Separate Security Concerns from Competition Concerns in Reviewing Acquisitions by Foreign Entities." *Tsinghua China Law Review* 3, no. 2 (2011): 247–248; Sun, Jin and Yu, Zhe. "The Ambiguity of China's Anti-Monopoly Regulation Regarding Mergers and Acquisitions of Foreign Investment: From the Standpoint of Prohibited Coca-Cola's Acquisition to Huiyuan." *Oriental Law* 3, no. 3 (2010): 99–103.
143 Sun, Zhangwei. "General Analyses of Coca-Cola's Acquisition of Huiyuan." *Management Review* 23, no. 1 (2011).

144 Li, Yuwen and Bian, Cheng. "A New Dimension of Foreign Investment Law in China: Evolution and Impacts of the National Security Review System." *Asia Pacific Law Review* 24, no. 2 (2016): 159.
145 Li, Yuwen and Bian, Cheng. "A New Dimension of Foreign Investment Law in China: Evolution and Impacts of the National Security Review System." *Asia Pacific Law Review* 24, no. 2 (2016): 160.
146 Li, Yuwen and Bian, Cheng. "A New Dimension of Foreign Investment Law in China: Evolution and Impacts of the National Security Review System." *Asia Pacific Law Review* 24, no. 2 (2016): 160.
147 Yi, Ding. "Yonghui Drops Plans to Increase Stake in Chinese Retailer after National." 2019. www.caixinglobal.com/2019-12-17/yonghui-drops-plans-to-increase-stake-in-chinese-retailer-after-national-security-probe-101495178.html.
148 Kot, Jan. "Jardine-Backed Yonghui Buys Controlling Stake in Wuhan Retailer for RMB 559M." 2019. www.mingtiandi.com/real-estate/china-retail-real-estate-news/jardine-backed-yonghui-buys-control-of-wuhan-retailer/.
149 Hernandez, Maria Teresa. "Amazon E-commerce Sales Soar Amid COVID-19." 2020. www.spglobal.com/marketintelligence/en/news-insights/blog/amazon-ecommerce-sales-soar-amid-covid19.
150 Herbert Smith Freehills LLP. "National Security Review Regime under the New Foreign Investment Law." www.lexology.com/library/detail.aspx?g=61793b05-6109-4a68-9d02-5cf3f7dae384; Trivium China. "Foreign Investment Comes Under Scrutiny-China Tip Sheet August 23, 2019." 2019. https://triviumchina.com/2019/08/23/foreign-investment-comes-under-scrutiny-china-tip-sheet-august-23–2019/.
151 Watts, Gordon. "China Moves to Close the Door on Opening-up." 2019. https://asiatimes.com/2019/08/china-moves-to-close-the-door-on-opening-up/.
152 Yi, Ding. "Yonghui Drops Plans to Increase Stake in Chinese Retailer after National." 2019. www.caixinglobal.com/2019-12-17/yonghui-drops-plans-to-increase-stake-in-chinese-retailer-after-national-security-probe-101495178.html; Herbert Smith Freehills LLP. "National Security Review Regime under the New Foreign Investment Law." www.lexology.com/library/detail.aspx?g=61793b05-6109-4a68-9d02-5cf3f7dae384.
153 Kot, Jan. "Jardine-Backed Yonghui Buys Controlling Stake in Wuhan Retailer for RMB 559M." 2019. www.mingtiandi.com/real-estate/china-retail-real-estate-news/jardine-backed-yonghui-buys-control-of-wuhan-retailer/; Herbert Smith Freehills LLP. "National Security Review Regime under the New Foreign Investment Law." www.lexology.com/library/detail.aspx?g=61793b05-6109-4a68-9d02-5cf3f7dae384.
154 Herbert Smith Freehills LLP. "National Security Review Regime under the New Foreign Investment Law." www.lexology.com/library/detail.aspx?g=61793b05-6109-4a68-9d02-5cf3f7dae384.
155 Lau, Nanda. "China-National Security Review Regime under the New Foreign Investment Law." 2020. www.conventuslaw.com/report/china-national-security-review-regime-under-the/.
156 Yu, Scott, Jiang, Frank, Li, Rachel and Xu, Emily. "National Security Review in China: Ready to Embrace a Change?" 2019. www.zhonglun.com/Content/2019/09-26/1645514465.html.
157 Measures, Article 3(2).
158 Brooks, Stephen G. and Wohlforth, William C. "Reshaping the World Order: How Washington Should Reform International Institutions." *Foreign Affairs* 88, no. 2 (2009): 49–63; Ikenberry, G. John. "The Rise of China and the Future of the West: Can the Liberal System Survive." *Foreign Affairs* 87, no. 1 (2008): 23–37.
159 Economy Watch. "China Economy." 2020. www.economywatch.com/world_economy/china/?page=full.
160 Blacknell, Robert Gray. "Trust Not Their Presents, Nor Admit the Horse: Countering the Technically-Based Espionage Threat." *Roger Williams University Law Review* 12 (2007): 838–839; Saha, Souvik. "CFIUS Now Made in China: Dueling National Security Review Frameworks as a Countermeasure to Economic Espionage in the Age

of Globalization." *Northwestern Journal of International Law & Business* 33, no. 1 (2012): 201.

161 Saha, Souvik. "CFIUS Now Made in China: Dueling National Security Review Frameworks as a Countermeasure to Economic Espionage in the Age of Globalization." *Northwestern Journal of International Law & Business* 33, no. 1 (2012): 201.

162 Globerman, Steven and Shapiro, Daniel. "Economic and Strategic Considerations Surrounding Chinese FDI in the United States." *Asia Pacific Journal of Management* 26 (2009): 174.

163 Blacknell, Robert Gray. "Trust Not Their Presents, Nor Admit the Horse: Countering the Technically-Based Espionage Threat." *Roger Williams University Law Review* 12 (2007): 841.

164 Kastner, Scott L. and Pearson, Margaret M. "Exploring the Parameters of China's Economic Influence." *Studies in Comparative International Development* 56 (2021): 18–44.

165 Wang, Yan. *Chinese Legal Reform: The Case of Foreign Investment Law*. London: Routledge, 2002, 1–2.

166 Mira, Wilkins. *The Maturing of Multinational Enterprise: American Business Abroad from 1914 to 1970*. Cambridge: Harvard University Press, 1974; Mira, Wilkins. *The History of Foreign Investment in the United States 1914–1945*. Cambridge: Harvard University Press, 1989.

167 Graham, Edward M. and Marchick, David Matthew. *US National Security and Foreign Investment*. Washington, DC: Institute for International Economics, 2006, 3.

168 50 U.S.C.A. § 2170(d)(2)(1988).

169 50 U.S.C.A. § 2170(d)(2)(1988).

170 Foreign Investment Security Act of 2005, S. 1797, 109th Congress, § 2(3) (2005); Kimmitt, Robert Comment, America Seeks to Balance Investment and Security. www.ft.com/content/c82d1056-8e9d-11da-b752-0000779e2340.

171 Foreign Investment Security Act of 2005, S. 1797, 109th Congress, § 2(3) (2005); Kimmitt, Robert Comment. *America Seeks to Balance Investment and Security*. www.ft.com/content/c82d1056-8e9d-11da-b752-0000779e2340.

172 Statement of Daniella Markheim in Testimony, House of Representatives Homeland Security, on 24 May 2006, 2.

173 Covington & Burling LLP. "CFIUS Update: FIRRMA Finalized, Nears Passage." 2018. www.cov.com/en/news-and-insights/insights/2018/07/cfius-update-firrma-finalized-nears-passage, 2–3.

174 Covington & Burling LLP. "CFIUS Update: FIRRMA Finalized, Nears Passage." 2018. www.cov.com/en/news-and-insights/insights/2018/07/cfius-update-firrma-finalized-nears-passage, 2.

175 Wang, Yan. *Chinese Legal Reform: The Case of Foreign Investment Law*. London: Routledge, 2002, 1.

176 Hearing before the Senate Committee on Commerce, Science and Transportation, 100th Congress, 10 (1988).

177 Jackson, James K. "The Committee on Foreign Investment in the United States (CFIUS)." https://fas.org/sgp/crs/natsec/RL33388.pdf, 1.

178 50 U.S.C. § 2170 (g)(1) (2007).

179 50 U.S.C. § 2170 (b)(3)(C)(iv)(II)(aa) (2007).

180 50 U.S.C. § 2170 (b)(2)(B)(i)(I) (2007).

181 50 U.S.C. § 2170 (b)(3)(B) (2007).

182 50 U.S.C. § 2170 (b)(3)(C)(iv)(II)(bb) (2007).

183 50 U.S.C. § 2170 (b)(3)(B) (2007).

5 A Comparative Study of Chinese and US National Security Reviews

5.1 Comparative Study on Substantive Attributes

5.1.1 Review Body

5.1.1.1 China

The Measures made significant changes to the review body. First, a permanent institutional arrangement, namely the Working Mechanism, was created for organizing, coordinating, and guiding foreign investment security review work. The Working Mechanism Office (WMO) was established accordingly, to undertake the routine responsibilities in relation to foreign investment security review under the legal regime of the FIL. Notably, pursuant to the Measures, the WMO is located in the NDRC and under the leadership of the NDRC and MOFCOM.[1] In the past, however, such responsibilities over national security review were undertaken by the Joint-Conference (JC). As the name indicates, the JC was an interministerial agency led by MOFCOM and NDRC, which convened only when cases arose for deliberation.[2] Compared with the Working Mechanism, whose sole responsibility was for enforcing national security review, the authority of the JC was considerably broader, involving analysis of inward investment in terms of national security implications and providing investigation reports on security-related complexities in the review processes of certain transactions, in addition to the enforcement of national security review.[3]

Second is the matter of the members of the WMO. In the Measures, it is clearly expressed that national security review is carried out by the WMO, and the decisions on that review are made by the WMO. It seems that other agencies would not participate in carrying out national security review together with the NDRC and MOFCOM. The WMO, moreover, is specifically required to be located in the NDRC and led by the NDRC and MOFCOM, giving rise to the suspicion that the functions of central ministries related to national security review and foreign investment have been clarified. As the Measures never mentioned any other agency in relation to national security review, presumably it is the NDRC and MOFCOM that jointly conduct national security review and make judgments on foreign investments on national security grounds. In the past, however, under the

DOI: 10.4324/9781003543749-5

institutional design of interministerial cooperation, JC, NDRC, and MOFCOM had to conduct national security review with other relevant ministries temporarily on a case-by-case basis.

Third, the WMO, which is responsible for the routine work of national security review, is located in the NDRC, constituting the sole difference between the roles of the NDRC and MOFCOM in national security review.[4] This means that the NDRC now serves as an interface for foreign investors to communicate with regulators, for such purposes as accepting national security review filings and notifying of results. It is not a surprising design, as the NDRC has was assigned, in NDRC Notice 4, in 2019, to take over the MOFCOM's responsibility for receiving application materials about national security review.[5]

Fourth is the leadership of national security review. In the past, foreign investment M&A transactions fell under the scrutiny of MOFCOM and its local bureaus. Local MOFCOM bureaus had to report to the MOFCOM regarding certain transactions which would fall within the scope of national security review,[6] and MOFCOM was the sole agency responsible for the receipt of applications for national security review, as well as the determining power on the issue of whether certain transactions fell within the scope of national security review.[7] Also, the MOFCOM was a prominent agency which always took national security into account in market access review for FIEs and foreign investment projects.[8] The NDRC, however, shared its regulatory power to review foreign investment projects in industrial sectors, and continued for several years to erode the MOFCOM's exclusive regulatory power on foreign investment.[9] State Council Notice 6 specifically assigned MOFCOM and the NDRC as conveners for the first time.[10] Although the subsequent State Council Notice 24 was silent on the lead role of the NDRC and MOFCOM, it stipulated that the JC consisted of the NDRC, MOFCOM and other relevant authorities in accordance with the areas involved in foreign investment and would conduct national security review.[11] This vigorous march into grabbing authority over enforcement was developed by unilaterally expanding from verification into a de facto approval with veto power in denying foreign investment.[12] Given the long-lasting competition between MOFCOM and the NDRC over jurisdictional power on foreign investment, a compromise was reached on the enforcement of security review under the leadership of the NDRC and MOFCOM, in order to ease the institutional tension between the two. Despite the power struggle between the MOFCOM and the NDRC, the NDRC's expansion in relation to security review has its own rationale in the context of China as a socialist market economy and in light of the purposes of covering a wider range of foreign investments.[13] When the FIL came into force to adopt the principle of pre-established national treatment, moreover, the MOFCOM's authority on approval review for FIE establishment was eliminated. The adjustment of departmental responsibilities that took place in 2018, however, resulted in the NDRC superseding MOFCOM in relation to the duty of accepting national security review filings.[14] As the authority for reviewing M&A transactions was transferred to a newly established SAMR as a result of this adjustment, the M&A review for foreign investment is no longer subject to MOFCOM's jurisdiction. There was no longer any convenience to MOFCOM in accepting national security review filings. This could also explain why the WMO is located in the NDRC and why it is the NDRC that accepts national security review filings in accordance with NDRC Notice 4 rather than, as in the past, MOFCOM.

5.1.1.2 The US

In the US, it is the CFIUS that reviews foreign investment which has posed or might pose a threat to national security.[15] The CFIUS was established in 1975, and its membership has been continuously developed. A series of executive orders, as well as the FINSA and the FIRRMA, eventually led to its current membership. Originally, the CFIUS comprised the head officials of nine statutory US departments and offices, namely, secretary of treasury, secretary of homeland security, secretary of commerce, secretary of defense, secretary of state, attorney general of the United States, secretary of energy, secretary of labor, director of National Intelligence (DNI), with the heads of any other executive departments, agency, or office, as the president or the secretary of the treasury determines appropriate, generally or on a case-by-case basis.[16] In a sense, the membership of the CFIUS is expanding to a potentially unlimited capacity.[17] Among the aforementioned nine statutory departments and offices, there are two members that hold *ex officio* positions in the CFIUS and do not possess voting power, namely, the secretary of labor and the DNI.[18] There are also five observers in the CFIUS who participate in and report to the president on CFIUS activities. They are the director of the Office of Management and Budget, the chairman of the Council of Economic Advisers, the assistant to the president for National Security Affairs, the assistant to the president for Economic Policy, and the assistant to the president for Homeland Security and Counterterrorism.[19] Under the reformed legal regime of the FIRRMA, through the addition of US Trade Representative and director of the Office of Science and Technology Policy among the CFIUS members, the composition of the current CFIUS amounts to 16 fixed members in total, including two nonvoting members, and five observer members.

It is the secretary of the treasury that is positioned as the chairperson of the CFIUS, with exclusive authority to act or communicate with the Congress and the public on behalf of the CFIUS.[20] To be specific, the chairperson is assigned the functions of the president to provide for the imposition of civil penalties for any violation, including those of any mitigation agreement or condition imposed on certain transactions, or to the extent possible, to minimize paperwork.[21] Additionally, the chairperson also coordinates a reporting requirement, with descriptions of factors that are considered in any national security review or investigation of a covered transaction, or requires parties to provide to the CFIUS the information necessary to consider such factors.[22] In terms of reporting obligations, the chairperson is empowered to coordinate the preparation of the annual report and transmit it to the Congress, with authority to assign the responsibility to any member of the CFIUS for conducting studies and providing analysis necessary for the preparation of the report, as the chairperson determines if it's appropriate and consistent with the law.[23] More importantly, designated by the president, the chairperson has the power of directing, subject to notice and comment, the issuance of regulations to carry out national security review.[24] Last but not least, the chairperson may designate at his or her own discretion, a member or members of the CFIUS to be the lead agency or agencies on behalf of the CFIUS, on a case-by-case basis and for each transaction, to undertake the responsibilities of negotiating any mitigation agreements or other conditions necessary to safeguard national security, and for all matters related to the monitoring of completed transactions, in order to ensure compliance with such agreements or conditions.[25]

The primary work of the chairperson has evolved from monitoring foreign investment activities to reviewing national security issues, which is now the most important function.[26] During the process of lawmaking for US national security review, however, several critics proposed changes to the arrangement of the chairperson in the CFIUS. The report "Defense Trade: Enhancements to the Implementation of Exon-Florio Could Strengthen the Law's Effectiveness" issued by the Government Accountability Office Report (GAO Report), for example, objected that "national security" as defined by the secretary of the treasury was too narrow to offer full protection from national security threats from foreign investment, and suggested the secretary of defense replace the former as chairperson of the CFIUS.[27] This arrangement, however, would have offered no advantage if it had come into force, as each CFIUS member enjoyed equal power to influence the CFIUS. Indeed, the secretary of the treasury continues to hold the position of chairperson in the CFIUS, signaling that the US still consistently holds an open policy and encourages foreign investments and that national security review will be triggered only when foreign investment endangers national security.[28]

In acting on behalf of the CFIUS, a lead agency or lead agencies would be obliged to negotiate, modify, monitor, and enforce, on behalf of the CFIUS, any mitigation agreement entered into or conditions imposed with respect to a covered transaction between parties and the CFIUS, based on its own expertise and knowledge, keep the CFIUS fully informed of its activities and notify the chairperson of any material action that the lead agency proposes to take.[29] It must also provide periodic reports to the CFIUS on any material modification of certain mitigation conditions and ensure that such a material modification be reported to the DNI and the Attorney General of the United States.[30]

The evolving US emphasis on national security in different periods is also reflected in the institutional design of the CFIUS. The involvement of the DHS, which was established immediately after the 911 attacks, in the CFIUS, for example, reflects the high US sensitivity of the time in seeking to prevent any potential risks to homeland security from foreign investment. Although certain fields, such as energy, telecommunications and transportation, had already been identified by the DHS as critical infrastructure to be subject to national security review, the introduction of the Department of Energy (DOE) as a member of the CFIUS through the FINSA took place in specific political and economic conditions, affected especially by the CNOOC–UNOCAL transaction in the energy industry, as one of the measures specifically taken by the US to ensure enhanced protection of critical infrastructure, especially energy resources, from foreign investment.[31]

The role of the DNI is quite different from that of other CFIUS members, as a nonvoting, *ex officio* member of the CFIUS holding a relatively independent position and serving no policy role in the CFIUS, other than to provide risk analysis in connection with a covered transaction.[32] To be specific, it can expeditiously carry out a thorough analysis with basic information regarding any threat to US national security posed by any covered transaction, seek and incorporate views of all affected or appropriate intelligence agencies with respect to the covered transaction, or provide an assessment of any operational impact of a transaction on the intelligence community and a description of any action that has been or will be taken to mitigate any such impact.[33] Such an analysis may be supplemented or amended, moreover, as the DNI considers necessary or appropriate, or upon a request for additional information by the CFIUS.[34] When entering into a mitigation agreement, such an analysis has to be updated with respect to a covered transaction, under the request of the lead agency.[35] The DNI's risk analysis and preliminary national security review are carried out in parallel, indicating the unique role of the DNI in protecting national security from foreign investment.

Similarly, the secretary of labor serves no policy role in the CFIUS and does not possess any voting right. The title holder participates in national security review on an ex officio basis, demonstrating that the US desires to protect labor rights.[36] In response to a request from the chairperson of the CFIUS, the secretary of labor could identify for the CFIUS any risk mitigation provisions proposed to or by the CFIUS that would violate US employment laws or require a party to violate US employment laws.[37] The consideration of whether there is any violation of employment law in the mitigation agreements demonstrates the issues perceived by the US as employment issues among the national security considerations.[38] A reinforced attempt by the CFIUS to define national security in a broader sense, such as the effects of foreign investment on employment or social stability, can therefore be implied.[39]

A number of observer members in the CFIUS participate in CFIUS activities as appropriate and report to the president. Unlike other CFIUS members, all of these observers work for the president, serving as powerless agents. This institutional arrangement of observers indicates an enhanced presidential attempt to engaged in the operational process of national security review conducted by the CFIUS, rather than blindly wait for the last layer of presidential decision based on the CFIUS's recommendation.

Table 5.1 indicates the CFIUS members with their typical tendency on the basis of their officially announced missions. It could be concluded that the CFIUS deliberately includes agencies with distinctive functions, in order to reach judgments that account for national security-related considerations on foreign investment.[40] Other than three members who are neutral on national security and foreign investment, there are seven who tend to advocate foreign investment promotion, while three of them are observers. There are six members who tend to advocate national security protection, and two of them are observers. As observers only participate in national security review in appropriate situations, there are four regularly voting members promoting foreign investment and, again, four protecting national

Table 5.1 Composition of the CFIUS, Year of Delegation, Tendency, and Legal Source

CFIUS Members	*Year of Delegation*	*Tendency*	*Legal Source*
Secretary of Treasury	1975	Advocate of foreign investment liberalization	Executive Order No. 11858, Sec.1 (a)(2)
Secretary of Commerce	1975	Advocate of foreign investment liberalization	Executive Order No. 11858, Sec.1 (a)(4)
Secretary of State	1975	Advocate of foreign investment liberalization	Executive Order No. 11858, Sec.1 (a)(1)
US Trade Representative	1980	Advocate of foreign investment liberalization	Executive Order No. 12188, Sec.1–102 (b)(1)
Director of the Office of Management and Budget	*1988*	*Advocate of foreign investment liberalization*	Executive Order No. 12661, Sec.3–301 (1)
Chairman of the Council of Economic Advisers	*1980*	*Advocate of foreign investment liberalization*	Executive Order No. 12188, Sec.1–102 (b)(13)
Assistant to the President for Economic Policy	*1993*	*Advocate of foreign investment liberalization*	Executive Order No. 12860, Sec.1
Secretary of Homeland Security	2003	Advocate of national security protection	Executive Order No. 13286, Sec.2
Secretary of Defense	1975	Advocate of national security protection	Executive Order No. 11858, Sec.1 (a)(3)
Attorney General of US	1988	Advocate of national security protection	Executive Order No. 12661, Sec.2–201(1)
Secretary of Energy	2007	Advocate of national security protection	Section 721 of the Defense Production Act of 1950, 50 U.S.C. § 2170 (as amended by the Foreign Investment and National Security Act of 2007), (k)(2)(G)
Assistant to the President for National Security Affairs	*1993*	*Advocate of national security protection*	Executive Order No. 12860, Sec. 1
Assistant to the President for Homeland Security and Counterterrorism	*2008*	*Advocate of national security protection*	Executive Order No. 13456, Sec. 3(c)(v)
Director of the Office of Science and Technology Policy	1993	Neutrality	Executive Order No. 12860, Sec. 1
Secretary of Labor	2007	Neutrality	50 U.S.C. § 2170 (k)(2)(H)
Director of National Intelligence	2007	Neutrality	50 U.S.C. § 2170 (k)(2)(I)

(*Note:* Fixed CFIUS members; *CFIUS observer members*; nonvoting CFIUS members ex officio)

security. This indicates that, on the composition of CFIUS members, the US not only involves a number of departments with various professions and areas of expertise, but also attempts to involve departments with conflicting interests. With this institutional design bringing it diverse and even controversial perspectives, the CFIUS can be exposed to a variety of opinions on national security implications and certain foreign investments, with the credibility to make much more comprehensive and objective determinations.

Even though the interministerial agency of the CFIUS on national security review provided an apparent reference in terms of the institutional layout to the design of China's review body, especially the former JC, there are significant differences.[41] Currently, both the CFIUS and the WMO are operational and statutory review bodies. It seems that the NDRC acts in a similar role to the chairperson of the CFIUS, responsible for communication and coordination issues. The WMO consists of two members, however, and the CFIUS has considerably more. While in China a general principle applies of comparing the positions of the NDRC and the MOFCOM in the WMO, moreover, the US provides detailed explanations and guidelines for each CFIUS member's authority. The results of national security review in China regarding foreign investment are expected to be made jointly by the NDRC and the MOFCOM, while the results in US national security review are determined by a wider range of members possessing diversified expertise and professional positions.

5.1.2 Review Scope

5.1.2.1 China

In FIL, "foreign investment" refers to any investment activity directly or indirectly conducted by a foreign natural person, enterprise, or other organization, to establish a foreign-funded enterprise independently or jointly with any other investor, to acquire shares, equities, property shares or any other similar rights and interests of an enterprise, to invest in a new project independently or jointly with any other investor, within the territory of China, or to undertake investment in any other way stipulated by laws, administrative regulations, or provisions of the State Council.[42] Foreign investment affecting or having the possibility to affect national security is subject to national security review.[43] A proposed transaction in any industry or sector would be subject to national security review, but the Measures highlight a number of sectors of focus which must be subject to national security review and are categorized into two types.[44]

First are industries relevant to national defense security, such as military industries and military supporting industries, or investments in areas close to military facilities and military industry facilities (Type I Foreign Investments).[45] Second is the situation in which a foreign investor acquires actual control of the investee company in industries relevant to national security, such as important agricultural products, important energy and resources, important equipment and manufacturing, important infrastructure, important transportation services, important cultural products and services, important information technology and internet products and services, important financial services, critical technologies, and other important industries (Type II Controlling Foreign Investment).[46] A foreign investment relating to national defense-related security is subject to review, regardless of whether a controlling power is sought, whilst a foreign investment in prescribed important sectors is subject to review only if the foreign investor seeks control of the Chinese target company. The WMO may request parties to submit national security review filings with respect to these two types of foreign investment.[47]

For Type II Controlling Foreign Investments, the Measures provide a detailed description of "actual control" in relation to three circumstances. First is the case of transactions acquiring more than 50 percent of shares.[48] Second is the case in which, when less than 50 percent of shares are acquired, voting rights that enable significant influence over the board of directors and shareholders' resolutions would also be understood to result in actual control.[49] Third is the case of transactions acquiring material influence over the business decisions, personnel, finance, and technology of the investee companies by other means.[50] In spite of these general conditions for actual control, the Measures failed to provide a detailed elaboration of "significantly influence" or "other means". Nor do they offer a definition of important industries or an exhaustive list of "actual control" scenarios. These unsolved issues create great ambiguity around foreign investments and make it difficult for foreign investors to determine whether their proposed investments would fall within these sectors of focus and trigger national security concerns. It is expected that the WMO could respond to these issues and provide relevant interpretation and explanation when enforcing national security review of foreign investments.[51]

5.1.2.2 The US

In accordance with the FIRRMA and its regulations which are effective currently, foreign investment subject to national security review could be summarized into the following five categories. First is the "covered control transaction", which is a traditional scope originally regulated in the earliest Exon-Florio Amendment, referring to any merger, acquisition or takeover that is proposed by or with any foreign person and which could result in foreign control of any US business.[52] In contrast to the vague descriptions of three circumstances of "actual control" in China's national security review, the US offers a rather detailed explanation of the key terminology of "control" and an exhaustive list of such control matters.[53] In examining questions of control in situations where more than one foreign person has an ownership interest in an entity, moreover, factors for assessing control are enumerated.[54]

Second is the non-controlling investment, that is, a direct or indirect investment, by a foreign person in an unaffiliated US business involved in certain critical technologies, critical infrastructure, or the sensitive personal data of US citizens, which is referred to as "TID US business".[55] Pursuant to the FIRRMA, TID US business means any US business that (i) produces, designs, tests, manufactures, fabricates, or develops one or more critical technology; (ii) performs functions with respect to covered investment critical infrastructure, such as management, operation, manufacture, or supply; or (iii) maintains or collects, directly or indirectly, sensitive personal data of US citizens.[56] The FIRRMA explains the term "TID US business" in detail. The scope of critical technologies, for example, is clearly identified and includes such items as defense articles or defense services included on the United States Munitions List set forth in the International Traffic in Arms Regulations, items included on the Commerce Control List, specifically designed and prepared nuclear equipment, parts and components, materials, software, and technology relating to assistance to foreign atomic energy activities, nuclear facilities, equipment, and material relating to export and import of nuclear equipment and material, select agents and toxins, and emerging and foundational technologies controlled under section 1758 of the Export Control Reform Act of 2018.[57] Unlike the controlling investment, foreign investment in this category does not need to meet the threshold of control, as long as it is in relation to TID US business, but must meet the following three conditions to trigger national security review: (i) access to any material nonpublic technical information in the possession of TID US business; (ii) membership or observer rights on, or the rights to nominate an individual to a position on, the board of directors or equivalent governing body of a TID US business; or (iii) any involvement, other than through voting of shares, in substantive involvement in the decision-making of US business with respect to the technology, infrastructure, or data.[58]

The third involves any change in the rights which could result in the aforementioned two types, that is, controlling investment or non-controlling investment in TID US Business.[59] The fourth type is greenfield real estate transactions, namely, the purchase or lease by, or a concession to, a foreign person of private or public real estate located in the US, and such a transaction is located within or functioning as part of specified ports, either airports or maritime ports, or in close proximity to military installations and other facilities of the US government.[60] The FIRRMA defines close proximity as within an area that extends outward one mile from the boundary of a military installation or another facility or property of the US government and further provides specific circumstances for determining "close proximity", such as whether it could reasonably provide the foreign person with the ability to collect intelligence on activities being conducted at such an installation, facility, or property, and whether national security activities would be exposed at such an installation, facility, or property to the risk of foreign surveillance.[61] The fifth type is any foreign investment which is designed or intended to evade or circumvent the regulatory mechanism of national security review.[62]

5.1.2.3 Comparison

The legal provisions of review scope concerning national security review in China and the US reveal the host country's ideas on national security and foreign investment. To be specific, the regulatory mechanism of national security review in the US attempts to satisfy its national security concerns, especially on foreign investment in relation to TID US business, no matter whether it obtains controlling stakes. Another difference is that the US provides detailed descriptions of foreign investment subject to national security review, such as the definitions of control, TID US business, lists of critical infrastructure, and lists of specific industries which are subject to export controls, while China's national security review merely prescribes sectors of focus regarding national security review in general.[63]

Both in Chinese and US jurisdictions, transactions subject to review are no longer limited to foreign M&As of domestic companies. In China, even though foreign investment subject to national security review was once confined to mergers, acquisitions, or takeovers, China has already reviewed other forms of foreign investment, such as the establishment of FIEs and other foreign investment projects through other approval reviews at the market access. Even in State Council Circular 24, which was promulgated in 2015, new projects or the establishment of new enterprises independently by foreign investors or jointly with foreign persons, as well as other methods of foreign investment, such as controlling agreements, trusts, reinvestment, overseas transactions, leases, subscriptions of convertible bonds, etc., have all fallen within the scope of national security review.[64]

Similarly, the tendency to expand the scope of national security review in the US seems to resemble China's traditional approach, which has placed regulatory scrutiny on all kinds of foreign investment on national security grounds, despite the fact that this was once achieved through various regulatory reviews at the market access. Before the FIRRMA, national security review was only triggered when an M&A resulted in foreign control of a US business which had posed or might pose a threat to US national security, while, under the FIRRMA, for the first time, review could be triggered by non-controlling foreign investment in TID US business and real estate transactions. Also, the sectors of focus in national security review have been expanded as well.[65] In the Exon-Florio Amendment, national security review mainly focused on national defense and defense production. In the FINSA, the sectors of focus expanded to critical infrastructure. In the FIRRMA, the sectors of focus were expanded greatly, becoming no longer limited to the defense field, but to emerging and fundamental fields, such as critical technology as well as sensitive personal data. In other words, the scope of foreign investment subject to national security expands and involves non-controlling investments in TID US business as well as certain greenfield real estate transactions. The criteria and circumstances of foreign investment subject to national security review, moreover, have been defined and explained clearly in the FIRRMA. Examples have even been added for a number of key terms, such as "control", "covered non-controlling investment", "covered transaction", "sensitive personal data" as well as "TID US business".[66] It can be concluded that the US has gradually brought more types of foreign investment into the scope of national security review so that it is not controlling only foreign investment M&A transactions which originally fell within the scope of such reviews.

In addition to the similar tendency towards a larger scope of national security, there are several significant differences between the two jurisdictions concerning the types of foreign investment subject to review. First, there are different focuses on controlling investments and non-controlling investments. Even though both Chinese and US national security reviews distinguish between controlling investments and non-controlling investments, there is a clear difference between their categories. In China, foreign investment relating to national defense security is subject to review, regardless of whether a controlling power is sought. That is to say, non-controlling investment is related to military fields, and is described as purely safeguarding military security or national defense security, whilst non-controlling investment in US national security review embraces a much broader range. Non-controlling investment in "covered investment critical infrastructure" is similar to that of China, mainly focusing on military security and national defense security. Non-controlling investment in relation to critical technology and sensitive personal data, which mainly attempts to maintain US technological leadership, however, indicates that, to some extent, technological security and security of data are regarded as the first priority in protecting national security. In China's national security review, foreign investment in important technology will be triggered only if it seeks actual control. This means that in terms of restricting foreign investment in important technology, China has established a much stricter restriction on launching a national security review, which highlights the fact that military security seems to be prioritized over security of technology in China. One possible reason is that US technology is much more advanced than China's, and the US is afraid that advanced technology might be obtained by China through Chinese investment, strengthening China's capability in challenging US technological leadership. The US is more sensitive than China on foreign investment in critical technology.

Another difference is reflected in the definition of control. China and the US respectively define the elements of control in quantitative and qualitative approaches. China adopts the quantitative condition as a principle, that is, de facto power on substantive matters, to determine whether control is sought in the target company. For example, China sets the threshold of control at 50 percent or more of shares in the target company, whereas a foreign takeover that is below 50 percent of shares in the Chinese company, but it would result in the substantive impact.[67] In general, however, foreign control is automatically assumed if a 10 percent threshold of shares acquired in the US entity is reached.[68] Even a transaction below 10 percent shares is not completely immune from national security review, unless the investor can prove that the investment is made solely for the purpose of passive investment.[69]

Apparently, it is clear that greenfield investments fall within the purview of China's national security review if they might impose national security risks. Such investment may be beyond the reach of the CFIUS, however, except in the scenario in which a foreign investor establishes a new US entity to conduct a merger and acquisition in the US.[70]

Last but not least, China and the US have adopted two different modes with regard to sectors subject to review. China has an exhaustive list of ten primary sectors subject to review, which suggests that, at least on paper, non-listed sectors should be excluded from a potential national security review. Such a list is not provided in the US, implying that all sectors are potentially under the purview of the CFIUS review.[71]

In addition, both China and the US cover an increasing number of sectors. When China started to allow foreign investment in its domestic market, it placed great emphasis on whether foreign investment would challenge political and economic independence. Even though China did not directly clarify sectors which were closed to foreign investment, therefore, approval reviews of foreign-invested enterprises at the market access indicated that a large number of sectors in China were closed to foreign investment. When China adopted the catalogue system to further guide foreign investment and protect national security, sectors of focus regarding national security considerations were reflected in the Catalogue List, especially from the restricted and prohibited items identified in the Catalogue List. Nowadays, the number of restricted and prohibited sectors has been gradually decreased. Indeed, China provides a general and vague list, while the US offers detailed definitions or explanations of key terms, even with attached examples for better guidance. Even though foreign investment in relation to important technologies and sensitive places is subject to national security review in China and the US, definitions of important technology in China are never offered, while critical technology and how to determine sensitive places can be found in the FIRRMA.

5.1.3 Review Criteria

5.1.3.1 China

The Measures under the legal regime of FIL issued in 2020 do not mention review criteria, that is, the factors which would be considered by the WMO in a national security review. This demonstrates that the WMO is playing a significant role in determining whether to prohibit certain foreign investment and to what extent a transaction may negatively influence national security. Arguably, the concept of national security would be interpreted in a very expansive manner under a holistic approach to national security proposed in China. In the review criteria provided in the previous rules on national security review, considerations which should be taken into account during a national security review were expressed in an ambiguous way, in the following six respects.

First is the impact on defense security, involving the domestic production capacity for the products required for national defense, domestic service delivery capacity, and relevant equipment and facilities.[72] Second is the impact on the stable running of the national economy.[73] Third is the impact on the basic order of social life.[74] Fourth is the impact on national cultural security and public morality.[75] Fifth is the impact on national cybersecurity.[76] Sixth is the impact on the R&D capability of critical technologies related to national security.[77] These terms, however, lacked any further clarification in terms of conceptual scope in the review criteria, such as "national economy", "social order of basic living", "cultural security", and "public morality".

5.1.3.2 The US

Unlike China, the US provides relatively detailed information for review criteria in its national security review. The CFIUS is required to focus on examining the following three matters during the whole process of national security review. First is whether the transaction is a covered transaction.[78] Second is whether there is credible evidence to support a belief that any foreign person party to a covered transaction might take action that threatens to impair the national security of the US.[79] Third is whether provisions of law, other than the laws on national security review, and the IEEPA, provide adequate and appropriate authority to protect US national security.[80]

There is a total number of 11 factors for the CFIUS, the president and the president's designee, as follows: first, the domestic production needed for projected national defense requirements;[81] second, the capability and capacity of domestic industries to satisfy the requirements of national defense, including the availability of human resources, products, technology, materials, and other supplies and services;[82] third, the control of domestic industries and commercial activity by foreign citizens as it affects the capability and the capacity of the US to meet requirements of national security;[83] fourth, the potential effect of the proposed or pending transaction on sales of military goods, equipment, or technology to any country identified by the Secretary of State as a country supporting terrorism,[84] or a country of concern regarding missile proliferation, or a country of concern regarding chemical and biological weapons, or identified by the secretary of defense as posing a potential regional military threat to the interests of the US, or listed on the Nuclear Non-Proliferation-Special Country List;[85] fifth, the potential effects of the proposed or pending transaction on US international technological leadership in areas affecting US national security;[86] sixth, the potential national security-related effects on US critical infrastructure, including major energy assets;[87] seventh, whether certain foreign investment imposes potential national security-related effects on US critical technologies;[88] eighth, whether the covered transaction is a foreign-government-controlled transaction, which could result in control of a US business by a foreign government or a person controlled by or acting on behalf of a foreign government;[89] ninth the current assessment of the adherence of the subject country to nonproliferation control regimes, the relationship of such country with the US, and the potential for transshipment or diversion of technologies with military applications, as appropriate, and particularly with respect to transactions requiring an investigation;[90] tenth, whether such a foreign investment is related to the long-term projection of US requirements for sources of energy and other critical resources and material;[91] eleventh, a miscellaneous provision to cover any potential risks to US national security from foreign investment, referring to other factors as the president or the CFIUS may determine to be appropriate, generally or in connection with a specific review or investigation.[92]

5.1.2.3 Comparison

With respect to review criteria for national security reviews in these two jurisdictions, there are great differences. The first apparent difference lies in the fact that China's national security review does not expressly describe review criteria, which results in a lack of transparency and predictability for foreign investment, while the US at least provides several factors which should be considered in national security review, indicating its specific worries on national security as regards foreign investment.

Second, the concept of national security in national security review was defined and interpreted broadly by China, while, for the purpose of allowing maximum flexibility in determining the outcome of a transaction, there is no relevant legal reference on defining national security in the process of national security review in the US.[93] The Measures were drafted in accordance with the FIL, National Security Law (NSL), and other relevant laws. Under the NSL, "national security" refers to a state in which national power, sovereignty, unity and territorial integrity, the people's well-being, sustainable economic and social development and other major national interests are relatively free from danger and free from internal and external threats, as well as to the ability to ensure continued security.[94] The NSL also requires national security tasks to comply with a holistic approach to national security (HANS) which plays a significant role in the formulation of national security review under the FIL.[95] Eleven types of national security enumerated in the HANS, namely, political security, homeland security, military security, economic security, cultural security, social security, science and technology security, information security, ecological security, resource security and nuclear security, will affect the review criteria considered in national security review. In contrast, even though the FIRRMA provides several factors which should be taken into account in national security review, it purposely avoids giving a clear definition of the core concept of national security.

Third, China and the US have different focuses on review criteria. Even though considerations by the WMO when enforcing national security review are not expressly addressed in the Measures, China has two distinctive considerations, namely, the impact on the stable operation of the national economy and the impact on China's basic order of social life, in accordance with previous rules on national security review. These two factors are hard to justify, as it is not feasible to treat the whole economy as a sector to be protected against foreign control for security-related purposes, and China's social order of basic living can easily be interpreted in an arbitrary way encompassing unlimited connotations. In the US, the impact on US international technological leadership is a significant factor to be assessed in national security review. This factor could also explain why China is a special origin when the CFIUS reviews foreign investment and why all prohibitions following national security reviews are related to China. Both China and the US, however, are expected to introduce a comprehensive range of review criteria. As China lacks review criteria for national security review, enforcement is under the discretion of the WMO, resulting in a lack of transparency and predictability. In the Exon-Florio Amendment, the impacts on national security were placed in the fields of military or national defense, while, in the FINSA, the impacts on critical infrastructure were added. Then, in addition to critical infrastructure, the potential implications on critical technology and personal sensitive data were addressed in the current FIRRMA. This demonstrates that the US attempts to expand consideration to almost every sector of the economy, rather than just to the context of traditional security.[96] The FIRRMA, moreover, contains a miscellaneous provision as a factor of determining whether to trigger national security review. The review criteria could be considered as open-ended and therefore quite similar to those in China.

5.2 Procedural Attributes

5.2.1 Pre-consultation

5.2.1.1 China

It is the foreign investors or the relevant Chinese entities (parties concerned) that are required to submit a notice to the WMO in a situation in which the terms of the foreign investment fall within the scope of industries subject to national security review, which is discussed in the previous section, prior to the investment.[97] The term "foreign investors" is defined as foreign natural persons, enterprises, or other organizations.[98]

The parties concerned may consult the WMO over relevant issues before submitting national security review filings.[99] This pre-consultation phase is optional for parties and is not necessary for submitting a formal application. It only provides an opportunity for foreign investors to communicate with the WMO in advance on relevant issues of national security review, though this is not legally binding.[100] The term "relevant issues" is not explained, leaving the suspicion that both procedural and substantive issues might be addressed during the pre-consultation. Under the previous rules, however, pre-consultation touched only upon procedural information. Whether "relevant issues" refers to procedural matters or substantial issues, or both, confuses applicants. Presumably, pre-consultation in the Measures may comply with that in the previous rules, which focus only on procedural issues. One highly possible reason for this assumption is that there is a 15-day process for the WMO to determine whether a national security review would be conducted, which could be regarded as a stage for considering substantial issues.[101]

5.2.1.2 The US

Quite unlike China's pre-consultation, which had focused or might only focus on procedural matters, the US pre-consultation involves all information and documentary material disclosed or submitted to the CFIUS by any party or parties at this consultation stage being deemed relevant to the proposed transaction itself or its national security implications, including substantive and procedural matters alike.[102]

Foreign investors in the US, moreover, are encouraged to consult with the CFIUS in advance of filing a formal notice and, in appropriate cases, to file with the CFIUS a draft notice or other appropriate documents, in stark contrast to the situation in China, where there is no signal of encouraging pre-consultation emerging as a stage in the national security review process. The main reason for this difference is that China's pre-consultation phase on national security review focuses only on procedural matters, in order simply to make foreign investors clear about the procedural aspects of national security review, such as the timeline, requirements for preparing filings and materials, and the fact that the relevant authorities might not obtain any important information about covered transactions. The CFIUS, however, could obtain both substantive and procedural information on proposed transactions and could have a first glance of the transaction in question. It would therefore be rational for the CFIUS to have an intent to encourage pre-notice consultation, in order to obtain more information on certain foreign investments in advance and to improve the efficiency of the possible review process.

5.2.1.3 Comparison

In addition to the significant differences mentioned previously on pre-consultation, there are some similarities. First, pre-consultation, both in China and the US, serves as an optional process for foreign investors, not a mandatory requirement. Second, with regard to the context of the pre-consultation and draft notice, the CFIUS does not issue advisory opinions as to whether a transaction might raise national security concerns or be considered a covered transaction subject to national security. In a sense, it can be regarded as merely a procedural stage providing no substantive judgement.

5.2.2 Initiation

5.2.2.1 China

There is one major way to trigger the process of national security review: voluntary submission by the foreign investors or parties concerned. The Measures clarifies reporting materials which should be submitted for national security review. A party which reports foreign investment to the WMO shall submit a written report, an investment plan, a statement on whether the foreign investment affects national security, and other materials required by the WMO.[103] The relevant departments of the people's governments of provinces, autonomous regions, and municipalities can be authorized by the WMO, as needed for work, to collect filing materials and transfer them to the WMO.[104] It is the WMO that decides whether a security review of the reported foreign investment is required and notifies the party in writing, within 15 working days of receiving the required materials as submitted by a party or transferred by the relevant departments of local governments.[105] Once the filing of the national security review is submitted, such a foreign investment may not be made prior to the decision of the WMO on whether to conduct a national security review.[106]

In addition to voluntary application for national security review by foreign investment parties, the Measures provide another provision, to the effect that, if the relevant authorities, enterprises, social organizations, and public deem that foreign investment affects or may affect national security, they may put forward suggestions to the WMO for the launching of a security review.[107] It is under the discretion of the WMO to determine whether to accept such suggestions to conduct a national security review.

5.2.2.2 The US

National security review in the US is triggered by either a voluntary notification submitted by any party to a covered transaction, or a unilateral notification submitted by any CFIUS member or the president of the US.[108] Through the voluntary submission of a written notice of the transaction to the Secretary of Treasury, by foreign investors or concerned parties to any covered transaction, a national security review of this transaction is initiated.[109] Such a voluntarily submitted draft or formal written notice should include a stipulation claiming that a transaction is a covered transaction, and the CFIUS has to make comments on the draft notice or accept the formal written notice of a covered transaction not later than 10 business days after the date of submission of the draft or formal written notice.[110] The parties to a transaction have to provide the information in detail, which must be accurate and complete with respect to all parties and to the transaction.[111] If it is deemed to be incomplete, the CFIUS shall notify the concerned parties in writing and provide an explanation of all material respects in which the notice is incomplete.[112] Any information and other documentary material provided by the parties to the CFIUS after the filing of a voluntary notice must be part of the notice.[113] The FIRRMA clearly lists the materials required in the voluntary notice.

A voluntary notice may state that the transaction is a covered transaction or a foreign government-controlled transaction, with a detailed accompanying description of the basis for such statements.[114] In such a situation, the CFIUS has to provide comments on a draft or formal written notice or accept a formal written notice submitted with respect to a covered transaction not later than ten business days after the date of submission of the draft or formal written notice.[115]

In addition, national security review can be unilaterally initiated by the president, or any deputy secretary or appropriate department or agency on behalf of the CFIUS, in a unilateral initiation of review.[116] In a case where no voluntary notice has been filed for a transaction and such a transaction has not been reviewed before, the staff chairperson, acting on the recommendation of the CFIUS, may request the parties to the transaction to provide the CFIUS with the information necessary to determine whether the transaction is a covered transaction and, if the CFIUS determines that it is, to file a notice of such covered transaction.[117] Unlike voluntary applications, which can be withdrawn, this unilateral initiation cannot be withdrawn by the CFIUS member, or members, or the president, but only by the member who initially put forward the request for notification.[118] Also, unilateral initiation of national security review is applicable to any covered transaction that has previously been reviewed or investigated, as long as either of the following conditions applies. The first is that any party to the transaction submitted false or misleading material information to the CFIUS in connection with the national security review or national security investigation, or omitted material information, including material documents, from information submitted to the CFIUS.[119] The other condition is that, for any covered transaction that has previously been reviewed or investigated, the concerned party or entity resulting from consummation of the transaction intentionally and materially breaches a mitigation agreement or condition, such breach is certified to the CFIUS by the lead department or agency monitoring and enforcing such agreement or condition as an intentional and material breach, and the CFIUS determines that there are no other remedies or enforcement measures available to address such breach.[120] In general, the time period for unilateral national security launched by CFIUS members for reviewed transactions is three years from the transaction completion date, with an exception where the CFIUS member has reason to believe it is a covered transaction and may raise national security considerations in consultation with other members of the CFIUS.[121]

The FIRRMA specifies two conditions for which the CFIUS requires a mandatory declaration.[122] The first is for the mandatory declaration for foreign-government-controlled investment in TID US business, that is, a covered transaction that results in the acquisition of substantial interest in a TID US business by a foreign person in which the foreign government, directly or indirectly, has a substantial impact.[123] The second is for covered investment which could result in foreign control of a TID US business that produces, designs, tests, manufactures, fabricates, or develops one or more critical technologies, and such critical technologies are utilized or designed in connection with TID US business in one or more industry.[124]

Like the written notice, the declaration can also be withdrawn. Parties to a transaction that have submitted a declaration may request in writing, at any time prior to the CFIUS taking action, that such declaration be withdrawn, and this request is required to be directed to the chairperson with statements explaining why the request is being made, and whether the transaction that is the subject of the declaration is being fully and permanently abandoned.[125] Generally, the withdrawal or re-filing of a declaration is made by concerned parties voluntarily, not requested by the CFIUS, with the exceptions that the CFIUS permits parties to a covered transaction to correct material errors or omissions, or describe material changes to the transaction, in the declaration submitted with respect to that covered transaction.[126]

Similar to written notice, the mandatory declaration also has a time limitation. To be specific, the CFIUS may not require a mandatory declaration to be submitted with respect to a covered transaction more than 45 days before the completion of the transaction, and it may not request or recommend that a submitted mandatory declaration be withdrawn and refiled, except to permit parties to a covered transaction to correct material errors or omissions in the declaration.[127] As in the case of written notice, neither the CFIUS nor the president are bound by such a stipulation offered by the concerned parties, nor does any such stipulation limit the ability of the CFIUS or the president to act on any authority provided in national security review with respect to any covered transaction.[128]

5.2.3 Review Process

5.2.3.1 China

According to the Measures, the security review of foreign investments is divided into two phases: general review and special review.[129] During these two review stages, the concerned parties cannot complete the investment.[130] If the WMO decides to conduct a security review of a reported foreign investment, it shall complete the general review within 30 working days of the decision.[131] Under the phase of general review, the WMO is able to announce that the security review is concluded, if it deems that the reported foreign investment does not affect national security, or if it decides to initiate a special review upon deeming national security is affected or is likely to be affected.[132] The party shall be notified in writing of the decision made by the WMO.[133] During this process, there are two possible results: either approval or a decision to enter the phase of special review.

If the WMO deems that such a foreign investment would impact or might impact national security, a decision to initiate a special investigation of such a reported foreign investment is made.[134] The special investigation can result in one of two possible outcomes. First, if the reported foreign investment does not affect national security, the WMO shall decide that the security review has been concluded.[135] Second, if the reported foreign investment affects national security, the WMO may decide to prohibit the investment, or provide an opportunity to impose conditions designed to eliminate the effect on national security for the parties to accept.[136] There are three possible results for foreign investments: approval, prohibition, or approval with conditions. Generally, the special review is to be completed within 60 working days, while an unlimited extension is provided under exceptional circumstances.[137] This makes the timeline for national security review unpredictable.

5.2.3.2 The US

The whole process of national security review can be divided into three stages: preliminary national security review, national security investigation, and presidential decision. Upon receiving a written voluntary notification or pursuant to a unilateral notification initiated by the president or the CFIUS, a national security review should be completed by the CFIUS before the end of the 45-day period beginning on the date of the acceptance of written notice or the date of the unilateral initiation, to determine the effects of the proposed transaction on the national security of the US.[138] There are three possible results of 45-day preliminary national security review. First, in the event that the covered transaction does not threaten national security, the whole review process will be completed, and the proposed takeover may proceed. Second, if the CFIUS determines that a covered transaction might threaten national security but that these threats can be mitigated, the approval will be issued to the foreign investment parties as long as they can reach mitigation agreement with the CFIUS to eliminate risks. Third, a national security investigation will be initiated if the CFIUS determines that the notified transaction would threaten US national security and that threat has not been mitigated during or prior to the national security review, or it is a foreign government-controlled transaction, or if the CFIUS member advises the chairperson that it deems the transaction to threaten US national security and that threat has not been mitigated, or the lead agency recommends that an investigation should be undertaken.[139]

If the CFIUS determines that the notified transaction meets the aforementioned conditions, the CFIUS should immediately undertake a national security investigation of the effects of a covered transaction on national security, no later than the end of the 45-day national security review, and take any necessary actions in connection with the transaction to protect national security.[140] Once a covered transaction enters into the national security investigation, it is subject to more comprehensive and rigorous scrutiny.[141] In extraordinary circumstances, arising from a *force majeure* event or to protect the national security of the US, national security investigations can be extended for one 15-day period, as appropriate and necessary and upon written request signed by the head of the lead agency.[142] Such an extension has to be made prudently, however, as the authority of the head of a lead agency to request the extension of an investigation may not be delegated to any person other than the deputy head or equivalent thereof of the lead agency.[143] In summary, there are three possible results of the phase of national security investigation. First, the CFIUS determines that a covered transaction does not pose a national security threats. Second, the CFIUS determines that a covered transaction might pose a national security threat and that such threat could be mitigated through agreement, and then attempts to reach a mitigation agreement with the foreign investors. If the CFIUS resolves to conclude all deliberative action with regard to a notified covered transaction without sending a report to the president, such action shall be concluded, and an official of the chairperson must promptly advise the parties in writing of the determination to conclude action.[144] Third, if the CFIUS decides to send a report to the president upon completion or termination of the investigation, or it is unable to reach a decision on whether to recommend that the president suspend or prohibit the transaction, the president is requested by the CFIUS to make a final determination concerning the transaction.[145] Relevant information, concerning whether there is credible evidence that led the president to believe that a covered transaction might involve conduct that threatens national security, or whether provisions of laws other than the rules of national security review and the IEEPA, do not, in the judgment of the president, provide adequate and appropriate authority for the president to protect national security in the matter before him or her. The CFIUS's recommendation on covered transaction is also submitted to the president.[146] In the event that the CFIUS fails to reach a decision to present a single recommendation to the president, the differing views among the CFIUS members must also be reported to the president by the chairperson.[147] The president shall consider, as appropriate, whether to take action to suspend or prohibit any covered transaction, on the basis of the analysis of whether there is credible evidence to believe that a covered transaction might impair national security, as well as the explanation as to why legal instruments other than national security review are inadequate and inappropriate to protect US national security.[148] The time period for the president to announce a final decision on whether or not to take action to suspend or prohibit the proposed transaction is 15 days.[149]

5.2.3.3 Comparison

In respect to the review process, China has once again made an attempt at referring to its US counterpart. China's general review and special investigation are identical to two successive US instances of preliminary national security review and national security investigation. There are, however, some significant differences between the review processes in the two jurisdictions. First, the US has an additional phase which is exclusive to the president. The authority over national security review was originally granted to the president, and the CFIUS's responsibility for conducting national security reviews and national security investigations stems from the president. It is rational for the president to make a final decision, to improve the efficiency of the normal review process on the one hand and, on the other, to show a prudent US attitude towards the blocking of foreign investment, a power confined to the highest executive level, the president.

Second, unlike China, whose principles for entering national security investigations are vague, the US provides a detailed explanation of whether a back-to-back special investigation shall be conducted. It is expressly stipulated, for example, that, in the US, foreign investment which is controlled by foreign government will automatically enter national security review, while in China, it could be approved at the stage of the first general review if it is deemed not to threaten China's national security. In practice, given the facts that both the general review and the special investigation are subject to explicit time limitations by statute, and the CFIUS needs more time to reach a final decision, the review body often pushes the review process into the special investigation phase.

Third, the timeframes of national security reviews adopted in China and the US are different. China's general review is completed within 30 working days, while the initial phase of the US national security review is completed within 45 working days. Usually, China's special investigation has to be completed within 60 working days, while US national security investigations are required to be completed within 45 working days. Both of these second-tier investigation phases, however, provide extensions for extraordinary cases. To be specific, US national security investigations can be completed within 60 working days in extraordinary cases, while there is no time limitation on extensions of China's special investigation. The two-step review procedure in China takes up to 90 business days, while the timeline of the three-tier US national security review allows for a maximum of 120 days, from the official launch of the review to the final decision of the president.

Fourth, even though mitigation agreements can be reached to achieve approval from the national security review in both China and the US, this occurs in a different manner in each jurisdiction. In China, approval with mitigation conditions will occur only in the second tier, namely, special investigation, while mitigation conditions can be reached throughout the process of US national security review, either preliminary national security review or national security investigation. That is to say that in China, if special review is not undertaken, approval with conditions will not transpire in the stage of general review. Also, in China, it is expressed in the Measures that if the party undertakes in writing to accept the imposed conditions, its transaction can be approved.[150] This indicates that mitigation conditions may be made neither by the parties themselves nor by the negotiations between the review body and the relevant parties. Rather, they may be made unilaterally only by the review body, the WMO.

5.2.4 Implementation of Review Decision

5.2.4.1 China

It is the WMO in conjunction with relevant departments and local people's governments that is responsible for supervising the implementation of review decisions.[151] For foreign investment that obtains an approval conditionally, the implementation of conditions may be verified by means such as requiring the provision of relevant supporting materials and conducting an on-site inspection.[152] Where any foreign investment passes security review conditionally but the party fails to make the investment in compliance with the imposed conditions, the WMO can order it to take corrective action. If it refuses to do so, the WMO will order it to dispose of its resultant equities or assets within a specified period and take other necessary measures to restore matters to the state before the investment was made and eliminate the effect on national security.[153]

5.2.4.2 The US

The mitigation agreement can be made at any time during the whole review process. There is a discretionary power for the CFIUS or a lead agency, on its behalf to negotiate, impose, and enforce any agreement or condition with any party to the covered transaction in order to mitigate any risk to US national security that arises as a result of the covered transaction.[154] Mitigation measures will not only be adopted for pending transactions but also for withdrawn deals, with attempts to avoid any potential risks to national security caused by withdrawal of foreign investment which might elude CFIUS scrutiny.[155]

The mitigation authority is exercised by the CFIUS. In addition to the CFIUS's power to recommend suspension of a covered transaction under national security investigation, the CFIUS's determination of whether to negotiate, enter into or impose, or enforce any agreement or condition is required to be made on a risk-based analysis.[156] This risk-based analysis involves an assessment of the threat, vulnerabilities, and consequences to national security related to the transaction.[157] It is worth noting that the risk-based analysis is quite different from the analysis which is made by the DNI. It is only made by certain CFIUS members to support their recommendations to suspend specific transactions, to refer to the president or to reach a mitigation agreement, and on the basis of the risk-based analysis, the mitigation measures must be reasonably necessary to address the risk.[158] The thorough analysis expeditiously made by the DNI, by contrast, involves any threat to US national security posed by a covered transaction.[159] In addition, the CFIUS undertakes the responsibility of developing and agreeing upon methods for evaluating compliance with the mitigation agreement or condition, as well as enforcing such compliance.[160]

Once the mitigation agreement or condition is reached, the lead agency is responsible for negotiating, modifying, monitoring, and enforcing, on behalf of the CFIUS, such an agreement or condition, on the basis of the designated department or agency's expertise and knowledge of the issues.[161] The lead agency may, at its discretion, seek and receive the assistance of other departments or agencies in fulfilling the purpose of eliminating national security risks.[162] In the event that a mitigation agreement is in effect in relation to a covered transaction, the CFIUS or lead agency, as the case may be, shall formulate, adhere to, and keep updated a plan for monitoring compliance with the agreement.[163]

The designated lead agency in connection with a mitigation agreement on a covered transaction shall provide periodic reports to the CFIUS on any material modification to any such agreement or condition imposed with respect to the transaction, and, in the meantime, ensure that any material modification to any such agreement or condition is reported to the DNI, the Attorney General of the US, and any other federal department or agency that may have a material interest in such modification.[164] If at any time after a mitigation agreement or condition is effective, the CFIUS or the lead agency determines that the concerned parties have not complied with the terms of the agreement or condition, actions may be taken, including negotiation of a plan of action for the party or parties, requiring that they submit a written notice or declaration, or seeking injunctive relief, in order to remedy the lack of compliance.[165] In terms of imposed mitigation agreement or condition, both the chairperson and the lead agency must periodically review its appropriateness, and promptly terminate, phase out, or otherwise amend it if it is no longer required in relation to the addressed threat.[166] This allows the CFIUS adequately to ensure compliance without unnecessarily diverting its resources from assessing any new covered transaction for which a written notice or declaration has been filed and, if necessary, reaching a mitigation agreement with or imposing a condition on a party to such covered transaction or any covered transaction for which a review has been reopened for any reason.[167]

5.2.4.3 Comparison

One area of apparent difference between the two jurisdictions is that the US provides detailed requirements on how to reach mitigation measures in practice and how to supervise their implementation, while China offers only a general principle. Another key difference is that, in China, authority for implementing and supervising mitigation measures rests with the WMO, and relevant departments and local governments, while in the US, it lies with the lead agency designated by the CFIUS. In addition, only in the US is there a decision-making role for the president. In order to implement and enforce presidential decisions, the attorney general of the US is directed by the president to seek appropriate relief, including divestment, in the US district courts, without any statutory ambiguities in stipulating that the presidential decision and the actions of the president are not subject to judicial review.[168]

5.2.5 Supervision

5.2.5.1 China

Similar to previous rules on national security review, the Measures in the legal regime of the FIL still fail to provide provisions on review supervision, indicating that the WMO is not subject to any bottom-up or top-down accountability mechanism. Unfortunately, the MOFCOM Draft FIL, which was the only legal document to address this—by establishing a mechanism for supervision of implementation of review decisions, a requirement to publish guidance on security review, and an annual report on security review—was ineffective in China.[169] In the absence of these rules, the WMO appears free from any political intervention or supervision by a higher authority.

5.2.5.2 The US

The Congress has continually played a significant ex post role in supervising national security review conducted by the CFIUS or the president, be it during the review process or in annual reporting requirements. To be specific, upon completion of a preliminary national security review that concludes action, the chairperson and the lead agency are required to transmit a certified notice and a certified written report on the results of the investigation to the specified members of Congress, unless the matter under investigation has been referred to the president for decision.[170] In the event of a request from any specified member of Congress and if deemed necessary by the sensitivity of the information the CFIUS must promptly provide the congressional staff of such a member of Congress having appropriate security clearance with briefings on such a transaction, or on compliance with a mitigation agreement or condition imposed with respect to such transaction, on a classified basis.[171]

In addition to the oversight on each reviewed investment conducted by the CFIUS, the Congress aims to enhance its supervision on the overall national security review situation through an annual reporting requirement. Under the FIRRMA, the chairperson is required to transmit a report on all of the reviews and investigations of covered transactions completed during the 12-month period to the chairman and ranking member of the committee of jurisdiction in the Senate and the House of Representatives, before July 31 of each year.[172] The comprehensive report covers the information with respect to all notifications, reviews, investigations, withdrawals, presidential decisions, and mitigations for the period, as well as a detailed discussion of all perceived adverse effects on US national security.[173] In order to assist the Congress in its oversight responsibilities with respect to the annual report, the latter must also provide the following three items: first, an evaluation of whether there is credible evidence of a coordinated strategy by one or more countries or companies to acquire US companies involved in research, development, or production of critical technologies for which the US is a leading producer;[174] second, an evaluation of whether there are industrial espionage activities directed or directly assisted by foreign governments against private US companies aimed at obtaining commercial secrets related to critical technologies;[175] third, a description of the technologies recommended by the chairperson for identification.[176]

5.2.6 Information Confidentiality

5.2.6.1 China

The Measures contain one provision about information confidentiality. Where the foreign investment security review works, any official of a state agency who abuses regulatory power, neglects duties, practices favoritism, makes falsifications, divulges a state secret, or divulges a trade secret to which he or she has access, shall be subject to disciplinary action in accordance with the CPC rules and, if the act is criminally punishable, be held criminally liable in accordance with the law.[177]

5.2.6.2 The US

With respect to the requirement of information confidentiality, any information or documentary material filed with the president or the CFIUS pursuant to national security review shall be exempt for disclosure, and no such information or documentary material may be made public.[178] The Congress, which holds the power of supervision, is subject to the same limitations on disclosure of information.[179] The following four exceptions provide for informational confidentiality. First, information relevant to any administrative or judicial action or proceeding;[180] second, information provided to Congress or any duly authorized committee or subcommittee of Congress;[181] third information important to national security analysis or actions of the CFIUS provided to any domestic governmental entity, or to any foreign governmental entity of a US ally or partner, under the exclusive discretion and authorization of the chairperson, only to the extent necessary for national security purposes, and subject to appropriate confidentiality and classification requirements;[182] fourth, information that the parties have consented to be disclosed to third parties.[183]

5.2.6.3 Comparison

As regards disclosure of information regarding the public announcement of review proceedings and outcomes, China's national security review incorporate no duty to disclose any information to the public. The provision that officials who divulge a state secret, or divulge a trade secret to which they have access shall be punished, however, indicates the principle of information confidentiality to some extent. In contrast, the US national security review has a comprehensive information disclosure requirement, involving the publication of legislation, executive orders, regulations, filing instructions, annual reports, as well as governmental speeches, all of which must be readily accessible in the public domain. Even though both China and the US stress the principle of information confidentiality during the review process, their purposes are quite different. In China, the purpose of information confidentiality is mainly to protect state secrets and commercial secrets, with greater emphasis on state secrets. In the US, informational confidentiality focuses on transaction details, which prevent commercial information from being disclosed to the public.

5.2.7 Effectiveness

Both China and the US have established safe harbors, which provide assurance for transactions already subject to national security review that such foreign investment will gain immunity to a reopening or a revisit by the review body in the future. In China, for example, the parties concerned may implement the investment if the WMO makes a decision to pass the security review with respect to such a foreign investment. In the US, if the CFIUS has advised a party or parties in writing that a particular transaction triggered by a voluntary notification is not a covered transaction, or parties have been advised in writing that the CFIUS has concluded all actions with respect to their proposed transaction, or the president has previously announced his decision not to exercise any of his authority pertaining to the transaction, neither the CFIUS nor the president has the statutory power to reopen a transaction already reviewed or cleared by the CFIUS.[184]

Evergreen provisions, however, are also provided to safeguard national security. In China, there is a possibility that foreign transactions which have been subject to a national security review and have been cleared by the review body in the past could be subject to a revisit.[185] To be specific, even if the review process is completed and the review decision made, such a decision might be revoked if the party concerned provides false materials or conceals relevant information to defraud the security review.[186] More importantly, where, after the WMO decides that a security review of a reported foreign investment is not required or a reported foreign investment passes the security review, the party amends its investment plan, affecting or being likely to affect national security, the party is also required to report anew to the WMO.[187] In this case, it seems that no matter what kinds of actions are taken, foreign investment transactions which have previously been reviewed and approved with conditions do not obtain immunity from scrutiny and will continuously be scrutinized in relation to national security concerns.

Similarly, in the US, a review of a transaction that has previously been reviewed could be initiated under either of the following extraordinary circumstances. First, if any party to the transaction submitted false or misleading material information to the CFIUS in connection with the CFIUS's consideration of the transaction, or omitted material information, including material documents, from information submitted to the CFIUS, a reviewed transaction which has already been completed must be reopened.[188] Second, if any party to the transaction or the entity resulting from consummation of the transaction materially breaches a mitigation agreement or condition, which is certified to the CFIUS by the lead department or agency monitoring and enforcing such agreement or condition as a material breach, and at the same time, the CFIUS determines that there are no other adequate and appropriate remedies or enforcement tools available to address such breach, national security review may be re-initiated.[189] It can be concluded that, both in China and the US, the reopening of review procedures may be triggered by either deliberate or negligent misconduct of foreign investors.

5.3 Exclusive Rules in the US

5.3.1 Funding

A fund known as the Committee on Foreign Investment in the United States Fund (Fund), which was introduced by the FIRRMA, is held by the Treasury and administered by the chairperson of the CFIUS and intended to perform the functions of the CFIUS and allow more resources to be allocated to the CFIUS.[190] To be specific, the chairperson may transfer any amounts in the Fund to any other department or agency represented on the CFIUS for the purpose of addressing emerging needs in carrying out activities under national security review.[191] The Fund will help the CFIUS to support the work of the Department of Treasury for CFIUS activities with the full complement of staff necessary to ensure that the CFIUS's notoriously heavy workload can be handled adequately.[192] It is recommended to allocate the fund to hire additional full-time staff for CFIUS activities.[193] Such a request in the government's annual budget would be made by the president, who is authorized to determine whether and to what extent the expansion of the CFIUS's responsibilities as a result of the additional duties designated by the FIRRMA requires additional resources.[194]

With the endorsement of the Fund, the DOJ has made an effort to request a significant budget increase for its national security division for review of foreign investments.[195] Its budget proposal for the fiscal year 2020, for example, requested an increase of US$5 million and 21 members of staff, including 16 attorneys for its national security division, to assist with reviewing foreign investment transactions, compared with nine attorneys within its existing budget level.[196] This implies increasing US desire to increase significantly its current staff working on national security matters concerning foreign investment, monitor a larger range of foreign investment activities, and better safeguard national security.

In addition, a fee schedule was accordingly introduced through the FIRRMA.[197] The CFIUS may assess and collect a fee in an amount determined by the CFIUS.[198] The amount of the filing fee assessed with respect to a covered transaction shall not exceed an amount equal to the lesser of 1 percent of the value of the transaction, or US$300,000 adjusted annually for inflation.[199] On the one hand, this arrangement attempts to enable filing fees to be collected from each reviewed transaction on a case-by-case basis, to provide sufficient resources to the CFIUS and its members and strengthen their capability when conducting the national security review. On the other hand, through a limited and reasonable filing fee, the US intends to maintain the attractiveness of its domestic market to foreign investment and reduce the investment burden as far as possible.

5.3.2 Penalties and Damages

The legal rule of penalties and damages is another exclusive feature of the US national security review. All information provided to the CFIUS by any party to a covered transaction is subject to the False Statements Accountability Act.[200] In any case of a material misstatement, omission, or a false certification accompanied with a declaration or notice, such party may be liable to the US for a civil penalty not to exceed US$250,000 per violation.[201] Precisely the same civil penalty also applies to failures to comply with the requirements of mandatory declaration, where the concerned party may be liable to the US for a civil penalty not to exceed the value of the transaction, whichever is greater.[202] Generally, the amount of the penalty imposed for a violation is determined in accordance with the nature of the violation.[203]

In addition, the mitigation agreement may include a provision providing for liquidated or actual damages for breaches of the agreement, with specific explanation on the amount of any liquidated damages that are caused by the breach of such agreement, as well as a provision that the CFIUS may consider the severity of the breach in deciding whether to seek a lesser amount than that stipulated in the agreement.[204] Once the determination to impose penalties is made by the CFIUS, the concerned party shall be provided with a notice of the penalty, including a written explanation of the conduct to be penalized and the amount of the penalty.[205] Upon receiving such a penalty notice, the subject person can submit to the chairperson a petition for reconsideration, including a defense, justification, or explanation for such penalized conduct, within 15 business days of receipt of such notice, for the CFIUS to review the petition and issue any final penalty determination.[206] This provides an opportunity for the CFIUS and the subject person to reach an agreement on an appropriate remedy at any time before the CFIUS issues any final penalty determination.[207]

Notes

1 Measures on Security Review for Foreign Investment (2020) (Measures), Article 3.
2 Circular of the General Office of the State Council on Issuing the Trial Measures for the National Security Review of Foreign investment in the Pilot Free Trade Zone (State Council Circular 24), Article 3(1).
3 Circular of the General Office of the State Council on the Establishment of Security Review System Regarding Merger and Acquisition of Domestic Enterprises by Foreign Investors (State Council Circular 6), Article 3(3).
4 Liu, Ziyu. "Security Review in the Evolution of Foreign Investment Law with Chinese Characteristics: Part I." *Business Law Review* 41, no. 5 (2020): 178.
5 Notice of the NDRC No. 4 (2019) (NDRC Notice 4).

6 Liu, Ziyu. "Security Review in the Evolution of Foreign Investment Law with Chinese Characteristics: Part I." *Business Law Review* 41, no. 5 (2020): 177.
7 State Council Circular 6, Article 4(1); MOFCOM Announcement of Provisions on the Implementation of the Security Review System for Mergers and Acquisitions of Domestic Enterprises by Foreign Investors (MOFCOM Announcement 53), Article 6.
8 Liu, Ziyu. "Security Review in the Evolution of Foreign Investment Law with Chinese Characteristics: Part I." *Business Law Review* 41, no. 5 (2020): 177.
9 Liu, Ziyu. "Security Review in the Evolution of Foreign Investment Law with Chinese Characteristics: Part I." *Business Law Review* 41, no. 5 (2020): 177.
10 State Council Circular 6, Article 3(2).
11 State Council Circular 6, Article 3(2); State Council Circular 24, Article 3(1).
12 Liu, Ziyu. "Security Review in the Evolution of Foreign Investment Law with Chinese Characteristics: Part I." *Business Law Review* 41, no. 5 (2020): 177.
13 Liu, Ziyu. "Security Review in the Evolution of Foreign Investment Law with Chinese Characteristics: Part I." *Business Law Review* 41, no. 5 (2020): 178.
14 NDRC Notice 4; Bian, Cheng. *National Security Review of Foreign Investment: A Comparative Legal Analysis of China, the United States and the European Union*. London: Routledge, 2020, 78.
15 Executive Order No. 11858.
16 50 U.S.C. § 4565 (k)(2); Executive Order No. 13456, Sec.3 (b).
17 Bian, Cheng. *National Security Review of Foreign Investment: A Comparative Legal Analysis of China, the United States and the European Union*. London: Routledge, 2020, 111.
18 50 U.S.C. § 4565 (k)(2).
19 Executive Order No. 13456, Sec 3 (c).
20 Executive Order No. 13456, Sec 3 (c). Sec 4 (c); 50 U.S.C. § 4565 (k)(3).
21 50 U.S.C. § 4565 (h)(2)(A); 50 U.S.C. § 4565 (h)(2)(B)(i).
22 50 U.S.C. § 4565 (h)(2)(C); 50 U.S.C. § 4565 (h)(2)(B)(ii); 50 U.S.C. § 4565 (h)(2)(D); Executive Order No. 13456, Sec.4 (a).
23 Executive Order No. 13456, Sec.4 (d).
24 50 U.S.C. § 4565 (h)(1).
25 50 U.S.C. § 4565 (k)(5).
26 Lewis, James A. "New Objective for CFIUS: Foreign Ownership, Critical Infrastructure, and Communications Interception." *Federal Communication Law Journal* 57 (2005): 457.
27 US Government Accountability Office. *Defense Trade: Enhancements to the Implementation of Exon-Florio Could Strengthen the Law's Effectiveness*. 2005. www.gao.gov/products/gao-05-686.
28 Byrne, Matthew R. "Protecting National Security and Promoting Foreign Investment: Maintaining the Exon-Florio Balance." *Ohio State Law Journal* 67, no. 4 (2006): 908–910.
29 50 U.S.C. § 4565 (l)(3)(A); Executive Order No. 13456, Sec.5 (b).
30 50 U.S.C. § 4565 (l)(3)(B)(i)(I)-(II).
31 Uniting and Strengthening America by Providing Appropriate Tools to Restrict, Intercept and Obstruct Terrorism Act of 2001 (Patriot Act).
32 50 U.S.C. § 4565 (b)(1)(C); 50 U.S.C. § 4565 (b)(4)(A) and (C); 50 U.S.C. § 4565 (b)(4)(E); Cox (see n 468), p. 310.
33 50 U.S.C. § 4565 (b)(4)(A)(i)-(ii); 50 U.S.C. § 4565 (b)(4)(B)(i); 50 U.S.C. § 4565 (b)(4)(F).
34 50 U.S.C. § 4565 (b)(4)(C).
35 50 U.S.C. § 4565 (l)(3)(A)-(B).
36 50 U.S.C. § 4565 (k)(2)(H).
37 31 C.F.R. Part § 800.602.
38 50 U.S.C. § 2170 (h) (3)(C); 31 C.F.R. Part § 800.508.

39 31 C.F.R. Part § 800.508; Graham and Marchick (see n 21), p. 30.
40 Graham, Edward M. and Marchick, David Matthew. *US National Security and Foreign Investment*. Washington, DC: Institute for International Economics, 2006, 35.
41 Bian, Cheng. *National Security Review of Foreign Investment: A Comparative Legal Analysis of China, the United States and the European Union*. London: Routledge, 2020, 195.
42 Foreign Investment Law (FIL), Article 2.
43 FIL, Article 35.
44 State Council Circular 24, Article 1(1).
45 Measures, Article 4.
46 Measures, Article 4; Pan, Cindy, Lian, Zhelong and Zhou, Zhenyi. "China: China Released New Measures on Security Review of Foreign Investment." 2021. www.mondaq.com/china/inward-foreign-investment/1021876/china-released-new-measures-on-security-review-of-foreign-investment.
47 Measures, Article 4.
48 Measures, Article 4.
49 Measures, Article 4.
50 Measures, Article 4.
51 Pan, Cindy, Lian, Zhelong and Zhou, Zhenyi. "China: China Released New Measures on Security Review of Foreign Investment." 2021. www.mondaq.com/china/inward-foreign-investment/1021876/china-released-new-measures-on-security-review-of-foreign-investment.
52 50 U.S.C. § 4565 (a)(4)(B)(i); 31 C.F.R. Part § 800.210.
53 31 C.F.R. Part § 800.208(a).
54 31 C.F.R. Part § 800.208(b).
55 50 U.S.C. § 4565 (a)(4)(B)(iii)(II) and (a)(4)(D)(i)(III)(bb); 50 U.S.C. § 4565 (a)(4)(B)(iii)(I) and (a)(4)(D)(i)(III)(cc); 50 U.S.C. § 4565 (a)(4)(B)(iii)(III) and (a)(4)(D)(i)(III)(aa).
56 50 U.S.C. § 4565 (a)(4)(D)(i)(III)(aa),(bb) and (cc); 31 C.F.R. Part § 800.248 (a)-(c); 31 C.F.R. Part § 800.248.
57 31 C.F.R. Part § 800.215.
58 31 C.F.R. Part § 800.211(a)(b).
59 50 U.S.C. § 4565 (a)(4)(B)(iv); 31 C.F.R. Part § 800.213(c).
60 50 U.S.C. § 4565 (a)(4)(B)(ii).
61 50 U.S.C. § 4565 (a)(4)(B)(ii).
62 31 C.F.R. Part § 800.213(d).
63 31 C.F.R. Part § 800, Appendix A; 31 C.F.R. Part § 800, Appendix B.
64 State Council Circular 24, Article 1.
65 Tzinova, Antonia I. and Bisk, Caroline D. "New CFIUS Regulation Finally Take Effect." 2020. www.hklaw.com/en/insights/publications/2020/02/new-cfius-regulations-finally-take-effect.
66 31 C.F.R. Part § 800.208(e); 31 C.F.R. Part § 800.211(d); 31 C.F.R. Part § 800.213(e); 31 C.F.R. Part § 800.241(c); 31 C.F.R. Part § 800.248(d).
67 State Council Circular 24, Article 1(3).
68 50 U.S.C. § 4565 (v)(IV)(bb)(BB); 31 CFR Part § 800.302 (b).
69 31 C.F.R. Part § 800.243.
70 Pan, Cindy, Lian, Zhelong and Zhou, Zhenyi. "China: China Released New Measures on Security Review of Foreign Investment." 2021. www.mondaq.com/china/inward-foreign-investment/1021876/china-released-new-measures-on-security-review-of-foreign-investment.
71 Bian, Cheng. *National Security Review of Foreign Investment: A Comparative Legal Analysis of China, the United States and the European Union*. London: Routledge, 2020, 187.

72 State Council Circular 24, Article 2(1); State Council Circular 6, Article 2(1).
73 State Council Circular 24, Article 2(2); State Council Circular 6, Article 2(2).
74 State Council Circular 24, Article 2(3). State Council Circular 6, Article 2(3).
75 State Council Circular 24, Article 2(4).
76 State Council Circular 24, Article 2(4).
77 State Council Circular 24, Article 2(6); State Council Circular 6, Article 2(4).
78 31 C.F.R. Part § 800.601(a)(1).
79 31 C.F.R. Part § 800.601(a)(2).
80 31 C.F.R. Part § 800.601(a)(3).
81 50 U.S.C. § 4565 (f)(1).
82 50 U.S.C. § 4565 (f)(2).
83 50 U.S.C. § 4565 (f)(3).
84 50 U.S.C. § 4565 (f)(4)(A)(i). It is under section 6(j) of the Export Administration Act of 1979 (section 4605(j) of 50 U.S.C.).
85 50 U.S.C. § 4565 (f)(4).
86 50 U.S.C. § 4565 (f)(5).
87 50 U.S.C. § 4565 (f)(6).
88 50 U.S.C. § 4565 (f)(7).
89 31 C.F.R. Part § 800.222.
90 50 U.S.C. § 4565 (f)(9).
91 50 U.S.C. § 4565 (f)(10).
92 50 U.S.C. § 4565 (f)(11).
93 Tzinova, Antonia I. and Bisk, Caroline D. "New CFIUS Regulation Finally Take Effect." 2020. www.hklaw.com/en/insights/publications/2020/02/new-cfius-regulations-finally-take-effect.
94 National Security Law (NSL), Article 2.
95 NSL, Article 3.
96 Bian, Cheng. *National Security Review of Foreign Investment: A Comparative Legal Analysis of China, the United States and the European Union*. London: Routledge, 2020, 203.
97 Measures, Article 4.
98 FIL, Article 2.
99 Measures, Article 5.
100 MOFCOM Announcement 53, Article 4.
101 Measures, Article 7.
102 Hartge, Cathleen Hamel. "China's National Security Review: Motivations and the Implications for Investors." *Stanford Journal of International Law* 49, no. 1 (2013): 116.
103 Measures, Article 6.
104 Measures, Article 6.
105 Measures, Article 7.
106 Measures, Article 7.
107 Measures, Article 15.
108 50 U.S.C. § 4565 (b)(1)(C)(i)(I); 50 U.S.C. § 4565 (b)(1)(D)(i).
109 50 U.S.C. § 4565 (b)(1)(C)(i)(I).
110 31 C.F.R. Part § 800.501(i).
111 31 C.F.R. Part § 800.501(a).
112 50 U.S.C. § 4565 (b)(1)(C)(i)(II)(bb).
113 31 C.F.R. Part § 800.501(h).
114 31 C.F.R. Part § 800.501(o).
115 50 U.S.C. § 4565 (b)(1)(C)(vi)(I); 50 U.S.C. § 4565 (b)(1)(C)(i)(II)(cc).
116 50 U.S.C. § 4565 (b)(1)(D)(i); 50 U.S.C. § 4565 (b)(F).
117 31 C.F.R. Part § 800.501(b).

118 Pudner, Stephen K. "Moving Forward from Dubai Ports World-The Foreign Investment and National Security Act of 2007." *Alabama Law Review* 59, no. 4 (2007): 1285.
119 50 U.S.C. § 4565 (b)(1)(D)(ii).
120 50 U.S.C. § 4565 (b)(1)(D)(iii).
121 31 C.F.R. Part § 800.501(c)(1)(i); 31 C.F.R. Part § 800.501(d).
122 50 U.S.C. § 4565 (b)(1)(C)(v)(IV)(aa).
123 31 C.F.R. Part § 800.401(b); 50 U.S.C. § 4565 (b)(1)(C)(v)(IV)(bb)(AA).
124 31 C.F.R. Part § 800.401(c)(1); 31 C.F.R. Part § 800.401(c)(2).
125 31 C.F.R. Part § 800.406(c).
126 31 C.F.R. Part § 800.406(d).
127 50 U.S.C. § 4565 (b)(1)(C)(v)(IV)(ff)(AA)-(BB).
128 31 C.F.R. Part § 800.404(e).
129 Measures, Article 8.
130 Measures, Article 9.
131 Measures, Article 8.
132 Measures, Article 8.
133 Measures, Article 8.
134 Measures, Article 8.
135 Measures, Article 9.
136 Measures, Article 9.
137 Measures, Article 9.
138 50 U.S.C. § 4565 (b)(1)(A)(i); 50 U.S.C. § 4565 (b)(1)(F).
139 50 U.S.C. § 4565 (b)(2)(B)(i)(I)-(III); 31 C.F.R. Part § 800.505(b)(1)-(3); 31 C.F.R. Part § 800.505(a)(1)-(2); 50 U.S.C. § 4565 (b)(2)(B)(ii).
140 31 C.F.R. Part § 800.507(a); 50 U.S.C. § 4565 (b)(2)(A)-(C); 31 C.F.R. Part § 800.505(a).
141 Bian, Cheng. *National Security Review of Foreign Investment: A Comparative Legal Analysis of China, the United States and the European Union*. London: Routledge, 2020, 117.
142 31 C.F.R. Part § 800.508(f); 31 C.F.R. Part § 800.508(e); 50 U.S.C. § 4565 (b)(2)(C)(ii)(I).
143 31 C.F.R. Part § 800.508(e), 50 U.S.C. § 4565 (b)(2)(C)(ii)(II).
144 31 C.F.R. Part § 800.508(d).
145 31 C.F.R. Part § 800.508 (b)(1)(3).
146 50 U.S.C. § 4565 (d)(4)(A)-(B); 31 C.F.R. Part § 800.508 (c).
147 31 C.F.R. Part § 800.508(c).
148 50 U.S.C. § 4565 (f); 50 U.S.C. § 4565 (d)(4).
149 50 U.S.C. § 4565 (d)(2).
150 Measures, Article 9.
151 Measures, Article 13.
152 Measures, Article 13.
153 Measures, Article 18.
154 50 U.S.C. § 4565 (l)(3)(A)(i),(iii).
155 50 U.S.C. § 4565 (l)(3)(A)(ii).
156 50 U.S.C. § 4565 (l)(4)(B)(ii)(I)-(II).
157 50 U.S.C. § 4565 (l) (4)(A).
158 50 U.S.C. § 4565 (l)(1)(B).
159 50 U.S.C. § 4565 (b)(4)(A)(i).
160 50 U.S.C. § 4565 (l)(3)(C)(i)-(iii).
161 50 U.S.C. § 4565 (l)(6)(A).
162 50 U.S.C. § 4565 (l)(6)(A).
163 50 U.S.C. § 4565 (l)(6)(C)(ii).
164 50 U.S.C. § 4565 (l) (6)(B).

165 50 U.S.C. § 4565 (l)(3)(D).
166 50 U.S.C. § 4565 (l)(3)(B).
167 50 U.S.C. § 4565 (l)(6)(G).
168 50 U.S.C. § 4565 (e)(1).
169 MOFCOM Draft FIL, Articles 67, 68, 69.
170 50 U.S.C. § 4565 (b)(3)(A)-(B).
171 50 U.S.C. § 4565 (g)(1).
172 50 U.S.C. § 4565 (m)(1).
173 50 U.S.C. § 4565 (m)(3).
174 50 U.S.C. § 4565 (m)(3)(A).
175 50 U.S.C. § 4565 (m)(3)(B).
176 50 U.S.C. § 4565 (m)(3).
177 Measures, Article 20.
178 50 U.S.C. § 4565 (c)(1).
179 50 U.S.C. § 4565 (g)(2)(A)-(B).
180 50 U.S.C. § 4565 (c)(2)(A).
181 50 U.S.C. § 4565 (c)(2)(B).
182 50 U.S.C. § 4565 (c)(2)(C).
183 50 U.S.C. § 4565 (c)(2)(D).
184 31 C.F.R. Part § 800.601(a); Cox, Jason. "Regulation of Foreign Direct Investment after the Dubai Ports Controversy: Has the US Government Finally Figured Out How to Balance Foreign Threats to National Security Without Alienating Foreign Companies?" *The Journal of Corporation Law* 34, no. 1 (2008): 303.
185 Measures, Article 17.
186 Measures, Article 17.
187 Measures, Article 14.
188 50 U.S.C. § (b)(1)(D)(ii).
189 50 U.S.C. § (b)(1)(D)(iii)(I)-(III).
190 50 U.S.C. § 4565 (p)(1).
191 50 U.S.C. § 4565 (p)(4).
192 Heck (see n 1101).
193 Heck, Denny. "Support Robust Funding for the Committee on Foreign Investment in the United States (CFIUS) in FY 2021." http://dearcolleague.us/2020/03/support-robust-funding-for-the-committee-on-foreign-investment-in-the-united-states-cfius-in-fy2021/.
194 Jackson, James K. "The Committee on Foreign Investment in the United States (CFIUS)." https://fas.org/sgp/crs/natsec/RL33388.pdf.
195 Dunn, Gibson. "CFIUS Developments: Notable Cases and Key Trends." 2019. www.gibsondunn.com/cfius-developments-notable-cases-and-key-trends/.
196 Dunn, Gibson. "CFIUS Developments: Notable Cases and Key Trends." 2019. www.gibsondunn.com/cfius-developments-notable-cases-and-key-trends/.
197 50 U.S.C. § 4565 (p)(3)(C)(i).
198 50 U.S.C. § 4565 (p)(3)(A).
199 50 U.S.C. § 4565 (p)(3)(B)(i)(I).
200 31 C.F.R. Part § 800.901 (h).
201 31 C.F.R. Part § 800.901(a).
202 31 C.F.R. Part § 800.901(b).
203 31 C.F.R. Part § 800.901(a) and (b).
204 31 C.F.R. Part § 800.901(d).
205 31 C.F.R. Part § 800.901(e).
206 31 C.F.R. Part § 800.901(f).
207 31 C.F.R. Part § 800.901(f).

6 A Constructivist Approach to China and US Investments in the Context of National Security Review

6.1 Chinese Investment and US National Security Review

China and the US have quite different political and social regimes, and China is not a strategic ally of the US. It seems hard or even impossible for China to cooperate with the CFIUS on national security review. According to Table 6.1 and Figure 6.1, the number of Chinese investments under US national security review has rapidly increased, from one in 2005, 1.56 percent of total investments reviewed, to 24 in 2014, or 16.32 percent.[1] Since 2012, China has accounted for the largest proportion of cases reviewed on national security grounds by the CFIUS, at an annual rate of around 20 percent for eight consecutive years.[2] From 2012 to 2014, China began to be ranked first in the world, with 68 transactions reviewed by the CFIUS, which reviewed a total of 358. It was followed by the UK with 45, Canada with 40, and Japan with 37.[3] Of the 552 transactions that the CFIUS reviewed between 2015 and 2017, over 25 percent, the most of any country, were Chinese investments.[4] In 2022, there were 36 cases, accounting for 12.59 percent of the total.[5]

Even though the year 2018 witnessed a decreased proportion of Chinese investments reviewed by US national security review, this does not indicate that Chinese investment is eluding US national security scrutiny. The main reason for this result was the serious economic conflicts referred to as "the trade war" which took place in 2018, resulting in the decrease in the total number of Chinese investments in the US. In 2019, for example, Chinese investment in the US dropped to US$5 billion, the lowest amount since the financial crisis in 2009.[6] From 2017 to 2020, however, the number of prohibited Chinese investments increased even as Chinese investments in the US decreased, demonstrating the US's improved oversight of Chinese investment.[7] As Table 4 appears to show, since the national security review for foreign investment was established in the US in 1988, presidential decisions have been made only in relation to seven acquisitions, one of which was connected to China, while the rest were all Chinese investments.

Table 6.2 shows US presidential actions on foreign investment from 1980 to 2020. Soon after the passage of the Exon-Florio Amendment, President George Bush issued the first presidential action in 1990 and ordered the CATIC, a state-run corporation in China producing aircraft for defense and export markets, to divest

DOI: 10.4324/9781003543749-6

Table 6.1 Chinese Investment in US National Security Review from 2005 to 2022

Year	*Total Number of National Security Review*	*Number of Chinese Investments Under National Security Review*	*Proportion*
2005	64	1	1.56
2006	111	0	0
2007	138	3	2.17
2008	155	6	3.87
2009	65	4	6.15
2010	93	6	6.45
2011	111	10	9.01
2012	114	23	20.18
2013	97	21	21.65
2014	147	24	16.32
2015	143	29	20.28
2016	172	54	31.40
2017	237	60	25.32
2018	229	55	24.02
2019	231	25	10.82
2020	187	17	9.09
2021	272	44	16.18
2022	286	36	12.59
Total	2852	407	14.27

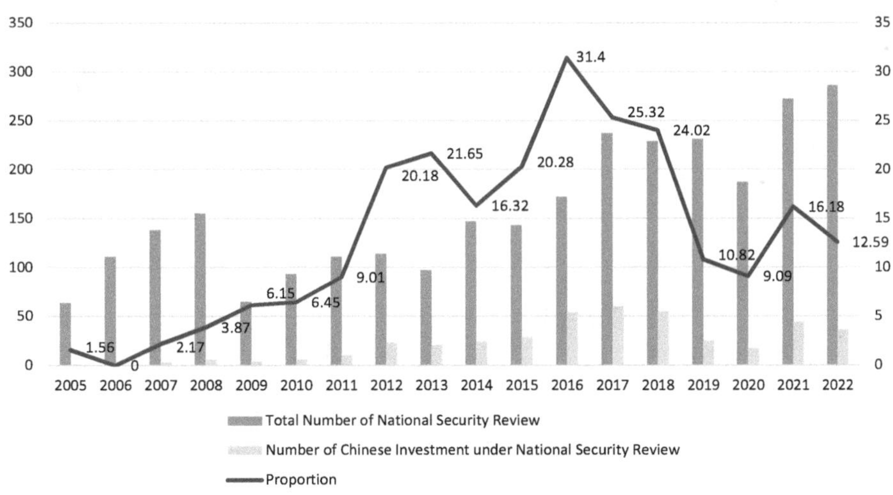

Figure 6.1 Chinese Investment in US National Security Review from 2005 to 2022

Table 6.2 US Presidential Actions on Foreign Investment from 1980 to 2020

Acquirer	*Target*	*Sector*	*Alleged Threat to US National Security*	*Year*	*President*
China National Aero-Technology Import and Export Corporation (CATIC)[13]	Mamco Manufacturing Inc.	Airplane component manufacture	The acquirer is likely to gain aircraft engine technology for military application	1990	George Bush
Ralls Corporation (US-based) and Sany Group (China-based)[14]	Terna Energy USA Holding	Wind farm	Target firm is in proximity to a naval weapons systems training facility	2012	Barack Obama
Grand Chip Investment GmbH (German-based) and Fujian Grand Chip Investment Fund LP (China-based)[15]	Aixtron, Inc, US business	Semiconductor	Acquirer may misuse the sensitive technology of missile defense systems held by the target company	2016	Barack Obama
Canyon Bridge Capital (US-based company, with a Chinese investor as its sole limited partner)[16]	Lattice	Semiconductor	Acquirer is foreign government controlled; Target company involved with technologies with potential military applications	2017	Donald Trump
Broaden (Singapore-based)[17]	Qualcomm	Semiconductor	Preserving US technology leadership in IT and communications	2018	Donald Trump
Stayntouch, Inc.	Beijing Shiji Information Technology Co., Ltd.	Software supplier to the hospitality industry	Sensitive nature of the data it collects in its software for the hotel, food service, retail, and entertainment industries	2020	Donald Trump
ByteDance Ltd[18]	Musical.ly (TikTok)	US social media app	Sensitive personal data	2020	Donald Trump

all interests in the Seattle-based aerospace manufacturer MAMCO.[8] The second was an action taken by President Obama in 2012 that directed Ralls to divest its interests in four wind farms in Oregon. President Obama also, in 2016, issued an executive order to prohibit Grand Chip Investment GmbH, a German entity owned by China's Fujian Grand Chip Investment Fund LP, from purchasing the US business of Aixtron SE, a German semiconductor equipment supplier.[9] Although most of the modifications in the FIRRMA came into effect in early 2020, Chinese investments had already been reviewed by the CFIUS, and some of them had ultimately failed national security reviews in the US. President Trump, for example, issued four executive orders during his presidency. To be specific, in September 2017, Canyon Bridge Capital Investment Limited, a US affiliate of China Venture Capital Fund Corporation Limited, was prohibited to acquire Lattice Semiconductor Corporation.[10] In March 2018, President Trump issued an executive order to prohibit Broadcom Limited from completing its attempted takeover of Qualcomm Incorporated.[11] The year 2020 saw two presidential orders on foreign investments, Beijing Shiji Information Technology's acquisition of StayNTouch in March, as well as the completed acquisition of Musical.ly by ByteDance.[12]

This number of presidential decisions on foreign investment does not show the full picture of US restrictions performed by the CFIUS, as, in practice and in many cases, before the CFIUS refers the transaction to the President for a final judgment, a large number of investors have already agreed to voluntarily divest their interest in a US business or abandoned their investment in many instances because of opposition from the CFIUS. From 2015 to 2019, for example, despite the fact that the president only formally made five presidential orders on foreign investment in the process of national security review, 56 transactions were abandoned in light of CFIUS-related national security concerns, including where the CFIUS imposed conditions that the parties found unacceptable, making no exception for Chinese investments.[19] The reformed national security review in the FIRRMA intended to address increasing national security concerns about Chinese investments, which might usher in a bitter winter for Chinese investment in the US.[20]

In practice, for example, ByteDance, a parent company of TikTok, is a well-known Chinese-owned technology firm, and in November 2017 it spent nearly US$1 billion to acquire the social video service Musical.ly, which is based in the US.[21] Clearance for this transaction, however, was not sought from the CFIUS.[22] When TikTok became the most downloaded application in the US, as a technology firm with over 100 million users both in the US and China, US concerns over cybersecurity—especially data security in relation to the collection and use of personal data—prompted the enforcement of a national security review into ByteDance. In August 2020, a pair of orders citing national security concerns were signed by President Trump to ban the application in the US and force ByteDance to sell its US assets. The orders alleged that TikTok captured information to threaten US national security as it offered the China's access to Americans' personal and proprietary information and potentially allowed China to track the locations of federal employees and contractors, build dossiers of personal information for blackmail, and conduct corporate espionage.[23] In terms of the second order that President Trump signed and which required ByteDance to divest from TikTok in the US, by November 12, 2020, an extension was granted by the CFIUS and confirmed by the Department of the Treasury, which has authority over acquisitions of US companies by foreign entities, and pushed the deadline 15 days from the original deadline.[24] This extension aimed to provide the parties and the CFIUS with additional time to resolve the case in a manner that complied with the order. TikTok had been working with the government to get approval in national security review, separating it somewhat from its Chinese parent company, ByteDance, and creating a new entity, TikTok Global, to include investments from Oracle and Walmart, with the hope of satisfying regulators' national security concerns.[25] Even as TikTok pursued a deal with US companies, it continued with a lawsuit against the Trump administration, asserting that the executive orders were unnecessary and unfair. This transaction illustrates that national security reviews conducted by the CFIUS may pay special attention to foreign investment, especially investments from China, on information and communications technology and services (ICTS), including data centers, mobile application services, and IT equipment providers.[26] Even more, an interim rule was issued by the Department of Commerce on implementing its sweeping new authority to block, unwind, or condition transactions in relation to ICTS, as a new lever in governing foreign investment and a distinct mechanism of import control entirely separate from export control review and national security review.[27]

6.2 Chinese Investors' Ideas on US National Security Review

Throughout three decades, from 1988 to 2019, the CFIUS received 3,428 applications, but 939 cases entered the investigation stage, accounting for 27.39 percent of the total number.[28] In the process of national security review, some transactions have been approved because there were no national security threats, and some deals were approved as they accepted the mitigation conditions set by the CFIUS, while only seven transactions were transferred to the president, accounting for 0.2 percent.[29] From 2016 to 2019, however, among 869 investments, 522 cases entered the investigation process, accounting for 60 percent.[30] This indicates that the scrutiny of foreign investment by national security review has been strengthened. A number of Chinese investments that have not been approved on national security grounds, or have even been prohibited by presidential order, resulted in China's external idea of discrimination by US national security review and being placed in a disadvantageous position.[31] In the Chinese view, national security reviews conducted by the CFIUS are one of the biggest obstacles facing Chinese investments in the US.

The Chinese perception of US national security review is significant to the point of determinative in relation to Chinese actions on whether to make national security review filings when investing in the US. It is therefore, necessary to explore the ideas of Chinese investors about US national security review. The business survey report on Chinese enterprises in the US (Survey) issued annually by the China General Chamber of Commerce (CGCC) serves as a reference for a partial analysis of Chinese investors' perceptions of US national security reviews, because the CGCC represented over 1,500 Chinese enterprises which invest and operate in the US, spanning a wide variety of sectors and locations, and such a report involved more than 500 distributed questionnaires.[32] The opinions found in this survey can be viewed as representative of the majority of Chinese investors in the US.[33]

It can be seen that nearly half of all Chinese enterprises investing in the US have no knowledge about the regulatory mechanism of national security review conducted by the CFIUS during the past years. In 2017, for example, 60 percent of Chinese investors were unaware of US national security review, while in 2019, 55 percent were not familiar with them.[34] Surprisingly, despite the news stories regarding the decline and failures of Chinese investment in the US because of the two countries' tense bilateral economic relations and reformed US national security review, as shown in Figure 6.2, around 55 percent of respondents in 2020 asserted their unfamiliarity with the national security review as updated in the FIRRMA.[35] The remaining respondents had knowledge about national security review, while nearly three quarters felt that they were politicized and opaque during these years.[36] In 2020, for example, only 11 percent of respondents viewed the national security review performed by the CFIUS as lawful and transparent.[37]

Against this background, the majority of the respondents did not consider filing notices with the CFIUS prior to investing in the US. As Figure 6.3 shows, both in 2014 and 2015, the majority of respondents did not consider applying for national security review when they made their investments, and this proportion increased to 60 percent in 2015, from 56 percent in 2014.[38] In 2015, only 7 percent of respondents had ever filed for national security review with the CFIUS, a 4 percent decline from the 2014 figure.[39] Based on the CGCC Survey, from 2014 to 2017, more than half of the respondents had not considered national security review, while the respondents who considered national security but thought it did not apply to them accounted for more than 20 percent.[40] The number of respondents that considered and did apply for national security review accounted for about 10 percent. Although there was a slight increase in filings with the CFIUS by Chinese investors, from 7 percent in 2015 to 13 percent in 2017, 64 percent of respondents did

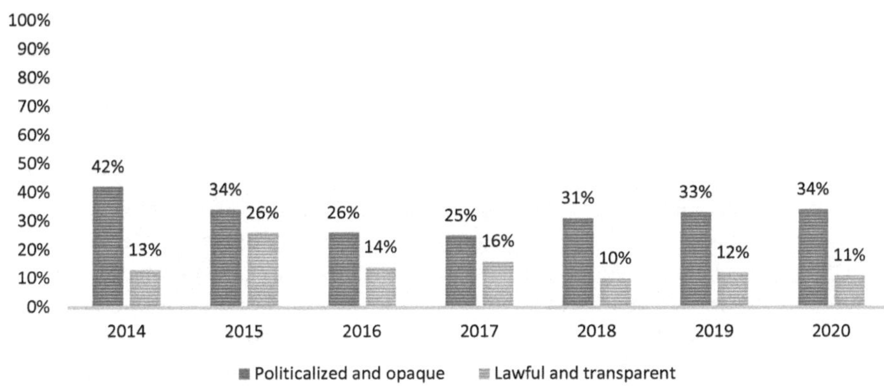

Figure 6.2 How Did Chinese Investors View CFIUS Review from 2014 to 2020?

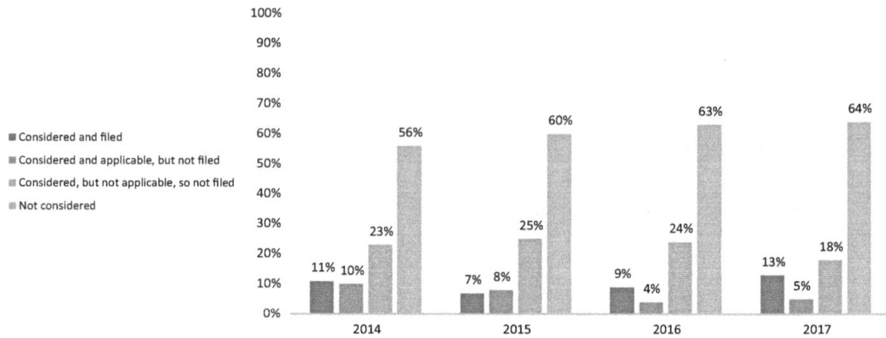

Figure 6.3 Percentages of Chinese Investors Who Considered Filing or Actually Filed for CFIUS Review from 2014 to 2017

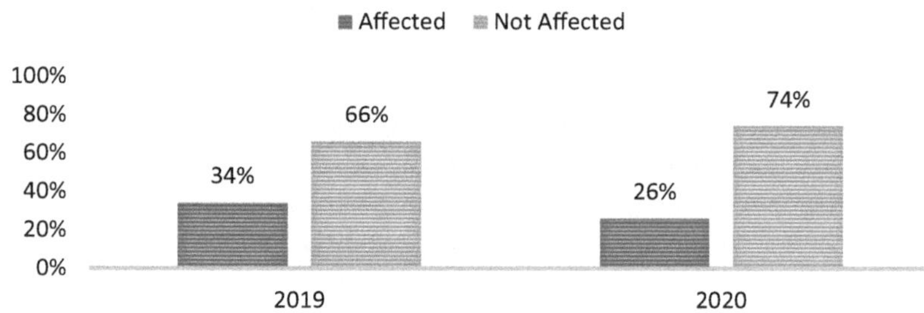

Figure 6.4 Implications of the CFIUS Review on Chinese Investment Plans from 2019 to 2020

not consider filing a notice with the CFIUS on national security review in 2017.[41] It can be concluded that the number of enterprises that have not applied for national security is as high as 90 percent of the total number of enterprises, and the number of enterprises that have carried out national security review accounts for only about 10 percent of the total number of respondents.[42] Although Chinese enterprises have invested in the US for several years, they have not paid enough attention to national security reviews conducted by the CFIUS, and more than 90 percent of respondents did not consider national security review to be a major barrier.[43]

Indeed, US national security review left a negative impression on Chinese investors. As demonstrated in Figure 6.4, in 2020, nearly one-third of respondents believed that their investment plans in the US were adversely affected by the CFIUS, whose heightened attention was paid to transactions involving Chinese companies.[44] Almost a quarter of respondents, however—74 percent—believed that US national security review did not cause any adverse impact to their businesses.[45]

Those who believe that US national security review will affect their investment plans hold the view that the role of the US national security review might be achieved by making them withdraw their investment plans, investment methods,

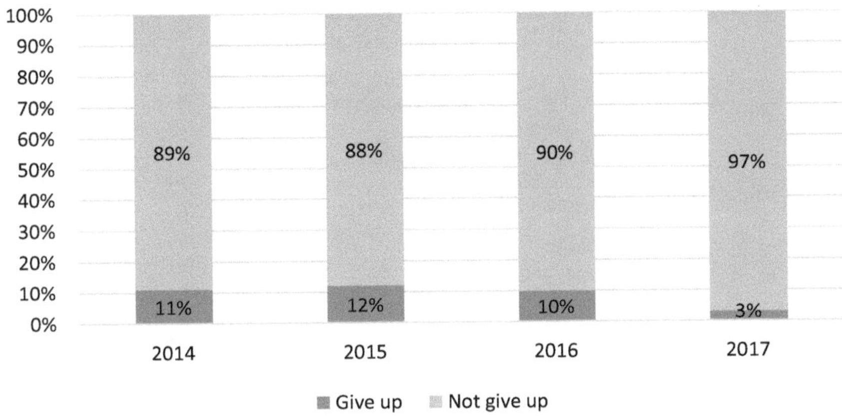

Figure 6.5 Chinese Investors' Response to CFIUS Review from 2014 to 2017

scale of investment or direction of business development in the US. According to the CGCC Survey, for example, in 2015, around 12 percent of respondents thought that they would even give up investment projects because of concerns about national security review, slightly 1 percent higher than those in 2014.[46] As Figure 6.5 shows, from 2014 to 2017, the percentage of respondents who decided not to pursue business in the US because of concerns about national security review remained low and decreased from 10 percent in 2016 to 3 percent in 2017, which is likely because the surveyed companies already operated in the US and were therefore less prone to pose any threat to US national security.[47] Although investing in the US presents a risk of national security review, only about 3 percent of Chinese enterprises would give up their investment plans because of fear of national security review, and nearly 97 percent of Chinese investors have not given up their investment in the US.[48] To some extent, this low proportion of investment plans abandoned because of national security review indicates that Chinese investors have not fully realized the significance and potential implications of US national security review for Chinese investment, prompting suspicion that Chinese investors have obtained little knowledge about the existing US legal regime of national security review.

As Figure 6.6 shows, however, in 2019, about 40 percent of respondents chose to withdraw their investment plans in the face of national security review in the US. Interestingly, 40 percent of respondents believed that they had to withdraw their investment plans, and 43 percent of respondents believed that they had to change the direction of business development in the US in 2019, while these proportions decreased to 17 percent and 29 percent in 2020. This indicates that in Chinese investors' perceptions, other viable measures still existed in spite of increasingly strict national security scrutiny. For major Chinese investors, the US national security review is not viewed as a regulatory layer which might completely close the market door to Chinese investment, as nearly half of the respondents entered the

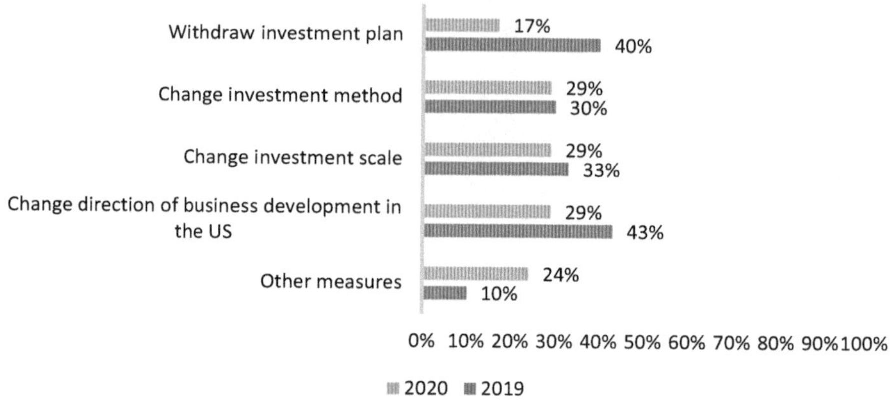

Figure 6.6 Responses of Chinese Investments to CFIUS Review from 2019 to 2020

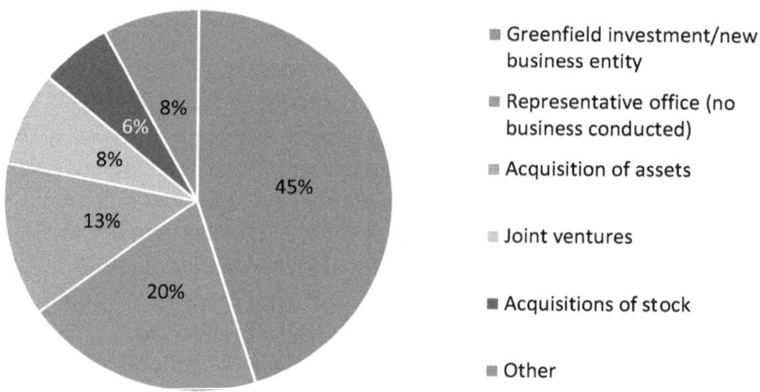

Figure 6.7 Methods of Chinese Investment in the US in 2020

US market by establishing a new business entity rather than acquiring an existing one, either by direct purchase of an entire corporate entity or of an entity's operating assets, which was accounted at 13 percent, as Figure 6.7 shows. Even though greenfield strategies may be the preferred method for Chinese investors starting a business in the US, greenfield investments are in general smaller than M&A investments in terms of scale, and M&As account for a larger proportion of Chinese investments in the US in terms of volume. The vast majority of Chinese capital invested in the US—as much as 90 percent—is invested in M&As, rather than greenfield investments. Also, the M&A investment method could offer Chinese investors access to the technical and managerial talent of acquired companies, and to the operating advantages and advanced capabilities of the acquired technologies and assets, and even, in certain circumstances, could enter US industries that have high barriers at the market access. Despite these advantages, Chinese investments that pursue M&A strategies might encounter the obstacle of national security review. Especially under the FIRRMA, which pays greater scrutiny to Chinese investment, enthusiasm for investing in the US through M&As has been decreasing. As we can see from Figure 6.8, 65 percent of respondents sought more acquisitions in the US in 2014, while only 39 percent had plans for conducting M&As in 2020.[49] Around 61 percent of respondents did not plan for M&As in 2020.[50] As illustrated in Figure 6.9, in 2018, nearly 11 percent of respondents chose greenfield investments with the purpose of avoiding national security review by the CFIUS.[51]

As discussed previously, the number of Chinese enterprises examined by the CFIUS in the process of investment activities is growing. Chinese enterprises have become the focus of national security review, while, at the same time, the majority of Chinese enterprises in the US fail to pay enough attention to this regulatory instrument, and fewer than one tenth of enterprises have applied for national security review as described previously. If Chinese enterprises continue to be unfamiliar with US national security reviews and fail to pay enough attention, the more national security reviews are conducted on Chinese investments, the greater the

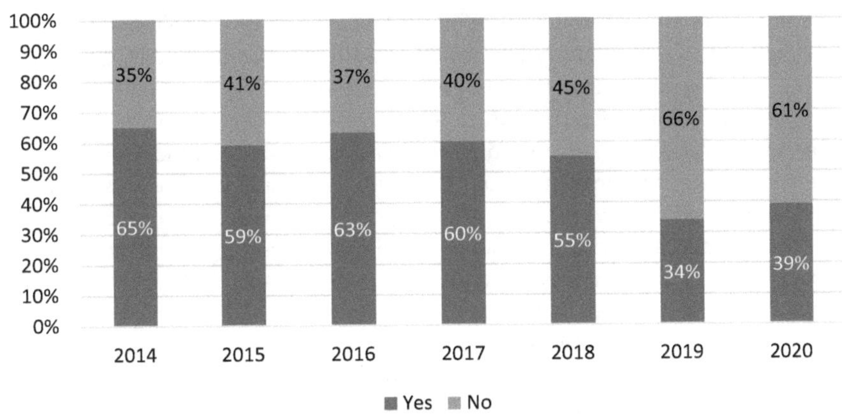

Figure 6.8 Chinese Investors' Ideas on Whether to Conduct M&As in the US from 2014 to 2020

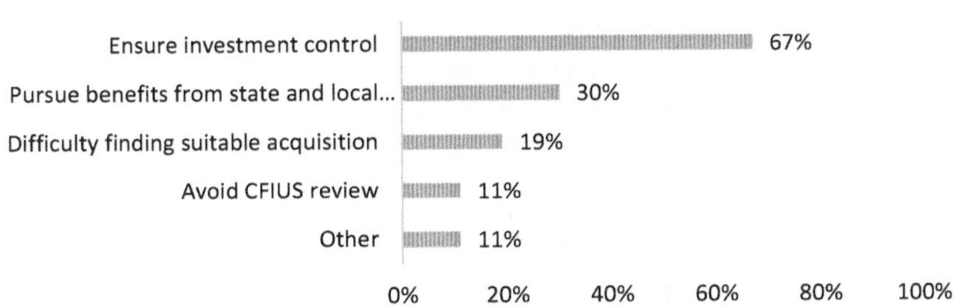

Figure 6.9 Primary Reasons for Chinese Greenfield Investment in the US in 2018

risks to those investments which might result in unpredictable national security reviews and increases in their investment costs. This being the case, prior to conducting investment plans in the US, it is necessary for Chinese enterprises to catch up with the updated rules on national security review in the FIRRMA, in order to avoid unnecessary trouble and losses by mistaking transactions subject to national security review for those which are not.

In addition to obtaining a general understanding of national security review in the US, Chinese investments should have a better understanding of key terms which are closely related to the procedure for initiating national security review. Under the FIRRMA, for example, the term "control" is no longer a necessary element in determining whether a foreign investment will be subject to national security review. Non-controlling foreign investment in TID US business could also initiate national security review. Even if the target of a Chinese investment is owned by foreigners, this transaction may still be subject to national security review as long as it is located in the US, because the national security review legal regime stipulates that "US business" refers to a person engaged in interstate commerce in the US, regardless of the nationality of the controlling person.[52] That is why the acquisition of British projects in the US by Dubai Ports World (DPW) was reviewed by the CFIUS. The term "foreigner" refers to foreign citizens, foreign governments, foreign entities, and any entity controlled or able to be controlled by foreign entities, and whether an entity is a foreigner is determined by the control element.[53] That is to say, it is not determined by whether the entity is established in the US, but by whether the entity is controlled by Americans or foreigners.[54] If the entity is controlled by a foreigner, it is considered a foreigner even if it is established in the US. That is why Sany's acquisition of wind farm projects in the US through its US affiliate, Ralls, fell within the scope of national security review, and Ralls was still regarded as a foreigner by the CFIUS, because its shareholders were Chinese, despite the fact that it is an American enterprise established in accordance with US laws. It is necessary for Chinese investment to be equipped with adequate knowledge about national security review in US foreign investment laws and practices.

The review criteria of national security review, moreover, should not be ignored, if investment costs and potential failures in the process of national security review are to be avoided. The US simply gives a number of general factors related to national security for the reference of the President or the CFIUS in their deliberations. The currently effective FIRRMA lists 11 factors regarding national security review to determine whether a covered transaction would impair US national security. We might summarize these factors, on the basis of the scope of the national security review and review criteria by observing the nature of American enterprises in which foreigners acquire control and the nature of foreigners who acquire control of American enterprises. If American enterprises which might be controlled by foreigners as a result of the proposed transactions meet any of the following conditions, the transaction might be prohibited or suspended by national security review: (i) if it provides products or services as general contractors, sub-contractor, or supplier of general contractor, to the federal government, state governments, and local government; (ii) if it has access to confidential information and material technology or obtains substantive decision-making power in relation to defense enterprises, security and security-related enforcement authorities, arms and ammunition production departments, aerospace systems, and radar systems, or TID US business; (iii) if it provides products and services to government agencies with functions related to national security; or (iv) if it is close to military installments and sensitive facilities of the US government. In addition to the nature of the American enterprises, the nature of the acquirers is also essential to the results of the national security review. Whether, for example, the foreigner is under the control of a foreign government, whether it has national security related records of the foreign country, and whether it seeks to cause the termination of the product and service contract between US business and the US government will affect the outcome of the national security review. In terms of review criteria, therefore, it is also necessary for Chinese investors to be equipped with comprehensive knowledge on review scope so that, prior to their investment in the US, they can find out whether their investment plans might meet these conditions.

On September 15, 2022, President Biden issued the Executive Order on Ensuring Robust Consideration of Evolving National Security Risks by the CFIUS, considering whether a covered transaction could reasonably result in future advancements and applications in technology that could undermine national security.[55] This is the first time in the CFIUS's nearly 50 year history that clear guidance has been officially provided on the risks that it should consider when conducting national security reviews on regulated transactions. In May 2023, the draft of the National Critical Capabilities Defense Act (NCCDA) was introduced. China was included in the list of countries of concern. This draft proposed to establish an inter-governmental agency, the Committee on National Critical Capabilities, similar to the CFIUS to govern US overseas investment. Accordingly, the Executive Order on Addressing United States Investments in Certain National Security Technologies and Products in Countries of Concern was issued by the Biden administration in September 2023, in a move representing significant progress in US investment in foreign countries (Reverse CFIUS).[56] Reverse CFIUS focuses on outward investment by US entities in key technology areas in countries of concern. This executive order referred to China as "special". Restricted investment areas include semiconductors, quantum computing, and artificial intelligence. If a US entity invests in entities located in, governed by, or owned by a Chinese entity in restricted investment areas, it may be ordered to prohibit transactions or required to declare by CFIUS. It is perceived by Chinese investors and the Chinese government that Chinese investments will undergo particularly strict oversight in the US on national security grounds.

6.3 The US Ideas on China's National Security Review

Not surprisingly, not only do Chinese investors make complaints about US national security review, but the US too is dissatisfied with China's foreign investment legal regime and its national security review. Even though a consolidated FIL was introduced that abolished the separate FIE laws governing foreign investment in the past decades, the absence of review criteria in the Measures leads to great ambiguity and uncertainty about enforcement, without predictability as to what extent foreign investment will be deemed as endangering national security, raising suspicions in the external structure that constitute negative external ideas on China's security review as designed by the FIL. To be specific, there are three prominent organizations concerned with US investment in China that have expressed deep concerns about the implications of China's national security review: the US General Chamber of Commerce (CGCC), the American Chamber of Commerce (AmCham) in China, and AmCham in Shanghai. They believe national security to be considered overly broadly in the enforcement of China's security review, in favor of interests that fall outside the widely recognized understanding of pure and essential national security concerns regarding foreign investment. Economic considerations, for example, are likely to feature in the national security review, raising fundamental questions about whether China's promised commitments to further reform and open its market to foreign investment will produce the intended results, as they believe the vague and broad sense of national security described in relation to security review under the FIL might contribute to a significant adverse impact on foreign investment in China and cause obstacles to the conclusion of Sino-US BIT because of its inconsistency with international investment principles such as nondiscrimination and transparency.[57]

According to the CGCC report, nearly half of respondents still feel less welcome in China, a trend that has risen by 11 percent since 2020 (Figure 6.10).[58] Some 38 percent of members reported that government policies and enforcement actions are applied unfairly to foreign companies. This marks the reversal of a three-year declining trend during which members were reporting less "unfair treatment" (from 37 percent in 2019 to 34 percent in 2020 and to 33 percent in 2021). Market access remains the top concern for 60 percent of members in 2022, albeit down 9 percent from 2021 (Figure 6.11).[59] Respondents considered whether the

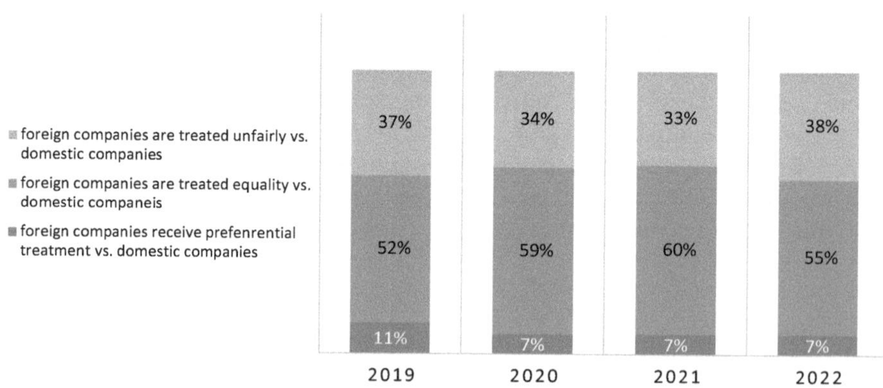

Figure 6.10 Compared to Domestic Companies, How Are Foreign Companies in Your Industry Treated by Government Policies and Enforcement Actions Compared to Domestic Companies?

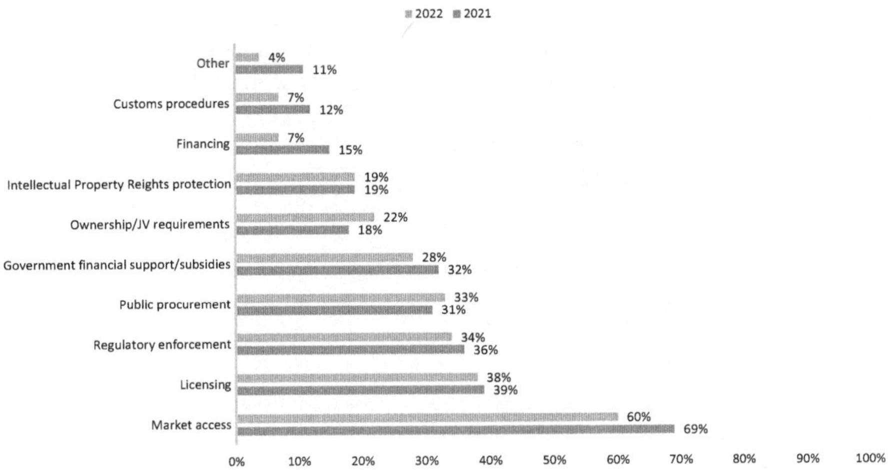

Figure 6.11 Areas of Unfair Treatment

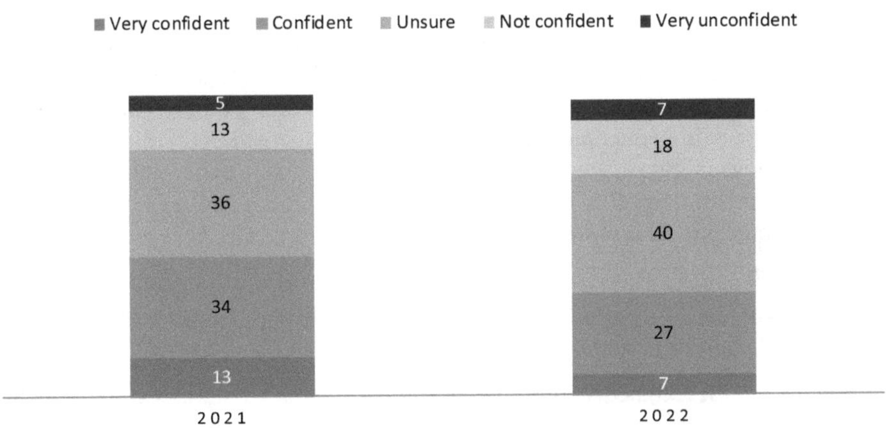

Figure 6.12 How Confident Are You that the Chinese Government Is Committed to Further Opening China's Market to Foreign Investment in the Coming Three Years?

Chinese government is committed to further opening its market to foreign investment, and uncertainty and lack of confidence rose (Figure 6.12).[60]

Responding to growing US complaints that China's foreign investment legal regime treats US investments unfairly, the Chinese government is emphasizing an open and friendly investment environment for foreign investment. In addition to the enactment of the FIL, the Law of Hainan Free Trade Port was promulgated on June 10, 2021, aiming to lay out a solid legal foundation for a much more liberalized investment environment, in line with international standards.[61] The Hainan government has been granted greater legislative and reform autonomy than governments of other areas to formulate local laws and regulations on trade, investment, and related management activities for the construction of Hainan Free Trade Port (FTP) in light of specific circumstances and actual needs.[62] Also, the Implementation Plan for Comprehensive Reform Pilot in Pudong New Area (2023–2027) was released in January 2024, with the purpose of achieving high-standards market rules for foreign investment.[63] It is expected that Hainan and Shanghai will be the first places to enforce national security review under the FIL and will make significant innovations.

Even though there are very few formal precedents in the enforcement of national security review in China, security review in areas not confined to foreign investment could be taken into consideration by foreign investors to facilitate an understanding of China's internal ideas on national security. The cybersecurity review, for example, could function as an appropriate channel for exploration of China's internal ideas on cybersecurity when reviewing foreign investment. It is worth noting that the Chinese Administration of Cyberspace conducted a cybersecurity review of Didi Chuxing Technology Co. (DIDI) and ordered stores selling the DIDI application to remove it from their platforms. This security review in the field of cyberspace and data was far-reaching and is expected to set a precedent for future national security probes in data collection, for the purpose of safeguarding cybersecurity. This demonstrates that China's perception of basic data collected by DIDI on road, transport and consumption habits is closely linked with national security. Even though a cybersecurity law has been enacted, it exists on paper only and has not been implemented. The cybersecurity review of DIDI indicates that big tech companies might face mounting regulatory pressures in cybersecurity. Foreign investment in similar fields might also enter the tough and complicated stage of national security review more easily than before.

6.4 Sino-US BIT Negotiations on Liberalizing Foreign Investment Legislation in China

Since the first BIT signed with Sweden in 1982, China's practices on BIT at the international level have evolved significantly.[64] In terms of the number of signed investment treaties, China is positioned second in the ranking, behind Germany.[65] To date, China has concluded a total of 145 BITs, and 108 of them are effective.[66] Because of China's attitude, which was more concerned with investment promotion than investment protection and because of its preference to retain its sovereignty in governing foreign investment, early BITs in China basically involved MFN treatment but neglected liberal national treatment provisions. As explained in China's internal structure, post-establishment national treatment had been adopted under the legal regime of the FIE Law for several decades, leading to heavy discrimination against foreign investment in favor of domestic investment.

Because of the role of process orientation, bilateral investment practices are promoted to constitute positive external ideas on other nations, in order to eliminate misunderstanding and mistrust, as national security reviews can be oriented to be similar to those of other countries through investment integration. Sino-US BIT negotiations play a significant role in eliminating investment conflicts on national security grounds. The formal talks pursuing a Sino-US BIT started in 2008, but one year later, these negotiations were halted, and little progress had been made. The reason for their suspension was to wait for the revised text of the 2012 US Model BIT with its greatly significant innovations, to revive BIT negotiations with China.[67] As China had never granted pre-establishment national treatment to foreign investment in past BITs, the breadth of national treatment coverage has become the most challenging topic for Sino-US BIT negotiations, as the revised 2012 US model advocated the principle of pre-establishment national treatment. Since July 2013, when China agreed to hold discussions on the promise of adopting the principle of pre-establishment national treatment with a negative list in FTZs, the Sino-US BIT negotiation has been on hold.[68] Both sides agreed to make commitments to apply the same rules and standards on national security and foreign investment as expeditiously as possible,[69] and exchanged negative lists three times between 2015 and 2016.[70]

In this regard, the approach of pre-established national treatment and negative lists has been tested in FTZs ahead of nationwide reform in foreign investment legislation before the enactment of the FIL in 2019. China once maintained ownership restrictions on foreign investment in about 100 wide-ranging sectors, including manufacturing, services, energy, and agriculture, while this list limiting access for foreign investment has been gradually whittled down since China first adopted a negative list in the Shanghai FTZ in September 2013. Although restricted sectors have been shortened by means of national negative lists and FTZ negative lists, critics in the external structure are still not satisfied with China's efforts. The European Chamber of Commerce in China, for example, pointed out that many industries and sectors on the negative list have been merely regrouped rather than removed.[71] Some US business groups believed that the modifications to China's negative list merely reflected a regulatory streamlining in terms of the guidance on foreign investment, rather than a significant liberalization of the internal investment market.[72]

In spite of the failure of Sino-US BIT, respondents to the CGCC report believed the Sino-US bilateral relationship to be key to growing their investments and business (Figure 6.13).[73] According to the report, among several external factors that have emerged as troubling the most Chinese members, the stalemate in bilateral relations between the US and China, subsequent trade friction between the two countries, and continuous inflation and subsequent trade friction were the top three concerns, at 81 percent, 68 percent, and 67 percent respectively (Figure 6.14).[74] Uncertain Sino-US relations represent the first challenge for investors in these two countries. If China or the US believes that investments from its opposite number need to be limited, screened, restricted, prohibited, or subjected to forced localization, the real purpose of Sino-US BIT may not ultimately succeed.[75]

Even though a Sino-US BIT is unlikely to change the national security review process because of the complicated political climate and relations between China and US,[76] such a BIT could bring clarity on national security review for both parties, as, both in China and the US, but especially China, it is expected to improve

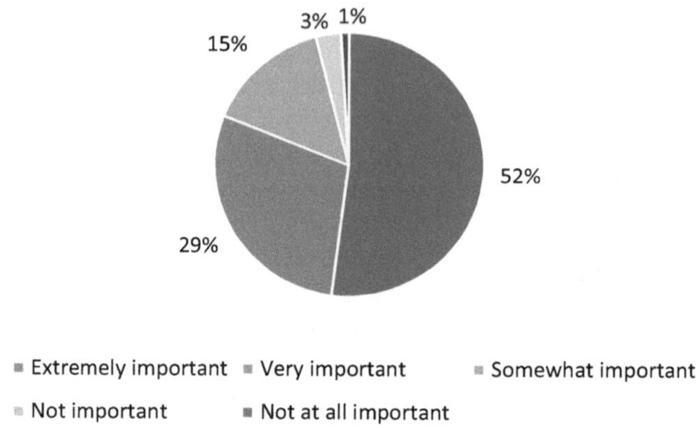

Figure 6.13 Importance of Positive Sino-US Relations to Business Growth in China

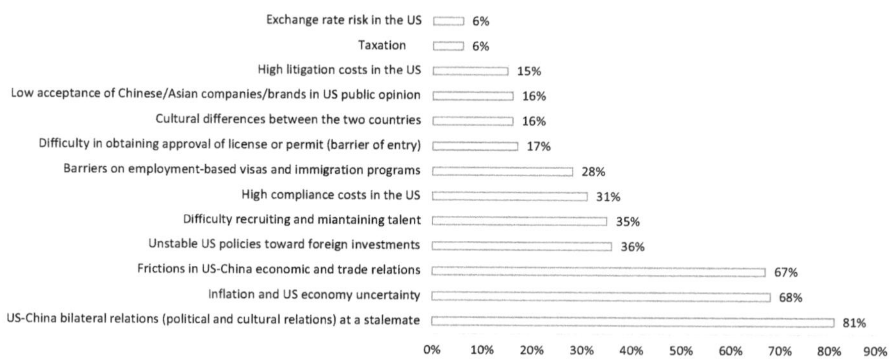

Figure 6.14 Challenges in the US Perceived by Chinese Companies

transparency and predictability for foreign investors in responses to national security review in each other's country.[77]

On the basis of process orientation analysis, it is suggested that the US recognize the great differences between the two nations' internal ideas on national security review, as they are developing at diametrically opposite starting points. It should be objectively recognized within the US that China's regulatory mechanism of national security review has already made great efforts to become oriented to the highly modernized and liberalized instrument boasted by the US, and China never hesitates to further liberalize foreign investment and limit national security concerns and intervention in investment practices. The existing differences and conflicts on national security reviews are historically and socially shaped by internal ideas, which are also closely correlated with institutions. It is suggested that the US study the underlying institutional and ideational reasons for such differences between national security reviews of Chinese and US foreign investment laws and practices, in order to eliminate misleading and discriminatory perceptions and reach a much more justified and rational understanding of China's regulatory mechanism and Chinese investment, rather than directly jumping to the ideational conclusions that Chinese investment will ultimately threaten US national security and China's national security review will treat US investment unfairly.

6.5 Cooperative External Ideas to Build Mutual Trust and Understanding

As the FIRRMA came into force in 2020, changes to the national security review process in law-making in the coming few years seem unlikely and consistency and stability of the rule of law are likely to be maintained. Mutual trust in a positive and friendly relationship between China and the US on investment issues could partly be achieved through the implementation of national security reviews. To be specific, when enforcing national security review, US regulators should comply with the nondiscrimination principle, through appropriate information disclosure to Chinese parties. The possibilities of mitigation agreements offered by the CFIUS, especially given the high proportion of mitigation agreements successfully reached by Chinese investors and the CFIUS, could also, to some extent, present opportunities for positive US gestures to Chinese investors on national security issues. In spite of the failure of Ralls' bid for Terna, for example, the court ruled that the US government should provide access to the unclassified evidence on which the decision was made.[78]

For China, the essential objective is to address potential US national security concerns about Chinese investment. First, it is suggested that reliable data and information about US investment activities in China be disclosed, especially data on transactions reviewed on national security grounds. There is an absence of case studies analyzing the impacts of US investment on China's economy and national security.[79] By contrast, the US has annually provided reports on national security reviews to the public, though the information is quite general, such as numbers of reviewed Chinese transactions, or related industrial sectors. Similarly, in the US, the lack of specific case studies on Chinese investments' impacts on the US economy and national security also impedes the ability of US regulators to shape a prospective BIT with China.

Second, in order to help the US constitute a positive external idea on China, the role of the Chinese government in the market economy should be constrained. On the one hand, inward investments, including those from the US, are subject to potential reviews by government authorities in China, in accordance with relevant industrial policies, competition policies, and national security review. As the Chinese government has exerted significant influence in industrial sectors which are viewed as strategically related to national security, such as telecommunications and autos, US investment in these industrial sectors might prompt Chinese nervousness on national security, leading to a stricter review by the Chinese government. On the other hand, the Chinese government is playing an active role in encouraging and supporting Chinese enterprises to go out into the global market. In particular,

Chinese SOEs are the main driver for these overseas investments, with robust subsidization programs and preferential policies.[80]

It is widely recognized that the "multiple ownership structure dominated by public ownership" is one of the Chinese characteristics, and this can be seen in the idea that foreign investment might endanger the survival of Chinese SOEs in the emerging FIE regime. Even though Chinese SOEs have completed transformation and reorganization as modern enterprises, these restructured SOEs are perceived to be under absolute control by the Chinese government. Given that Chinese SOEs are always offered strong financial support and sufficient government-backed resources, the US perception of Chinese SOEs as a potential threat to US national security is not inadequately addressed by antidumping or other countervailing measures, other than the regulatory mechanism of national security review. It is therefore necessary for China to carry out SOE reform, to eliminate negative US impressions of Chinese SOEs. In 2020, there were approximately 473,600 SOEs in China, 97 of which were central SOEs directly under the control of central government, while the municipal or provincial governments owned the rest.[81] Indeed, in an effort to allay US concerns on the role of government in economic activities, China proposes a strategy on mixed-ownership reform (MOR) of SOEs.[82] The continuously further deepening reform of SOEs is an appropriate way to allay US criticisms over excessive intervention of the Chinese government in the market and eliminate US sensitivity about Chinese investment conducted by SOEs.

For Chinese SOEs investing in the US, the updated legal regime of national security review under the FIRRMA will play a significant role, as foreign investments connected to foreign governments, irrespective of the possibility of control, will undergo national security review. Also, the CFIUS will focus on whether the foreigner is controlled by the foreign government, the extent to which foreign investors make investment decisions on the basis of commercial considerations, and the extent to which foreign investors exercise investment decision-making and to which management rights are independent of the government. Suspected governmental control behind Chinese SOEs, therefore, will undoubtedly raise US national security concerns, and their investment in the US might encounter great obstacles caused by national security reviews conducted by the CFIUS. This is not an insurmountable obstacle, however, as this challenge could be significantly addressed through further deepening of economic reform, especially the existing MOR on SOEs in China. On the basis of China's basic economic regime, it is impossible to completely privatize the existing SOEs for the sole purpose of successfully investing in the US. Highlighting the commercial aspect of the SOEs, however, is one of the ways to deepen the equity reform of such enterprises, reducing direct governmental intervention and minimizing the risks of national security review during the process of their investments in the US. SOEs could be transformed into mixed ownership enterprises, weakening their governmental background and highlighting their commercial character. In addition to MOR, it is suggested that a reasonable equity incentive mechanism be established for the executives and employees of SOEs, as an important part of the companies' remuneration packages, in accordance with the rules of the market, to highlight the commercial nature of such an enterprise which pursues commercial profits, and to encourage the executives and employees to manage and operate the company better.

Simultaneously, in an attempt to make its enterprises more technologically advantageous and internationally competitive in the global market amid the trend of foreign investment liberalization, China promotes a "going out strategy" to encourage private enterprises and SOEs to invest abroad, which signals China's efforts toward the expected shift of its priority in BIT negotiations from investment promotion to investment protection. Against this background, Chinese negotiators on Sino-US BIT are concerned with the implications of Chinese SOEs in the US, which feel vulnerable in the face of the CFIUS, and would become more willing to reach a BIT with clear definitions and explanations on investment through SOEs, in order to facilitate investment solutions to investment conflicts. If this was achieved, US external ideas on Chinese SOEs would be improved. Through an increasing number of successful bilateral investment practices between China and the US, both nations would constitute positive external ideas on the other and the other's investments, as well as on the other's national security review in relation to its investments. A consensus could be much easier to achieve, and a cooperative idea on national security review and foreign investment could be collectively shared, with national security review no longer perceived as a merely political and retributory tool.

Third, it is necessary for China to distinguish the regulatory techniques of competition policy from national security review for foreign investment. The US perceives that China's competition policies under the AML are not only employed purely to protect competition, but also to pursue other objectives that have no place in a fair and open market-based economy. According to the survey conducted by the US-China Business Council in 2014, more than 80 percent of companies were concerned with the enforcement of the AML and complained about the lack of transparency and due process, as well as requirements of technology transfer.[83] The US views China's AML as one of numerous mechanisms to lower the value of foreign-owned patents and benefit Chinese companies with access to foreign technology.[84] In the Sino-US BIT negotiating process, worries regarding China's investment restrictions and discrimination in competition policies have been raised at the highest level, but giving cause for optimism, there is significant cooperation and coordination on competition policies. US officials from the Federal Trade Commission and the Department of Justice, for example, have consistently engaged in consultation, training, and exchanges about AML enforcement with Chinese antitrust officials.[85] In practice, however, China's anti-monopoly review has frequently been adopted for national security reasons, which would eliminate the rationality and objectivity of the results of anti-monopoly review. It is therefore suggested that China distinguish between national security review and anti-monopoly reviews regarding foreign investment, to truly achieve the purpose of national security review and to protect the functions and benefits of anti-monopoly reviews.

Fourth, it is suggested that provisions of the Investor-state Dispute Settlement (ISDS) be adopted in the 2012 US Model BIT and that an investment dispute mechanism be established in a potential Sino-US BIT, serving as a tool to limit the discretionary ability of the host country to block or unravel foreign investment from the other country.[86] The 2012 US Model BIT, however, includes a security exception clause that is broad enough for the CFIUS and the president to review investment transactions considered necessary for the protection of its essential security interests, while in practice, this principle has never been tested, leaving unresolved the question about whether adverse CFIUS decisions could be subject to an ISDS challenge.[87] Additionally, one of the concerns is the extent to which the ISDS would truly function as expected. On the one hand, the US might be less willing to apply the ISDS, as there are some critics who perceive the ISDS to weaken national sovereignty and accelerate the pace at which companies transfer industries abroad.[88] On the other hand, China is relatively disadvantaged in the ISDS, with quite weak enforcement advantages in its international practices. Also, China and the US have not yet reached a BIT. The possibility of their resolving their bilateral investment disputes through the ISDS is therefore quite low, and the ISDS might not be the best option for coordinating investment conflicts between China and the US.

Instead, the bilateral assessment and dispute settlement arrangement in the Economic and Trade Agreement between China and the US signed on January 16, 2020, which requires both parties to establish a trade framework group to conduct high-level discussions on economic and trade issues, could make contributions to facilitate resolutions to investment conflicts undergoing national security review.[89] This diplomatic channel is highly pragmatic. As due process and transparency are required, national security review conducted either in China or the US regarding the other's investment could fulfil the obligations of fairness and nondiscrimination in the review process. Also, the review body could communicate with the other through the high-level trade framework group and explain results made in national security reviews, which could largely eliminate misunderstandings and mistrust caused by information asymmetry surrounding national security reviews and investments. This approach could lay a cooperative foundation by constituting positive external ideas on the other through investment integration, which might play a significant role in the enforcement of national security review regarding bilateral investment activities. When necessary, moreover, China and the US could go beyond the individual case itself, expand the scope of convergence of mutual interests and cooperate in other areas to reach a consensus on the settlement of disputes. Thus, they could reach a package agreement on several disputes to achieve a balance of mutual interests as a whole, rather than focusing only on an individual case. It is worth noting, however, that this diplomatic-centered suggestion might make the enforcement of national security review in relation to foreign investment a purely political event through frequent adoption. On this issue, the diplomatic approach through such a trade framework group should be prudently employed. Also, it is suggested that it be used in a large number of successful investments approved in national security review or approved investments that reach mitigation conditions with the other's review body. That is to say that the review body could use the trade framework group as a channel to actively explain its considerations and results in relation to the other's investment and national security review. In this way, both China and the US would obtain adequate and fresh knowledge on the other's enforcement of national security review, largely eliminating suspicions and negative feelings. This knowledge, along with hopeful and promising information and explanations on the enforcement of national security reviews would shape the cooperative idea shared between China and the US, by means of mutual understanding and mutual trust in bilateral investments affected by national security concerns.

In terms of diplomatic considerations, in order to be equipped with objective and justified perceptions on national security reviews conducted by the CFIUS on Chinese investment, China should observe and admit that the debate over investment from China and national security review is not the first instance in which anxiety and hostility have been directed toward a single nation. Investments from both Germany and Japan were once viewed as harmful and paid great scrutiny by national security review in the US. Even though it seems that neither China nor the US is listening to the other or being heard by the other, there would be cause for optimism and hope if both were willing to gain a deeper knowledge and appreciation of their differences caused by internal ideas and similarities oriented by external process. It is necessary for them to recognize the significance and oriented role of process through bilateral investment to facilitate solutions to investment conflicts undergoing national security review. When continuously promoting reform and opening up, China should also give a clear and accurate description and explanation of its strategic intention, in order to avoid a misleading and negative impression caused by false translation and vague expression. To be specific, the Chinese side should frankly put forward its real national security concerns on foreign investment during the course of communication with the US, to show a positive sign to the US and then facilitate a positive US external idea on China. In this way, mutual understanding and mutual trust can easily be strengthened. As to the US, it must recognize that China's security is people-oriented security and China's developmental aim is to pursue high living standards for its citizens, rather than to challenge US hegemony and overthrow US-led international rules. Investment integration with China is essential for orienting China's national security review towards similarity with US national security review with increasing transparency and predictability. Similarities caused by process orientation offer a platform for China and the US to explain and understand differences caused by internal ideas and create great scope for potential cooperation. The US could gain positive perceptions of Chinese investment in relation to national security through continual investment practices.

Because of the role of process orientation, it is likely that China and the US will have chances of future coordination and cooperation, as long as the two sides stay patient and far-sighted about recognizing the differences dominated by internal ideas and similarities oriented by processes of investment. Great efforts could be made in the area of process orientation to pursue normal or friendly relations between China and the US. The Pudong New Area Decision and Law on Hainan Free Trade Port is evidence that further deepened reform and opening up are expected in China. This shows a positive sign for foreign investors which are hesitating to enter China's market. Interestingly, the State Council Circular on Supporting High-level Reform and Opening Up, of June 2021, consolidates into one provision the aims of strengthening the fundamental role of competition policies, fully achieving a pre-establishment national treatment and negative list, positively promoting MOR and protecting legal interests of foreign investors. This reveals Chinese policymakers' perception that MOR and antitrust review are closely related to the liberalization of foreign investment, which is in line with the aforementioned recommendations to further promote MOR and distinguish antitrust review from national security review.

Overall, idea dominance and process orientation in explaining and comparing national security reviews in Chinese and US foreign investment laws and practices from a constructivist perspective may have practical value and be worthy of policy reference both for China and the US.

Notes

1 "CFIUS Reports and Tables." https://home.treasury.gov/policy-issues/international/the-committee-on-foreign-investment-in-the-united-states-cfius/cfius-reports-and-tables (CFIUS Reports and Tables).
2 CFIUS Reports and Tables.
3 US-China Economic and Security Review Commission. "Policy Considerations for Negotiating a US-China Bilateral Investment Treaty." 2016. www.uscc.gov/research/policy-considerations-negotiating-us-china-bilateral-investment-treaty, 16.
4 Walshe, Taylor and Tan, Shining. "TikTok on the Clock: A Summary of CFIUS's Investigation into ByteDance." www.csis.org/blogs/trustee-china-hand/tiktok-clock-summary-cfiuss-investigation-bytedance.
5 CFIUS Reports and Tables.
6 Walshe, Taylor and Tan, Shining. "TikTok on the Clock: A Summary of CFIUS's Investigation into ByteDance." www.csis.org/blogs/trustee-china-hand/tiktok-clock-summary-cfiuss-investigation-bytedance.
7 CFIUS Reports and Tables.
8 55 Fed. Reg. 3935 (1990); Schaus, John. "President Obama's Second Order on CFIUS." www.csis.org/analysis/president-obamas-second-order-cfius; Mir, Aimen, Laciak, Christine and Melanson, Sarah. "United States: CFIUS Review." 2021. https://globalcompetitionreview.com/review/the-antitrust-review-of-the-americas/2021/article/united-states-cfius-review#footnote-036.%20%20www.csis.org/analysis/president-obamas-second-order-cfius.
9 77 Fed. Reg. 60281 (2012); Mir, Aimen, Laciak, Christine and Melanson, Sarah. "United States: CFIUS Review." 2021. https://globalcompetitionreview.com/review/the-antitrust-review-of-the-americas/2021/article/united-states-cfius-review#footnote-036.%20%20www.csis.org/analysis/president-obamas-second-order-cfius; 81 Fed. Reg. 88607 (2016); Covington & Burling LLP. "President Obama Blocks Chinese Acquisition of Aixtron SE." 2016. www.cov.com/-/media/files/corporate/publications/2016/12/president_obama_blocks_chinese_acquisition_of_aixtron_se.pdf.
10 82 Fed. Reg. 43665 (2017).
11 83 Fed. Reg. 11631 (2018).
12 Clark, Harry. "President Trump Orders Divestment of US Company; CFIUS Clears Semiconductor Transaction." 2020. www.orrick.com/en/Insights/2020/03/President-Trump-Orders-Divestment-of-US-Company-CFIUS-Clears-Semiconductor-Transaction; Broadman, Harry G. "Trump's TikTok Tactics Provoke China's Countering CFIUS as New Data Portend Decoupling." 2020. www.forbes.com/sites/harrybroadman/

2020/08/31/trumps-tiktok-tactics-provoke-chinas-countering-cfius-as-new-data-portend-decoupling/?sh=449510867d85; Caparelli, Christopher M. "Taking on TikTok: CFIUS on the Front Page (and in the Fine Print)." 2020. www.torys.com/insights/publications/2020/09/taking-on-tiktok.

13 The White House. "Order on the China National Aero-Technology Import and Export Corporation Divestiture of MAMCO Manufacturing, Incorporated." 1990. www.presidency.ucsb.edu/documents/order-the-china-national-aero-technology-import-and-export-corporation-divestiture-mamco.

14 The White House. "Order Signed by the President Regarding the Acquisition of Four U.S. Wind Farm Project Companies by Ralls Corporation." 2012. https://obamawhitehouse.archives.gov/the-press-office/2012/09/28/order-signed-president-regardingacquisition-four-us-wind-farm-project-c.

15 The White House. "Presidential Order Regarding the Proposed Acquisition of a Controlling Interest in Aixtron SE by Grand Chip Investment GMBH." 2016. https://obamawhitehouse.archives.gov/the-press-office/2016/12/02/presidential-orderregarding-proposed-acquisition-controlling-interest.

16 The White House. "Order Regarding the Proposed Acquisition of Lattice Semiconductor Corporation by China Venture Capital Fund Corporation Limited." www.whitehouse.gov/presidential-actions/order-regarding-proposed-acquisition-latticesemiconductor-corporation-china-venture-capital-fund-corporation-limited/.

17 The White House. "Presidential Order Regarding the Proposed Takeover of Qualcomm Incorporated by Broadcom Limited." www.whitehouse.gov/presidential-actions/presidential-order-regarding-proposed-takeover-qualcomm-incorporated-broadcom-limited/.

18 The White House. "Order Regarding the Acquisition of Musical.ly by ByteDance Ltd." www.whitehouse.gov/presidential-actions/order-regarding-acquisition-musical-ly-bytedance-ltd/.

19 Mir, Aimen, Laciak, Christine and Melanson, Sarah. "United States: CFIUS Review." 2021. https://globalcompetitionreview.com/review/the-antitrust-review-of-the-americas/2021/article/united-states-cfius-review#footnote-036.%20%20www.csis.org/analysis/president-obamas-second-order-cfius.

20 Walshe, Taylor and Tan, Shining. "TikTok on the Clock: A Summary of CFIUS's Investigation into ByteDance." www.csis.org/blogs/trustee-china-hand/tiktok-clock-summary-cfiuss-investigation-bytedance.

21 Walshe, Taylor and Tan, Shining. "TikTok on the Clock: A Summary of CFIUS's Investigation into ByteDance." www.csis.org/blogs/trustee-china-hand/tiktok-clock-summary-cfiuss-investigation-bytedance.

22 Walshe, Taylor and Tan, Shining. "TikTok on the Clock: A Summary of CFIUS's Investigation into ByteDance." www.csis.org/blogs/trustee-china-hand/tiktok-clock-summary-cfiuss-investigation-bytedance.

23 Caparelli, Christopher M. "Taking on TikTok: CFIUS on the Front Page (and in the Fine Print)." 2020. www.torys.com/insights/publications/2020/09/taking-on-tiktok; Lerman, Rachel. "TikTok Gets Short Extension before It Must Be Sole." 2020. www.washingtonpost.com/technology/2020/11/13/tiktok-sale-extension-cfius/; Altieri, Richard and Rocca, Benjamin Della. "Trump Signs Ban on TikTok, WeChat; US Officials Report Chinese Election Interference." 2020. www.lawfareblog.com/trump-signs-ban-tiktok-wechat-us-officials-report-chinese-election-interference.

24 Lerman, Rachel. "TikTok Gets Short Extension Before It Must Be Sole." 2020. www.washingtonpost.com/technology/2020/11/13/tiktok-sale-extension-cfius/.

25 Lerman, Rachel. "TikTok Gets Short Extension before It Must Be Sole." 2020. www.washingtonpost.com/technology/2020/11/13/tiktok-sale-extension-cfius/.

26 Barker, John P., Lee, Ronald D., Rhee, Soo-Mi, Perkins, Nancy L., Townsend, Nicholas L., McSorley, Tom, Anderson, Shira V. and Schmitt, Trevor G. "Beyond TikTok: Commerce Issues New CFIUS-Like Review Rule for Transactions Involving Information

and Communications Technologies and Services." 2021. www.arnoldporter.com/en/perspectives/publications/2021/02/beyond-tiktok.

27 Barker, John P., Lee, Ronald D., Rhee, Soo-Mi, Perkins, Nancy L., Townsend, Nicholas L., McSorley, Tom, Anderson, Shira V. and Schmitt, Trevor G. "Beyond TikTok: Commerce Issues New CFIUS-Like Review Rule for Transactions Involving Information and Communications Technologies and Services." 2021. www.arnoldporter.com/en/perspectives/publications/2021/02/beyond-tiktok.

28 CFIUS Reports and Tables.

29 CFIUS Reports and Tables.

30 CFIUS Reports and Tables.

31 Shackelford, Scott J. "Using BITs to Protect Bytes: Promoting Cyber Peace by Safeguarding Trade Secrets through Bilateral Investment Treaties." *American Business Law Journal* 52, no. 1 (2015): 43.

32 China General Chamber of Commerce. www.cgccusa.org/en/.

33 China General Chamber of Commerce. "2017 Annual Business Survey Report on Chinese Enterprises in the US." 2017. www.bjreview.com/pdf/2017/survey-report.pdf.

34 China General Chamber of Commerce. "2017 Annual Business Survey Report on Chinese Enterprises in the US." 2017. www.bjreview.com/pdf/2017/survey-report.pdf, 28.

35 China General Chamber of Commerce. "2020 Annual Business Survey Report: Chinese Enterprises in the United States." 2020. www.cgccusa.org/wp-content/uploads/2020/08/CGCC-2020-Annual-Business-Survey-Report.pdf.

36 China General Chamber of Commerce. "2020 Annual Business Survey Report: Chinese Enterprises in the United States." 2020. www.cgccusa.org/wp-content/uploads/2020/08/CGCC-2020-Annual-Business-Survey-Report.pdf.

37 China General Chamber of Commerce. "2020 Annual Business Survey Report: Chinese Enterprises in the United States." 2020. www.cgccusa.org/wp-content/uploads/2020/08/CGCC-2020-Annual-Business-Survey-Report.pdf.

38 China General Chamber of Commerce. "2015 Annual Business Survey Report: Chinese Enterprises in the United States." 2016. www.cgccusa.org/wp-content/uploads/2016/01/Survey-Report-2015.pdf, 16.

39 China General Chamber of Commerce. "2015 Annual Business Survey Report: Chinese Enterprises in the United States." 2016. www.cgccusa.org/wp-content/uploads/2016/01/Survey-Report-2015.pdf, 16.

40 China General Chamber of Commerce. "2018 Annual Business Survey Report: Chinese Enterprises in the United States." 2018. www.docdroid.net/YIGTPK8/cgcc-report-0611181-pdf.

41 China General Chamber of Commerce. "2018 Annual Business Survey Report: Chinese Enterprises in the United States." 2018. www.docdroid.net/YIGTPK8/cgcc-report-0611181-pdf.

42 China General Chamber of Commerce. "2018 Annual Business Survey Report: Chinese Enterprises in the United States." 2018. www.docdroid.net/YIGTPK8/cgcc-report-0611181-pdf.

43 China General Chamber of Commerce. "2018 Annual Business Survey Report: Chinese Enterprises in the United States." 2018. www.docdroid.net/YIGTPK8/cgcc-report-0611181-pdf.

44 China General Chamber of Commerce. "2020 Annual Business Survey Report: Chinese Enterprises in the United States." 2020. www.cgccusa.org/wp-content/uploads/2020/08/CGCC-2020-Annual-Business-Survey-Report.pdf.

45 China General Chamber of Commerce. "2020 Annual Business Survey Report: Chinese Enterprises in the United States." 2020. www.cgccusa.org/wp-content/uploads/2020/08/CGCC-2020-Annual-Business-Survey-Report.pdf.

46 China General Chamber of Commerce. "2020 Annual Business Survey Report: Chinese Enterprises in the United States." 2020. www.cgccusa.org/wp-content/uploads/2020/08/CGCC-2020-Annual-Business-Survey-Report.pdf; China General Chamber of Commerce. "2018 Annual Business Survey Report: Chinese Enterprises in the United States." 2018. www.docdroid.net/YIGTPK8/cgcc-report-0611181-pdf.

47 China General Chamber of Commerce. "2020 Annual Business Survey Report: Chinese Enterprises in the United States." 2020. www.cgccusa.org/wp-content/uploads/2020/08/CGCC-2020-Annual-Business-Survey-Report.pdf; China General Chamber of Commerce. "2018 Annual Business Survey Report: Chinese Enterprises in the United States." 2018. www.docdroid.net/YlGTPK8/cgcc-report-0611181-pdf.
48 China General Chamber of Commerce. "2020 Annual Business Survey Report: Chinese Enterprises in the United States." 2020. www.cgccusa.org/wp-content/uploads/2020/08/CGCC-2020-Annual-Business-Survey-Report.pdf; China General Chamber of Commerce. "2018 Annual Business Survey Report: Chinese Enterprises in the United States." 2018. www.docdroid.net/YlGTPK8/cgcc-report-0611181-pdf.
49 China General Chamber of Commerce. "2020 Annual Business Survey Report: Chinese Enterprises in the United States." 2020. www.cgccusa.org/wp-content/uploads/2020/08/CGCC-2020-Annual-Business-Survey-Report.pdf.
50 China General Chamber of Commerce. "2020 Annual Business Survey Report: Chinese Enterprises in the United States." 2020. www.cgccusa.org/wp-content/uploads/2020/08/CGCC-2020-Annual-Business-Survey-Report.pdf.
51 China General Chamber of Commerce. "2020 Annual Business Survey Report: Chinese Enterprises in the United States." 2020. www.cgccusa.org/wp-content/uploads/2020/08/CGCC-2020-Annual-Business-Survey-Report.pdf, 9.
52 50 U.S.C. § 4565 (a)(13); 31 C.F.R. Part § 800.252.
53 31 C.F.R. Part § 800.224.
54 31 C.F.R. Part § 800.223–224.
55 The White House. "Executive Order on Ensuring Robust Consideration of Evolving National Security Risks by the Committee on Foreign Investment in the United States." 2022. www.whitehouse.gov/briefing-room/presidential-actions/2022/09/15/executive-order-on-ensuring-robust-consideration-of-evolving-national-security-risks-by-the-committee-on-foreign-investment-in-the-united-states/.
56 The White House. "Executive Order on Addressing United States Investments in Certain National Security Technologies and Products in Countries of Concern." 2023. www.whitehouse.gov/briefing-room/presidential-actions/2023/08/09/executive-order-on-addressing-united-states-investments-in-certain-national-security-technologies-and-products-in-countries-of-concern/.
57 US Chamber of Commerce, American Chamber of Commerce in China, and American Chamber of Commerce in Shanghai. "Joint Submission to the State Council on the Trial Measures for the National Security Review of Foreign Investments in China's Pilot Free Trade Zones and Revised Free Trade Zone Negative List." www.amchamshanghai.org/ftpuploadfiles/insight/Security%20Reviews%20and%20Neg%20List.pdf, 1.
58 American Chamber of Commerce in the PRC. "China Business Climate Survey Report 2023." 2024. www.amchamchina.org/wp-content/uploads/2024/01/AmCham-China-2024-China-Business-Climate-Survey-Report.pdf.
59 American Chamber of Commerce in the PRC. "China Business Climate Survey Report 2023." 2024. www.amchamchina.org/wp-content/uploads/2024/01/AmCham-China-2024-China-Business-Climate-Survey-Report.pdf.
60 American Chamber of Commerce in the PRC. "China Business Climate Survey Report 2023." 2024. www.amchamchina.org/wp-content/uploads/2024/01/AmCham-China-2024-China-Business-Climate-Survey-Report.pdf.
61 HKTDC Research. "China Enacts Hainan Free Trade Port Law." https://research.hktdc.com/en/article/Nzc1MDU1MzE4; Kawate, Iori. "China Passes Law to Make Hainan Free Trade Haven." https://asia.nikkei.com/Politics/China-passes-law-to-make-Hainan-free-trade-haven.
62 Xinhua Net. "China Focus: China Passes Law on Hainan Free Trade Port." www.hellenicshippingnews.com/china-focus-china-passes-law-on-hainan-free-trade-port/.
63 Implementation Plan for Comprehensive Reform Pilot in Pudong New Area (2023–2027), Article 1. www.gov.cn/govweb/zhengce/202401/content_6927505.htm.

64 Cohen, Tyler and Schneiderman, David. "The Political Economy of Chinese Bilateral Investment Treaty Policy." *The Chinese Journal of Comparative Law* 5, no. 1 (2017): 110–128.

65 US-China Economic and Security Review Commission. "Policy Considerations for Negotiating a US-China Bilateral Investment Treaty." www.uscc.gov/research/policy-considerations-negotiating-us-china-bilateral-investment-treaty, 9; Li, Yuwen and Bian, Cheng. "A New Dimension of Foreign Investment Law in China: Evolution and Impacts of the National Security Review System." *Asia Pacific Law Review* 24, no. 2 (2016): 503–551.

66 "International Investment Agreements." https://investmentpolicy.unctad.org/international-investment-agreements/countries/42/china.

67 Office of the US Trade Representative. "Bilateral Investment Treaties." https://ustr.gov/trade-agreements/bilateral-investment-treaties; Sachs, Wayne. "The New U.S. Bilateral Investment Treaties." *Berkeley Journal of International Law* 2, no. 1 (1984): 192; Gantz, David A. "Challenges for the United States in Negotiating a BIT with China: Reconciling Reciprocal Investment Protection with Policy Concerns." *Arizona Journal of International & Comparative Law* 14, no. 3 (2015): 216; US Department of State and Office of the U.S. Trade Representative. "2012 U.S. Model Bilateral Investment Treaty." www.state.gov/documents/organization/188371.pdf; US-China Economic and Security Review Commission. "Policy Considerations for Negotiating a US-China Bilateral Investment Treaty." www.uscc.gov/research/policy-considerations-negotiating-us-china-bilateral-investment-treaty, 8.

68 Shen, Weiduo. "China-US BIT Terms May be Included in Phase Two Trade Talks: Source." www.globaltimes.cn/content/1177341.shtml.

69 White House Office of the Press Secretary. "Fact Sheet: U.S.-China Economic Relations." https://obamawhitehouse.archives.gov/the-press-office/2015/09/25/fact-sheet-us-china-economic-relations (visited 25 April 2021).

70 US-China Economic and Security Review Commission. "Policy Considerations for Negotiating a US-China Bilateral Investment Treaty." www.uscc.gov/research/policy-considerations-negotiating-us-china-bilateral-investment-treaty, 13;

71 European Union Chamber of Commerce in China. "China Free Trade Zones 2015 Update: European Chamber Initial Assessment." 2015. www.europeanchamber.com.cn/en/national-news/2269/china_free_trade_zones_2015_update_european_chamber_initial_assessment.

72 Office of the US Trade Representative. "Remarks by Ambassador Michael Froman to AmCham China and the US Chamber of Commerce." 2015. https://ustr.gov/about-us/policy-offices/press-office/speechestranscripts/2015/april/remarks-ambassador-michael.

73 American Chamber of Commerce in the PRC. "China Business Climate Survey Report 2023." 2024. www.amchamchina.org/wp-content/uploads/2024/01/AmCham-China-2024-China-Business-Climate-Survey-Report.pdf.

74 American Chamber of Commerce in the PRC. "China Business Climate Survey Report 2023." 2024. www.amchamchina.org/wp-content/uploads/2024/01/AmCham-China-2024-China-Business-Climate-Survey-Report.pdf.

75 Donnelley, Shaun. "A Business Perspective on a China-US Bilateral Investment Treaty." 2014. http://ccsi.columbia.edu/files/2014/01/FDI_90.pdf.

76 Hufbauer, Gary Clyde, Miner, Sean and Moran, Theodore. "Committee on Foreign Investment in the United States and the US-China Bilateral Investment Treaty: Challenges in Meeting China's Demands." In *Toward a US-China Investment Treaty*. Washington, DC: Peterson Institute for International Economics, 2015, 39.

77 US-China Economic and Security Review Commission. "Policy Considerations for Negotiating a US-China Bilateral Investment Treaty." www.uscc.gov/research/policy-considerations-negotiating-us-china-bilateral-investment-treaty, 15.

78 Chon, Gina. "Chinese Group wins CFIUS Legal Case." www.ft.com/content/0fd071ea-0d03-11e4-bf1e-00144feabdc0; Dockery, Stephen. "Chinese Wind Company Settles with U.S. in CFIUS Battle." www.wsj.com/articles/BL-252B-8393;

79 US-China Economic and Security Review Commission. "Policy Considerations for Negotiating a US-China Bilateral Investment Treaty." www.uscc.gov/research/policy-considerations-negotiating-us-china-bilateral-investment-treaty, 23.
80 Chinese University of Hong Kong. "China's State-Owned Enterprises Reform: Will It Work?" https://cbkcuhk.wordpress.com/2016/01/05/china-state-owned-enterprises-reform-will-this-time-work/; US-China Economic and Security Review Commission. "2013 Annual Report to Congress." www.uscc.gov/sites/default/files/annual_reports/Complete%20 2013%20Annual%20Report.PDF.
81 State-owned Assets Supervision and Administration Commission of the State Council. "List of the Central State-owned Enterprises." www.sasac.gov.cn/n2588035/n2641579/n2641645/index.html; Zhuang, Shu and Miller, Matthew. "China Plans Mergers to Cut Number of Big State Firms to 40—State Media." www.reuters.com/article/china-soe-idUSL4N0XO4FD20150427; Sina Finance. "Development into the Fast Lane, The Number of State-owned Enterprises Increased to 460,000." https://baijiahao.baidu.com/s?id=1646761734403301601&wfr=spider&for=pc.
82 Irwin, Amos. "Crossing the Ocean by Feeling for BITs: Investor-State Arbitration in China's Bilateral Investment Treaty." Boston University Global Economic Governance Initiative Working Paper (2014): 3; Wildau, Gabriel. "China SOE's Restructuring Leaves State Ownership Intact." www.ft.com/content/902826f4-c878-11e4-8617-00144feab7de.
83 US Chamber of Commerce. "Competing Interests in China's Competition Law Enforcement." www.uschamber.com/report/competing-interests-chinas-competition-law-enforcement-chinas-anti-monopoly-law-application, 1.
84 Martina, Michael and Miller, Matthew. "As Qualcomm Decision Looms, U.S. Presses China on Antitrust Policy." 2014. www.reuters.com/article/qualcomm-china-antitrust/as-qualcomm-decision-looms-u-s-presses-china-on-antitrust-policy-idUSL3N0TW2SF20141216.
85 US-China Economic and Security Review Commission. "Policy Considerations for Negotiating a US-China Bilateral Investment Treaty." www.uscc.gov/research/policy-considerations-negotiating-us-china-bilateral-investment-treaty, 19.
86 US-China Economic and Security Review Commission. "Policy Considerations for Negotiating a US-China Bilateral Investment Treaty." www.uscc.gov/research/policy-considerations-negotiating-us-china-bilateral-investment-treaty, 25; Chow, Daniel C. K. "Why China Wants a Bilateral Investment Treaty." *Boston University International Law Journal* 33 (2015): 118.
87 2012 US Model BIT, Article 18; US-China Economic and Security Review Commission. "Policy Considerations for Negotiating a US-China Bilateral Investment Treaty." www.uscc.gov/research/policy-considerations-negotiating-us-china-bilateral-investment-treaty, 25.
88 Warren, Elizabeth. "The Trans-Pacific Partnership Clause Everyone Should Oppose." www.washingtonpost.com/opinions/kill-the-dispute-settlement-language-in-the-trans-pacific-partnership/2015/02/25/ec7705a2-bd1e-11e4-b274-e5209a3bc9a9_story.html.
89 Economic and Trade Agreement between the Government of the United States of America and the Government of the PRC, Chapter 7. https://ustr.gov/countries-regions/china-mongolia-taiwan/peoples-republic-china/phase-one-trade-agreement/text.

Index

Page numbers in *italics* indicate a figure and page numbers in **bold** indicate a table on the corresponding page.

FSC
www.fsc.org
MIX
Papier | Fördert
gute Waldnutzung
FSC® C083411

Kolibri 360 GmbH
Ferdinand-Jühlke-Straße 7
99095 Erfurt, Deutschland
produktsicherheit@kolibri360.de